The Stab-in-the-Back Myth and the Fall of the Weimar Republic

The Stab-in-the-Back Myth and the Fall of the Weimar Republic

A History in Documents and Visual Sources

Edited by George S. Vascik and Mark R. Sadler

Bloomsbury Academic
An imprint of Bloomsbury Publishing Plc

BLOOMSBURY
LONDON · OXFORD · NEW YORK · NEW DELHI · SYDNEY

Bloomsbury Academic
An imprint of Bloomsbury Publishing Plc

50 Bedford Square
London
WC1B 3DP
UK

1385 Broadway
New York
NY 10018
USA

www.bloomsbury.com

BLOOMSBURY and the Diana logo are trademarks of Bloomsbury Publishing Plc

First published 2016

© George S. Vascik and Mark R. Sadler, 2016

George S. Vascik and Mark R. Sadler have asserted their right under the Copyright, Designs and Patents Act, 1988, to be identified as Editors of this work.

All rights reserved. No part of this publication may be reproduced or transmitted in any form or by any means, electronic or mechanical, including photocopying, recording, or any information storage or retrieval system, without prior permission in writing from the publishers.

No responsibility for loss caused to any individual or organization acting on or refraining from action as a result of the material in this publication can be accepted by Bloomsbury or the authors.

British Library Cataloguing-in-Publication Data
A catalogue record for this book is available from the British Library.

ISBN: HB: 978-1-4742-2780-3
PB: 978-1-4742-2779-7
ePDF: 978-1-4742-2781-0
ePub: 978-1-4742-2782-7

Library of Congress Cataloging-in-Publication Data
Names: Vascik, George S., editor. | Sadler, Mark R., editor.
Title: The stab-in-the-back myth and the fall of the Weimar Republic :
a history in documents and visual sources / edited by
George S. Vascik and Mark R. Sadler.
Description: London : Bloomsbury Academic, 2016.
Identifiers: LCCN 2015043343 | ISBN 9781474227803 (hardback) |
ISBN 9781474227797 (paperback) | ISBN 9781474227810 (ePDF) |
ISBN 9781474227827 (ePub)
Subjects: LCSH: World War, 1914-1918–Political aspects–Germany–Sources. |
Germany–Politics and government–1918-1933–Sources. |
Germany–History–1918-1933–Sources. | World War,
1914-1918–Peace–Sources. | BISAC: HISTORY / Europe / Germany. |
HISTORY / Modern / 20th Century. | HISTORY / Military / World War I.
Classification: LCC D651.G3 S73 2016 | DDC 943.085–dc23
LC record available at http://lccn.loc.gov/2015043343

Cover design: Catherine Wood
Cover image: German Federal Archives

Typeset by Integra Software Services Pvt. Ltd.

For our mentors
Jay W. Baird
and
John Dolibois

For her tireless help and support
Charlene C. York

CONTENTS

List of Illustrations viii
List of Charts x
Preface xi
Acknowledgments xiv

Introduction 1

1 The Food Problem 9

2 Blockade 27

3 The Labor Question 39

4 The January Strikes 49

5 Military Collapse 63

6 Whose *Dolchstoß*? 77

7 Did an English General Start the Myth? 93

8 The Hindenburg Testimony 109

9 The Ebert Libel Trial 129

10 The Munich *Dolchstoß* Trial 159

11 A *Dolchstoß* Consensus? 177

12 The *Dolchstoßlegende* and the Fall of the Weimar Republic 203

Notes 208
Bibliography 220
Index 227

LIST OF ILLUSTRATIONS

1.1 Berlin delicatessen looted during 1916 Bread Riot (Imperial War Museum) 19
1.2 Dead horse butchered for food during December 1918 street fighting (Imperial War Museum) 22
2.1 Comparison of daily meal before (the front rows) and during Great War (the rear row) (Imperial War Museum) 32
3.1 Wilhelm Groener (Bundesarchiv Bildarchiv) 39
3.2 Volunteer strike breakers (Imperial War Museum) 43
4.1 Frederich Ebert (Bundesarchiv Bildarchiv) 50
4.2 Philipp Scheidemann (Bundesarchiv Bildarchiv) 51
6.1 Meeting of Congress of People's Deputies in the *Reichstag* chamber (Bundesarchiv Bildarchiv) 78
6.2 Karl Liebknecht speaking to a crowd in the Tiergarten, December 1918 (Bundesarchiv Bildarchiv) 81
6.3 A Guard Corps marching down *Unter den Linden*, December 10, 1918 (Bundesarchiv Bildarchiv) 87
6.4 The Council of People's Deputies (Bundesarchiv Bildarchiv) 87
6.5 Friedrich Ebert welcoming troops as they pass through the Brandenburg Gate and down *Unter den Linden*, December 10, 1918 (Alamy) 88
7.1 Sir Frederick Barton Maurice (National Portrait Gallery) 93
8.1 Celebration of Hindenburg's 70th birthday (Imperial War Museum) 110
8.2 Poster for the 7th War Loan featuring Hindenburg (Bundesarchiv Bildarchiv) 110
8.3 Karl Helfferich, Paul von Hindenburg and Erich Ludendorff at Helfferich's villa after the generals' testimony (Alamy) 113
8.4 German Everyman washing his dirty laundry in public, *Kladderadatsch*, November 23, 1919 (University of Heidelberg Digital Newspaper Collection) 123
8.5 An antisemitic interpretation of Hindenburg's testimony, *Kladderadatsch*, November 30, 1919 (University of Heidelberg Digital Newspaper Collection) 124
9.1 *Ulk*, January 9, 1925, "Vergiftete Waffen" (University of Heidelberg, University Library digitized historical literature collection) 135
9.2 *Lachen Links*, November 7, 1924, "Dolchstoß von Hinten" (University of Heidelberg, University Library digitized historical literature collection) 136

9.3 *Ulk*, January 1, 1925, "Ansaubere Hände" (University of Heidelberg, University Library digitized historical literature collection) 148
9.4 *Lachen Links*, November 7, 1924, "Regimentsfeier" (University of Heidelberg, University Library digitized historical literature collection) 149
9.5 *Lachen Links*, November 7, 1924, "Die Folgen der Dolchstoßlegende" (University of Heidelberg, University Library digitized historical literature collection) 153
10.1 *Lachen Links*, November 7, 1924, "der Dolchstoß bewiesen" (University of Heidelberg, University Library digitized historical literature collection) 160
10.2 *Ulk*, November 20, 1925, "Der 'letzte' Kronzeuge" (University of Heidelberg, University Library digitized historical literature collection) 161
10.3 DNVP poster December 1924 election (Bundesarchiv Bildarchiv) 173
10.4 DNVP poster 1920 election (Bundesarchiv Bildarchiv) 174
10.5 SPD December 1924 Prussian election (Bundesarchiv Bildarchiv) 176

LIST OF CHARTS

1.1 Food riots in 1916, by city 17
1.2 Select food prices 1914–1915 in Berlin 25
1.3 Impact of price controls calculated in shillings and pence per pound 25
2.1 Weight change for Americans leaving Germany, April 1917–January 1918 35
2.2 Length of stay of Americans leaving Germany, April 1917–January 1918 35
2.3 Former residence of Americans leaving Germany, April 1917–January 1918 36
2.4 Number of deaths attributable to the blockade 36
2.5 Number of deaths attributable to the blockade by age cohort, 1917 36
11.1 Members of the Subcommittee, 1919–1927 200
11.2 Members of the Subcommittee by blocs 201
11.3 National Assembly and *Reichstag* elections, January 1919–December 1924 201

PREFACE

The Stab-in-the-Back Myth—in its many manifestations—had a profound and pernicious impact on the course of Germany's first democracy. Scholars reflecting on German history between 1919 and 1933 are unanimous that the demonization and search for scapegoats that grew out of Germany's defeat in the First World War colored political debate and solidified anti-Republican sentiment among Germans inhabiting both the political Right and Left. Just as the centenary of the beginning of the Great War prompted a flood of reflection and debate on the origins of the war, so it can be expected that 2018 will bring renewed focus on the war's end.

This reader is designed to place a tool in the hands of instructors seeking to lead students in a discussion of the Stab-in-the-Back. We have adopted a "choose it and use it" philosophy that affords instructors maximum flexibility. We have broken what were originally three sections into twelve easily assigned chapters. Each chapter begins with a contextualization of the documents. At the end of each documents section, we have included "sources for further reading" that can be used as a launch pad for research papers, analytical charts and tables where applicable, and document-based thought questions that can serve as the basis for reflective essays or group discussions. We have also designed a website (http://www.dolchstosslegende.com) to supplement (but not supplant) the use of this reader. In this way, we hope to expand the breadth of our offerings and create a venue for materials (especially visual) that could not fit within the word constraints of this volume.

Authors assembling a reader on the Stab-in-the-Back have a wealth of primary documents at their disposal, most in the German language, if one has the time and language skill to access them. First and foremost are the eight published volumes of documents created for the Subcommittee of the *Reichstag* to examine the causes of the collapse in 1918.[1] The Subcommittee held 104 formal hearings (most of them not open to the public) between 1919 and 1927, collected masses of documentation, took affidavits, solicited long depositions from leading experts with vastly differing political perspectives, and invited members of parliament to debate the value of the evidence. We read through the entire corpus, selected and translated extracts that we thought were particularly useful.

We were assisted in this effort by four sets of published documents selected by Ralph Haswell Lutz, for years the director of the Hoover Institution on

War, Revolution and Peace at Stanford University.[2] *Collapse of the German Empire* contains excerpts from the officially authorized translation of the Subcommittee report. In some cases, most notably in Chapter 5, we have incorporated these translations into the text. Otherwise, we used *Collapse* to select documents from the German edition of the Subcommittee report, which we then translated ourselves.

We similarly used *The Fall of the German Empire* to lead us to contemporary German newspaper sources, which we then, unless otherwise indicated, translated from the original. This process took us to newspaper collections at the *Institut für Zeitungsforschung* Dortmund, the *Staatsbibliothek zu Berlin* and the Library of Congress. We also acquired numerous editions via interlibrary loan through Rentschler Library at Miami University.[3]

Although we have used the month-day-year system in our text, where a different format appeared in our documents we retained that out of fidelity to our sources. While we translated our German news sources into contemporary English, we have retained archaic forms (aero-plane, to-day) found in the English language sources. For these, we selected *The Times*, the *New York Times*, the *New York World*, the *Washington Evening Star*, the *Chicago Daily Tribune*, and several newspapers from the Midwestern German belt. We found this to be a special learning experience on the quality of contemporary sources. The reporting in *The Times* was uniformly detailed and entertaining. When students read these selections, they will immediately recognize that they are reading a quality paper that devoted considerable resources to following events in Germany. The *New York Times*, on the other hand, had clearly not emerged as the American "paper of record." It frequently relied upon the Associated Press feed for its news coverage, only rarely dropping in a "special correspondent" to give their stories "local color." Unlike the *New York Times*, the *Chicago Daily Tribune*, frequently published reports from correspondents of the Tribune News Service that were always insightful and clearly written by native German speakers. We also included articles extracted from county newspapers where large numbers of German-Americans lived. These newspapers frequently published articles transmitted across the United Press wire by Carl Groat, who later went on to edit the *Cincinnati Post* and play an important role in the Scripps newspaper chain.

Some instructors might be troubled by the relative absence of non-elite voices from this reader. This was intentional on our part. Recent translations from German of works by Bernd Ullrich and Benjamin Ziemann would make their inclusion redundant. We refer readers interested in this perspective to those works. Moreover, in the course of its investigation, the *Reichstag* Subcommittee collected a raft of letters and diaries from soldiers at the front. The Social Democratic Party, which collected similar material, opened their archives to the investigation. We will be posting these on our website as they become available and we have time to translate them.

We have also mounted other materials (such as documents relating to the infamous *Judenzählung*, the census of Jewish soldiers' service in the war), and speculative mini-chapters on our website (i.e., did Ludendorff suffer a nervous breakdown in September 1918) that have less documentation but are inherently interesting. Those interested in exploring the voluminous German-language literature are referred to the site as well.

A note on our use of German terminology and capitalizations

We have used the German term *Dolchstoß* in the text interchangeably with Stab-in-the-Back and *Dolchstoßlegende* with Stab-in-the-Back Myth. We have retained the German symbol for "double s"—ß—because it is uniformly used in contemporary sources and the German language secondary literature. On our website URL we have dropped the "double s" in favor of *Dolchstoss* because of the difficulty students might experience if their web browser is not properly set to display German symbols.

We have attempted to follow the *Chicago Manual of Style* rules for capitalizations, using Collapse when referring specifically to the phenomenon the Germans universally referred to as the *Zusammenbruch*. We have capitalized Subcommittee throughout when referring to the 4th subcommittee of the *Reichstag* investigative committee on the causes and end of the war. When Nationalist is spelled with a capital "N" it refers to members specifically of the German National People's Party; when the word is used with a lowercase "n," it refers to the broader bodies of nationalists.

Translating the words for prejudice toward and hatred of Jews poses a particular set of problems. Current English language usage suggests a preference for antisemitic over the previously ubiquitous anti-Semitic. When using the term, we use antisemitic as an adjective and Antisemitic as a proper noun. We have also most frequently translated the German word *völkisch* as antisemitic, although that term conveys a whole set of notions and its own distinct political style.

ACKNOWLEDGMENTS

The authors divided their tasks as follows: both authors selected the documents used in this volume. Vascik wrote the text. He chose (and where necessary translated) the documents in Chapters 1–4, the second half of Chapters 6 and 7–11, chose the majority of the illustrations and created the tables and graphs. Sadler selected and translated the documents in Chapters 5 and the first half of Chapter 6. He chose Figures 10.1–10.4 and populated the ancillary website, which includes his translations of documents concerning Hitler's experience of the Great War, the NSDAP and the *Dolchstoß*, and historians on the Stab-in-the-Back. Both authors collaborated on the bibliography.

Librarians and archivists at the *Institut für Zeitungsforschung* Dortmund, the *Staatsbibliothek zu Berlin*, the University of Heidelberg Digital Collection, the Imperial War Museum (London), the Library of Congress, and the US National Archives provided invaluable support. Polly Whitaker, Hannah Radford, and Mark Shores at Rentschler Library, Miami University, deserve special mention for their assistance in tracking down and acquiring sources. Connie Webb was always eager to lend a hand in the reams of copying this project required.

We would like to thank the Board of Trustees of the Leland Stanford Jr. University for permission to use *The Fall of the German Empire, 1914–1918* and *The Causes of the German Collapse in 1918: Sections of the Officially Authorized Report of the Commission of the German Constituent Assembly and of the German Reichstag, 1919*, both edited by Ralph Haswell Lutz. The scholars who read our proposal for Bloomsbury Publishing made numerous useful comments and recommendations. Richard Levy read the entire manuscript with great attention to detail and offered a plethora of suggestions that we have integrated into the text. Jay Baird provided encouragement throughout the project and read the final manuscript. Martin Burke read drafts and offered invaluable editorial advice. Our thanks as well to Rhodri Mogford, Emma Goode, and the staff of Bloomsbury Publishing for their support in this endeavor.

Lastly, we must thank Charlene C. York, who put aside her own work for six weeks to assist us during a critical phase of the project. She meticulously edited footnotes and bibliography, proofread the text, and helped secure permissions. Her superior organizational skills helped us bring this volume to a successful conclusion.

Introduction

Since the origin of our discipline, historians have wondered why wars begin. From Herodotus's *"historia"* of how the Greeks and the Persians came into conflict to the contemporary debate over the origins of the First World War, we have tried to understand how the natural conflicts between nations and peoples escalate into war. No doubt this is because of the human toll that wars inevitably extract, a toll that seems to rise with each advance in technology. The ways that wars end is consequential as well. What price do the winners exact from the losers? Loss of sovereignty? The extinction of a people and culture? And what price do the victors pay in terms of their own future well-being? If it is rightfully said that the seeds of the next war are planted with the conclusion of the first, what does that say about the proper way to make peace?

One might argue that the way the Great War ended for Germany generated a disaster that was unprecedented in European history, not least because of the different ways that Germans came to understand their defeat. Press censorship had assured that during the war, civilians were unable to accurately assess the true situation; body counts were distorted, labor troubles and food shortages troubles—for the most part a phenomenon of the large cities—were minimized, and victory was near. Convinced by military propaganda that their country was fighting a defensive war and that the German army was victorious in the field, the majority of the German populace found the turn of events in October 1918 psychologically devastating. They had suffered physical deprivation and sacrificed loved ones in what all agreed was an unprecedented war effort. There had been political debates about war aims; strikes, bread riots, and rumblings of discontent for eighteen months, but still defeat came as a shock.

As the immediacy of the traumatic events of November 1918—January 1919 receded into memory, Germans of all political persuasions and faiths needed to create a personal narrative that could explain what they had witnessed. Their conclusions varied, as had their lived experience. For many, a sense of betrayal took root. At one extreme, supporters of the imperial regime who thought that the army and navy had been stabbed in the back by domestic traitors; at the other, Communists and Independent Social Democrats who believed that Friedrich Ebert and the Majority Social Democrats had betrayed the cause of proletarian revolution. Across society in endless permutations, people came to wonder whether—as Hagen in Wagner's *Götterdämmerung* had stabbed Siegfried in the back—their own individual hopes had somehow been similarly betrayed.

Few people in February 1919 would have reflected back on the events of the preceding five months and not been able to find indicators, whether contained in letters from loved ones at the front, handbills covertly distributed on street corners and in factories or the disturbing news that a loved one had fallen on the field of battle. Fewer still could have been unaware of mutineers.[1] Units that had maintained discipline and marched in orderly fashion to the Rhine bridgeheads melted away as large numbers of front line troops did not even wait to be formally demobilized, a process complete with discharge letter, a last pay and a new suit of civilian clothes. Those trains that were not overloaded with returning wounded and ranks hanging from the side were piloted by the feared "red marine" mutineers, carrying revolution from the North Sea ports far inland and raising the red flag over innumerable city halls. Even in the sleepiest parish rectories, young children feared the coming of the "fearsome Spartacists."[2]

In his review of Boris Barth's comprehensive work on Stab-in-the-Back Myths, Laird Easton quotes Claude Levi-Strauss that "The purpose of myth is to provide a logical model capable of overcoming a contradiction."[3] For German nationalists who believed the military's propaganda of a victorious army, it was difficult to comprehend how all the Fatherland's sacrifice had come to naught. From seeds already planted during the political debates of 1917 and 1918 over strikes in the war industries and radical Socialist agitation against the war, the thought emerged that the German army must have been betrayed by enemies of the imperial regime and the "customary moral order."[4] In its crudest form, one version of the nationalist Stab-in-the-Back Myth held that the "victorious" German army had been defeated, not by the Allies, but by treason on the Home Front.[5]

Within the Nationalist camp, however, there were a startling number of variations on the *Dolchstoß* theme. "Moderate" *Dolchstoß* proponents, such as Hermann von Kuhl (second in command of the 8th Army Corps and a respected military historian), believed that the German army could no longer win the war by late summer 1918—because of a combination of Allied manpower superiority and the "poisoning" of the army's morale through revolutionary propaganda—but insisted that it could have withdrawn to a more defensible line where it might have forced the Allies to consider honorable terms to end the war.[6] According to the German Admiralty, the hitherto ineffective High Seas Fleet could have sailed forth and defeated the British navy in the Channel, winning the war, if ranks and Communist "red marines" in Kiel had not mutinied.[7] Nationalists, supporters of the imperial regime and Supreme Command generals like Erich Ludendorff blamed a range of politicians, union officials, and Jews to varying degrees at varying times to different audiences.[8] The most radical adherents of *Dolchstoß* Theory, led by pre-war Antisemites and the radical right wing newspaper *Deutsche Tageszeitung*, blamed Jews and a Jewish conspiracy for Germany's defeat.[9]

What makes matters more complex was that there were a seemingly endless number of backs—not just nationalist—being stabbed. One might be tempted to dub this a phenomenon of "every man his *Dolchstoß*." The most prominent alternative *Dolchstoß* laid the blame for the way that events unfolded in 1918/19 on the shoulders of Social Democratic leaders Friedrich Ebert, Philipp Scheidemann, and Gustav Noske who, rather than support the autogenerated and authentic workers' and soldiers' councils as an alternative source of power to maintain the revolutionary regime, chose the path of parliamentary republicanism. In this interpretation, Ebert entered into a secret, sinister bargain with the forces of the Right (fragments of the old officer corps and newly created *Freikorps* units) to suppress first the red marines in December 1918 and then the Spartacists in January 1919.[10]

All told, the contested memory of the war's end had a profound impact on Weimar politics. It was a central issue in the "victory" of the "black-white-red" (anti-Republican) parties in the 1924 elections. It divided the German National People's Party and made its participation in either "Bourgeois" or "Grand Coalition" cabinets problematic. It tore apart the Social Democratic movement and ultimately strengthened the anti-Republican Communist party.[11]

Given the intensity of the Stab-in-the-Back debate between 1919 and 1933, and the use that the Nazis made of "their" version of the *Dolchstoß*, it is perhaps surprising that the concept largely disappeared after 1945, living on only in the apologetic memoirs of German generals seeking to explain why they failed to support the military resistance to Hitler and why they stood by the regime to the bitter end. The topic was clearly not a priority for the Marxist historians of the German Democratic Republic, nor did it seem to excite their bourgeois counterparts in the West, many of whom had survived the terrible "Brown Years" and wished to return to "pure" history. It was only in 1963 that simultaneous extended essays were published on the topic, one in the Federal Republic and the other in the GDR. Friedrich Freiherr Hiller von Gaertringen (historian and son-in-law of Weimar-era Nationalist politician Cuno von Westarp) published what was in retrospect an extremely balanced account of the origins of *Dolchstoß* theory, its permutations in the course of a generation and its impact on the Nazi-era German officer corps.[12] More frequently cited in English-language scholarship has been an intense intellectual excavation of the origins and uses of the *Dolchstoß* concept written by Joachim Petzold, a Marxist scholar at the Institute for History of the Academy of Science in (East) Berlin.[13]

There the discussion stood for a generation. The *Dolchstoßlegende* was a topic of instruction in the schools of both German states, as it is still in a unified Germany. The general contours of the contemporary popular consensus are clear. The German army had clearly lost the war by the fall of 1918 and could no longer continue. The loss and deprivation brought about by the war gave rise to popular discontent (particularly in the cities and among factory workers) that was increasingly radicalized and revolutionary. The imperial government collapsed under the weight of Allied military pressure, American demands, and events that outpaced anyone's ability to control them. This consensus view—dramatized in "*Der Gewaltfrieden*," a two-episode television documentary produced in 2010 by "*Bayerischer Rundfunk*", is flexible enough to leave room for variation and emphsasis.[14] Some prefer to focus on Ludendorff's actions, the Ebert-Groener Pact, or the insurrection of January 1919 without full reference to the context of those events.[15]

In the past twenty years, aspects of the events of 1918 and 1919 have been the subject of voluminous specialist and popular literatures. Of the breakdown on the army alone, Bernd Ullrich, Benjamin Ziemann, Wolfgang Kruse, John Horn, and Christopher Jahr have greatly expanded our scope of knowledge.[16] By 2000, sufficient scholarship had been generated that Gerd Krumeich, one of the most respected historians in the debate on the origins of the Great War, published a new overview of literature on the *Dolchstoß*.[17] Krumeich's essay appeared, interestingly enough, on the eve of a new era, when the Myth itself would once more become the topic of scholarly note. The year 2003 witnessed the publication of Boris Barth's professorial thesis (*Habilitationsschrift*) completed at the University of Constance and Rainer Sammet's dissertation at the University of Freiburg.[18] Barth's work is an incredibly dense 560 pages that has not found universal applause from English-language reviewers, but it is an important milestone in a revived consideration of the *Dolchstoß* question.[19] Barth has also published an essay that details the main points of this work.[20] Sammet is some ways breaks new ground through a detailed study of discussions of the Stab-in-the-Back through a multitude of national, regional, and local newspapers and posits that the issue fell from public notice after 1925.

In its contours, the estimation of the Stab-in-the-Back Myth in the English-speaking world is similar to the general German popular understanding. Several recent examples illustrate this. In *Weimar Germany. Promise and Tragedy*, Eric Weitz has written, "Avoiding public responsibility for its own actions, the military would quickly claim that Germany was robbed of its victory by traitors at home, the Social Democrats and Jews and even Catholics like Erzberger. The infamous legend, which would be used to stunning effect by Adolf Hitler, was launched even before the armistice had been signed."[21] Richard Evans, in his widely read *The Coming of Nazi Germany*, asserts that

> The harshness of the Armistice terms was thrown into sharp relief by the fact that many Germans refused to believe that their armed forces had actually been defeated. Very quickly, aided and abetted by senior army officers themselves, a fateful myth gained currency among large

sections of public opinion in the centre and on the right of the political spectrum .... [this myth held] that the army had been the victim of a "secret, planned, demagogic campaign" which had doomed all its heroic efforts to failure in the end.[22]

The importance of the Stab-in-the-Back Myth is not in dispute. Larry Eugene Jones calls the Stab-in-the-Back legend, "along with Germany's defeat, the threat of Bolshevism ... and runaway inflation, a significant factor in a veritable explosion of anti-Semitism."[23] For Richard Bessel, "The image of the demobilized hero of the trenches coming home to an unappreciative, disrespectful, scornful home-front formed an important element in the political vocabulary of the Weimar Republic, particularly on the Right."[24]

While Anglo-American scholars agree that the *Dolchstoßlegende* played an important role in German memory of the Great War and the unraveling of the Weimar Republic, as late as five years ago one needed to refer to the German literature and possess a strong reading knowledge of that language to explore the specifics.[25] That too has changed with the new century. Jeffrey Verhey has written a field-changing book on the myth of the spirit of August, the surge of patriotic feeling the Germans were long thought to have experienced at the start of the Great War.[26] The scholarship of Belinda Davis, Scott Stephenson, and Thomas Weber has expanded their specific fields in new and innovative ways.[27] Nor has impact of the war on the intensification of antisemitism been overlooked, as books by Tim Grady, Peter Applebaum, and Brian Crim testify.[28]

This growing wave of specialist literature has sparked a series of English-language translations that should be very useful to undergraduates who do not have grounding in German. This is particularly the case in the work of Benjamin Ziemann, one the most prolific and innovative specialists in the field.[29] Ziemann's collaboration with Bernd Ullrich in the publication of diaries and letters that German soldiers wrote home from the field should spark thoughtful work.[30] Students interested in the revolution also benefit from the translation of Pierre Broué's Marxist analysis of the revolution, Ralf Hoffrogge's biography of Revolutionary Shop Steward leader Richard Müller, and Gabriel Kuhn's set of documents on the council movement.[31]

For the average American university student who is asked to research the *Dolchstoß* and follows the now current adage, "when in doubt, Google it out," the pickings are scarce. If they search through several screens—past Wikipedia and assorted dross—they will find Harold Marcuse's review of Barth's *Dolchstoßlegenden*. Marcuse has created a colorful, interesting page that not only displays his review (and German-language reviews of the book) but also inserted footnotes, illustrations, Internet links, and a short bibliography of works on the Stab-in-the-Back. He also adds images of the posters that Rainer Sammet included in his dissertation. All in all, it is a good place to begin serious study.[32] He does not, however, take his readers to document collections. This a small quibble really when one considers the innovative nature of the posting and Marcuse is to be commended for e-publishing such an important resource.

This reader has been written in such a way as to aid instructors and students needing access to the primary documents at the root of the *Dolchstoß* debate. We have translated chosen documents from German that we think are helpful and representative. Where English translations of our documents already existed, we have retranslated them to suit modern English usage. Throughout we have indicated where additional documents can be found and what secondary sources students might find useful in developing a deeper understanding of the issues involved.

In the first two chapters, we discuss Germany's inability to feed its own people in the course of the Great War and the impact that failure had on the war effort and civilian morale. Chapter 3 looks at growing labor unrest within the war economy. The focus of Chapter 4 is on the nationwide munitions workers strike that occurred in January 1918 on the eve of the last great German offensive. This strike would become an important event in the *Dolchstoß* narratives of both the nationalist right and the communist left. It was a particularly intense memory for Adolf Hitler, not only embittering him toward the betrayal at home, but also influenced his elaborate attempts to forestall a reoccurrence domestic unrest during the Third Reich. Chapter 5 presents a series of documents on the military collapse and Chapter 6 deals with the revolutionary events of November 1918–January 1919 that were at the center of later contestation.

The following five chapters explore the creation of the nationalist Myth. One of the foundation stones of the nationalist *Dolchstoßlegende* was that "an English general" was the first to recognize that the German army—undefeated in the field—was brought low by the collapse of the Home Front. We explore the origins of this lie and suggest how it might have taken root in Chapter 7. Chapter 8 focuses on a seminal moment in the creation of the *Dolchstoßlegende*: the testimony that Field Marshal Paul von Hindenburg gave in November 1919 before the initial *Reichstag* Committee created to investigate the origins, conduct, and conclusion of the Great War. In his brief testimony, only days after the one year anniversary of the Armistice, the most respected man in Germany declared that the German army had been stabbed in the back, although he refused to name the guilty parties.

Subsequent to this botched initial phase when most of the leading figures in the imperial government were called to testify, the *Reichstag* parties decided that it would be best to set up four separate subcommittees to investigate the discrete issues involved. The fourth subcommittee was charged with investigating the military and internal causes of the Collapse. It met a total of 104 times, mostly in closed session, and only issued its final conclusions in November 1927. In Chapter 11, we have translated abridged versions of selected depositions, testimony, and the final reports.

We argue that by the time this authoritative report was issued, most minds were made up as to whether there was a Stab-in-the-Back, whose back was stabbed and who did the stabbing. Central to the formation of the various *Dolchstoßlegenden* were two high-profile trials. In Chapter 9, we present documents from the defamation lawsuit brought by Friedrich Ebert, the president of the republic, against Erwin Rothardt, publisher of a minor antisemitic newspaper in Prussian Saxony. What began as a trial against Rothardt's libelous remarks was transformed into a circus orchestrated by Nationalist circles in which Ebert had to prove that he was not a traitor because he participated in the January 1918 strike of Berlin munitions workers. The decision of the county court the Ebert had legally committed treason, based on a tortured reading of the law and evidence that was certain to be overturned on appeal, was fodder for the Nationalist claims that the Social Democrats had betrayed the Fatherland. An unexpected consequence of the trial was that President Ebert, having delayed surgery for an appendicitis attack so as not to seem that he was seeking public sympathy, died of peritonitis six weeks after the verdict was announced.

Chapter 10 recounts a second infamous *Dolchstoß* trial that took place in Munich in the autumn of 1925. In the spring of 1924, Paul Nicholas Cossmann published two volumes of virulently nationalistic, antisemitic essays on the Stab-in-the-Back and continued thereafter to publicize them in his monthly *Süddeutsche Monatshefte*. When the editor of Munich's Social Democratic newspaper accused Cossmann of "historical falsification" (throwing in libelous references to Cossmann's Jewish heritage), Cossmann initiated legal action. The three-and-a-half week trial featured testimony from former German military figures (especially from the navy), Social Democratic participants in the events of 1918 and "experts" who had prepared depositions for the investigative Subcommittee. The highpoint of the trial was provided by the testimony of former general Wilhelm Groener, who revealed that Independent Socialist leader Hugo Haase promised that he would work against revolution and do his best to prevent strikes in the war industries. More significantly, Groener detailed his agreement with Friedrich Ebert to provide military support for the Council of People's Deputies if Ebert dismissed the Independent members of the Council and suppressed the Communists. This "Groener-Ebert Pact" was seen by advocates of the leftist *Dolchstoßlegende* as proof positive that Ebert "betrayed" the revolution. We conclude, in Chapter 12, with a discussion of the ways in which the memory of 1918 impacted the Weimar years. We contend that the issue faded into the background in the period of stabilization that followed 1925, only to resurface as a keystone of Nazi propaganda with the onset of the economic depression.

1

The Food Problem

Institutional context

The German Empire (*Reich*) was a federal union of twenty-seven states. The states represented a broad range of forms: kingdoms, principalities, grand duchies, duchies, and free cities. Each possessed its own laws, legislatures, and army, as well as its own internal system of administration. The states ceded control over foreign affairs, currency, and limited areas of lawmaking and taxation to the *Reich*, but retained broad powers over health, education, transportation, and agriculture. They also retained control of the most lucrative sources of tax revenue—such as the land tax—since prior to the First World War and the founding of the Weimar Republic; the *Reich* did not assess direct taxes. As we will see in the documents below, this system of dispersed control created problems for the central administration of scarce resources.

The most powerful state within this system was the Kingdom of Prussia, which accounted for two-thirds of both the Empire's land mass and its population and its greatest concentration of wealth and industrial production. The Prussian legislature was firmly under the control of the ruling classes as its members were elected by a weighted franchise that favored wealthy landed and business élites at the expense of the middle and lower classes. The inequity of this system would emerge as a major complaint of striking workers in Berlin in 1917.

At the imperial level, power was symbolized in the person of the Emperor (*Kaiser*), who was simultaneously King of Prussia. The Chancellor and the civilian government that he led were responsible only to the Emperor and did not require a parliamentary majority. Under the constitution created by Otto von Bismarck, federal legislative power was vested in two institutions—the *Bundesrat* (or council of state governments) and the Imperial Diet (the *Reichstag*). Each member state had a foreign minister who represented his state's interest in the *Bundesrat*, which initiated most federal legislation and validated all laws passed by the imperial legislature. Members of the *Reichstag* were elected by universal, adult (over 25 years of age) male suffrage. It had very little power over the conduct of the war. *Reichstag* approval of "war credits" was necessary so that the government could finance the war and while it did hold hearings on aspect of the war effort (and on July 19, 1917, passed a resolution calling for a negotiated end to the war), it had next to no direct input over the conduct of the conflict and was mostly kept in the dark by both civilian and military authorities.

The food problem

In January 1919, Germans went to the polls to elect a National Assembly charged with writing a constitution for the new republic that would replace the disintegrated imperial regime. Among the many tasks this constituent assembly undertook was determining the circumstances under which Germany went to war in 1914 and why the war effort and the imperial regime so spectacularly collapsed in November 1918. It set up a committee for this purpose, with a special Subcommittee charged with investigating the collapse. While the Subcommittee members and the experts from whom they heard testimony sharply disagreed on the causes of the military collapse, they were unanimous in defining the internal causes. The members shared the view that in August 1914, all Germans (save a handful of radical Social Democrats) were united in the defense of the Fatherland in the face of Russian aggression, a phenomenon contemporaries referred to as the "Spirit of August." As part of this *Augusterlebnis*, the political parties agreed to suspend their disagreements for the duration and work in harmony to win the war, the so-called domestic truce or *Burgfrieden*.

Reflecting upon when and why this unity began to fracture, the Subcommittee was convinced that domestic unity began to fray when the government encountered difficulties supplying the civilian population with food. "Under the influence of war profiteering and serious abuses in the food supply," the deputies agreed, "the idea of class antagonism and the will to class struggle rose once again among the working masses …. Discontent grew with the unexpectedly long duration of the war and through the massive loss of life and strength due to the [Allied] blockade."[1]

Both the food problem and the blockade came as a surprise to German war planners on the General Staff. The famous Schlieffen Plan for fighting a war on two fronts was predicated on the concept of a short war. Consideration did not have to be taken of the impact of mass militarization on the labor force or on the supply of food necessary to sustain military and civilian needs. Nor did the planners imagine that, if hostilities lasted beyond the expected three months, the British navy would be able to enforce a blockade and deny Germany essential food imports from the United States and Argentina.

Initial difficulties

As the war extended beyond Christmas, the imperial government began in a haphazard way to manage scarce food resources. In January 1915 it created an Imperial Grain Board, whose task was to ascertain the amount of bread and fodder grains available and coordinate food policy across the sovereign federal states. The Board set nominal prices for cereals delivered to millers and bread sold in bakeries. It asked the federal states to issue ration cards that would entitle each citizen to a weekly amount of bread at a set price.[2] Some of these policies were spectacular failures, such as the infamous Pig Massacre (*Schweinemord*) that occurred when bureaucrats in the Prussian Agricultural Ministry, fearing that there was insufficient grain to both feed the people and sustain Germany's sizable pig herd, ordered the slaughtering of most of the country's pigs.[3]

The government sought to reassure the anxious population with its limited initial steps. Prussian Minister of Agriculture Clemens von Schorlemer granted an interview to an Italian newspaper that he knew would be translated and republished in the German press (see Document 1.1). Schormeler's optimistic words, while meant to reassure, reflected the government's unwillingness to address the issue in a systematic fashion. Ministers and bureaucrats alike preferred to address the looming food problem on an ad hoc basis. Creating a global policy meant entering the thicket of competing consumer and producer interests, something the government was loath to do in the hopes of maintaining internal unity.

1.1 AN OPTIMISTIC OFFICIAL PROGNOSIS, FEBRUARY 11, 1915[4]

I can assure you that we are not dependent on foreign countries for our food. We need only meat, corn, and potatoes to feed our people. Our stocks of cattle have continually increased in the past years, so that we can provide meat for our people at normal prices. The shortfall of fodder imports will be made good this year by a bountiful hay harvest and by using beet sugar as fodder. Moreover, we need provide for only a few months—and for these our supplies are adequate—as in May the cattle can go out to grass. In 1913 we had an extraordinarily good harvest. That for 1914 a very good one as well. The English, who think they can starve us out, forget that since the outbreak of war a hundred thousand foreigners have left our country, and that three million of our soldiers are fed in foreign countries from food available in the theater of operations. We can, therefore, provide very well for prisoners of war, whose number now reaches almost a million. We have a sufficiency of field labor available in Germany; if need be, POWs can be used for field labor.

Reassuring platitudes, such as those uttered by Schoerlemer, could not hide mounting concern within both middle- and working-class sections of the population. The Social Democratic Party—through an editorial published by its newspaper *Vorwärts* (see Document 1.2)—complained that the creation of the Grain Board was too-little-too-late. An article (Document 1.3) that appeared in the progressive, mass-circulation *Berliner Tageblatt* the first week of February is a second example of the growing public anxiety. The *Tageblatt* had a reputation for tweaking the noses of noble estate owners in eastern Germany, so the fact that they expressed concern over the food supply without belittling large producers is significant. Similarly, the liberal *Frankfurter Zeitung* (Document 1.4) expressed concern about the distribution of food to middle class consumers. In line with the *Burgfrieden*, the normal class-conscious critique of both papers softened into complaints of the protection of special interests in the countryside.

1.2 SOCIAL DEMOCRATIC CRITICISM OF THE GOVERNMENT'S DELAY IN FORMULATING A PLAN FOR THE FOOD SUPPLY, JANUARY 27, 1915[5]

It has taken fully five months for the government finally to decide on the measures that we have demanded from the beginning of the war. These are absolutely necessary if we are to provide the people with sufficient food. We are not going to reiterate our opinion why the measures have been adopted so late, or who was responsible for the delay. The difficulties that will inevitably arise could have been avoided if the new regulations had been in place from the beginning. Now the state grain monopoly has been put into effect and it turns out that a solution to the complicated problem of providing bread is simple, provided that all participants involved are willing to facilitate its enforcement. This has been demanded in the decree of the State Ministry .... The grain monopoly, with its restrictions on private business, stands alone in an economy which is completely built up in all other respects upon business initiative, interests, and needs. These restrictions can and will lead to all sorts of disturbances, some planned and some spontaneous. Unfortunately the present regulations have been presented as a temporary emergency measure, although they can only be effective if they are permanent.

As far as the organization of the grain monopoly is concerned, the regulation of consumption is entrusted to a supreme board, the *Reich* Distribution Board in Berlin. The *Reich* Distribution Board has the task of providing for the distribution of the supply at hand of grain and flour in cooperation with the municipalities and the "War Grain Company." Municipal bodies are to distribute the supply they receive .... Imprisonment and fines are threatened for producers who do not declare their inventory properly or who fail to deliver goods. The competent central boards must purchase stocks at a "reasonable price." Where maximum prices have been fixed, they are to be observed.

The decree does not say anything about the selling prices of flour and grain. Municipalities will have to secure supplies as cheaply as possible, since many of the advantages of state regulation might be lost if flour and grain cost too much. Working with non-profit food cooperatives will help. The decree offers our [Social Democratic] representatives on city councils the opportunity for oversight, input, and cooperation with civil authorities.

1.3 A LIBERAL PERSPECTIVE ON THE IMPACT OF THE WAR ON AGRICULTURE, FEBRUARY 2, 1915[6]

No segment of the economy has been more affected by the onset of the war than agriculture. Farmers now work under completely altered conditions: their supply of important raw materials has been restricted, their markets and the consumption of their products are being hampered by legal measures. Their labor supply and beasts of burden have been seriously reduced in number …. Although the demands on farmers are now greater than in peacetime, they have been compelled to sacrifice a considerable part of their livestock due to lack of fodder. Thus, in the case of the 25 million pigs that Germany now possesses … about 12 million will have to be slaughtered in the near future. A shortage of pork will be felt in the coming years, but fortunately pig breeding can be quickly expanded …. The proposal to reduce the national cattle herd, however, is very unfortunate. It will take years to restore the stocks to the pre-War level, and the impact upon butter and milk production will be disastrous.

The deficiency of fodder is already apparent in the lower output of dairy products, which has resulted in higher butter prices. Food prices are rising daily. Demands that the government take decisive steps are mounting, spurred on by the problems presented by unscrupulous profiteers. For some time the representatives of labor and others have appealed to the government for redress. The dissatisfaction with the … official agencies is obviously increasing even among the middle classes and the less highly paid officials. It is high time to take vigorous measures …. It is not from lack of the necessary food but from unscrupulous speculation that the situation has reached the point where people will be threatened with hunger unless we take decisive steps.

1.4 THE *FRANKFURTER ZEITUNG* ON THE IMPORTANCE OF SOLVING AGRICULTURE'S PROBLEMS, JULY 15, 1915[7]

At the moment no task is more urgent, if we are to maintain war production, than lessening the oppressive burden of the food shortage. In truth, it is no longer a mere question of a more or less agreeable and comfortable mode of life. It is the most important task the government must fulfill .... It must ensure that the wives and children of the men in the field suffer no harm, that the will to persevere remains alive in the country, that unity continues unimpaired, and that we do not present to our enemies ... a sorry picture of strikes and wage disputes in the midst of war. The war is felt by all levels of society, not merely because of the material sacrifices that it imposes but also because of the exasperating impression that a minority is profiting at the expense of the majority. All this has been made clear with increasing emphasis to the government in the press, in protest meetings and petitions.

A last and more ominous concern was added by complaints from *Vorwärts* (Document 1.5) regarding profiteering. Workers felt the first pinch as prices rose and goods became scarcer. For Social Democrats, this anger was directed specifically at farmers, large landowners, and the Conservative establishment. This sentiment fit easily within the context of European social thought since the French Revolution, where scarcities and rising food prices were perceived by an angry public not as the result of normal market forces but of greed and cupidity. In the German context, especially among the middle class but also among farmers and workers, scarcity and "price gouging" were frequently blamed on Jews, who played an important role as middlemen in the agricultural food chain.

1.5 SOCIAL DEMOCRATIC COMPLAINTS ABOUT PROFITEERING, OCTOBER 16, 1915[8]

The General Committee of the Trade Unions and the Executive Committee of the Social Democratic Party have recently submitted to the Chancellor a memorandum that states:

> The undersigned take this occasion to direct the attention of our Excellency to the unbearable rise of prices in our food products. The people face a serious danger that it is our policy to avert. The

> sacrifices that the German people are making today are unavoidable. Nonetheless, we still hear the opinion expressed that the people must be taught to economize and that this can only be done through higher prices. We reject this opinion.

More problems

There the matter sat through the winter months of 1915–1916. Protest continued unabated; prices continued to rise. As one problem was "solved," others emerged. The ability of government officials to accurately account for the amount of available grain proved to be a problem. Estimates based on harvest projections did not match with the amount of grain on hand. There were suspicions that throughout the supply chain, producers and wholesalers were under-reporting their inventory—wholesalers (usually typecast as Jews) in order to have undeclared stores to sell on the black market, farmers to keep consumable grain back as fodder for their livestock. The president of the War Grain Board, Georg Michaelis, addressed this problem in a speech to the Prussian House of Deputies (Document 1.6).

1.6 REMARKS OF GEORG MICHAELIS TO THE PRUSSIAN PARLIAMENT, FEBRUARY 16, 1916[9]

Various statements have been published with reference to the results of the revisions of our inventory. In July we undertook an estimate of the grain harvest. The figure arrived at was 10 million tons, an exceptionally low figure in view of the fact that a good harvest yields from 14 to 15 million tons. It was hoped at the time that the yield would in the end turn out to be higher. An inventory was carried out on 16 November, and everyone expected that a higher amount would be shown. The very opposite proved to be the case. The yield was found to fall short of the needs of the country, so the authorities found themselves obliged to enact measures to reduce consumption in order to adjust our supplies to our needs.

At the same time the reported inventories were proofed and it was found that in many cases there had been understatements. We have now made a complete revision, and we're satisfied to find that the supposed deficit previously shown is fully covered .... This extra quantity is necessary in order to provide against a deficit. We know fairly accurately the amount of our requirements and we cannot be again misled on this point .... This correction, however, does not mean that reason for anxiety of the food supply is past.

Crisis

Bread, however, was not the only staple that was in short supply. Emanuel (alternatively Immanuel) Wurm, a Social Democratic member of the Berlin City Council and the party's food specialist in the *Reichstag*, complained of a lack of meat and fats such as butter (Document 1.7). His comments indicate the extent to which civil cohesion was beginning to break down as class antagonisms grew.

1.7 SPEECH BY SOCIAL DEMOCRAT WURM IN BERLIN CITY COUNCIL, SPRING 1916[10]

What measures does the Municipal Council intend to adopt for procuring and regulating the supply of meat for the Berlin population? Only a few weeks ago we [Social Democrats] had to call attention to the unsatisfactory supply of provisions for Berlin, especially for the poorer classes. At that time, the problem was the dearth of potatoes and the Council's failure to take measures to insure the necessary amount of potatoes was released to the market. At present there is a scarcity of fat, butter and meat. You all know the trouble that people must go through in order to procure those few provisions accessible to them. They have to wait for hours in front of the stores only in the end to face the well-known, "Sold out!" ... How can women employed on war work find time to stand before the shops and actually beg food for their families? At the same time these faulty arrangements entail a waste of productive power and a danger to health in the weather we had last week. And yet the proper authorities fail to take the necessary steps.

We [Social Democrats] demand that the Municipal Council inform the responsible imperial and state authorities that this mismanagement can no longer be tolerated. We must demand a central organization headed by a man who will be fairer to the cities than has been the case to date. We need an imperial department that has the right to confiscate provisions and to deliver them to the municipal authorities [who distribute food].

Wurm's comments came as the situation in the cities was rapidly deteriorating. According to official statistics (which could well be understated), in 1916 there were three food riots in January, four in February, five in March, and three in April (Chart 1.1).

The government recognized the danger and responded by establishing the War Food Office in May 1916 (Document 1.8). Talented individuals from throughout the military—such as Wilhelm Groener—and the civilian bureaucracy were seconded to the Office, as were individuals from the private sector. One of the first accomplishments of the War Food Office was the creation of a national meat ration card as a means of allocating that commodity (Document 1.9).

CHART 1.1 *Food riots in 1916, by city*

Month	#	City
January	3	Berlin, Chemnitz, Leipzig
February	4	Berlin, Cologne, Halle, Hannover
March	5	Berlin, Dusseldorf, Frankfurt, Munich, Munster
April	3	Berlin Dresden, Jena
May	0	
June	17	Aachen, Berlin, Breslau, Brunswick, Charlottenburg, Chemnitz, Coblenz, Cologne, Dresden, Duisberg, Dusseldorf, Essen, Kiel, Leipzig, Magdeburg, Munich, Nuremberg
July	0	
August	5	Berlin, Cologne, Dresden, Hamburg, southern Alsace
September	3	Brunswick, Hamburg, suburban Hamburg
October	6	Berlin, Bremen, Kiel, Leipzig, Munich (8 times), Stuttgart
November	2	Dresden, Hamburg (constant)
December	6	Breslau, Hamburg, Kiel, Lübeck, Munich, Posen

Source: Archibald C. Bell, *A History of the Blockade of Germany and the Countries Associated with Her in the Great War* (London: Her Majesty's Stationary Office, 1961), pp. 572–573.

1.8 DECREE ESTABLISHING A WAR FOOD SUPPLY DEPARTMENT, MAY 23, 1916[11]

A sufficient food supply for the people has been assured and will not be endangered by any blockade, however unscrupulous, and however long the war lasts. But the necessity of matching our consumption to the poor harvest of 1915 has led, as everybody knows, to a lack of food .... For months the federal government, together with the state governments and municipalities, has endeavored to meet the various difficulties and to secure a continuous, sufficient, and uniform food supply for the people. It has become, however, more and more evident that the present system of state organization stands as an obstruction in the way of full success of these efforts.

This necessitates the creation of a War Food Supply Department. The president of this department is given the power to regulate of all kinds of food and the raw materials and other things necessary for the food production, as well as of all food for animals. His powers include the regulation of sale and consumption (if necessary also the right of expropriation), the right of importing and exporting, as well as through the regulation of prices. In order to assure its enforcement, violations are punishable by an imprisonment of one year and by a maximum fine of 10,000 marks. The president is empowered to give orders to state authorities in case of imminent danger .... Experienced men of all important groups of economic interests—commerce and industry, military administration, and consumers—will co-operate in the War Food Supply Department. All decisions, however, will rest entirely with the president. The representatives of the state governments, of the military authorities and of the war companies will have a voice. The *Reichstag* Advisory Council on Food Supply will continue to function alongside of the newly established organization.

1.9 REPORT ON THE NEW MEAT RATIONING SYSTEM, AUGUST 23, 1916[12]

By the order of the president of the War Food Department the weekly maximum ration of 250 grams (0.55 lbs.) of meat will everywhere be apportioned in full, even to places that now get much less. Uniform rationing throughout the Empire will enable the authorities to allocate full supplies as quickly was possible. Inhabitants of districts that have so far received more than 250 grams weekly will have to comfort themselves with the knowledge that their reduced ration will benefit other districts that have previously been deprived .... Every person is to receive one meat card every four weeks. Children younger than six years old will receive half rations only.

Bureaucracies, however effective, cannot control the weather. The winter of 1916–1917 was particularly bad. Food was in short supply and bread riots became a common feature of urban life (Figure 1.1). Germans referred to the period as the Turnip Winter, when it seemed that turnips were the only commodity in plentiful supply. The Supreme Command was well aware of the problem and through its propaganda apparatus offered future visions of plenty when the resources of the conquered territories in the East were effectively exploited. They especially cast covetous eyes upon Romania and undertook a massive canalization project on the Danube to bring grain up river to Germany.

Of course any food from the Balkans had to transit Austria-Hungary, which if anything was in even worse nutritional shape than Germany. Not only did Germany's effective military *supremo* Erich Ludendorff demand

FIGURE 1.1 *Berlin delicatessen looted during 1916 Bread Riot (Imperial War Museum)*.

foodstuffs from starving Vienna, he also informed his allies that meat and dairy products from the Netherlands, Denmark, and Sweden would not be allowed to transit Germany to Austrian buyers (see Ludendorff's letter in Document 1.10). A memo from the Austrian ambassador in Berlin on the food situation (Document 1.11) that provides us with a non-German account of the severity of the situation.

1.10 LUDENDORFF'S DEMANDS TO THE AUSTRO-HUNGARIAN FOREIGN MINISTER, MARCH 25, 1917[13]

The food situation in Germany has recently grown much worse. Our agricultural food will be consumed before the next harvest. It is expected that our supply of potatoes will not carry us through the month of May. When the supply of potatoes was recently stopped for weeks by the heavy frost, it was possible for us to make up for it by increasing the rations in flour and other foodstuffs. In this way we shall be able to get along up to May, but no longer. The supply of cereals at the disposal of the *Reich* has never been as low as it is at present.

This supply is being replenished so slowly that it is very questionable whether or not we shall be able to maintain the rations at the present rate. The difficulties that we are bound to encounter with the coming of spring can probably be met only by increasing the meat rations. It has been proposed to increase the number of cattle to be slaughtered, yet we dare not decrease our livestock substantially or it will endanger our agricultural productivity through lack of manure.

It is therefore necessary that our meat supply be increased. Austria-Hungary is in a position to assist us materially in this respect. It cannot be denied that in many parts of Austria, and above all in Hungary, there is a much greater stock of cattle, especially of hogs, and that conditions there are far more favorable than in Germany. Austrian authorities have admitted this.

I therefore consider it essential that Austria-Hungary should relinquish its claims on any livestock, meat, and meat preserves received from the neutral countries and that it should turn over to Germany, from its own supplies, beef and pork to the extent of several millions of kilograms.

1.11 THE AUSTRIAN AMBASSADOR TO GERMANY ON THE FOOD SITUATION IN BERLIN, APRIL 20, 1917[14]

The previously announced change in the distribution of rations has now come into effect. The daily ration of flour was decreased from 200 grams to 170 grams [1 cup to 3/4 cup; about 4 slices of bread]. All supplementary allowances granted previously are abolished .... The quota of flour so far apportioned ... for men doing hard labor in the factories has been cut by 25 percent; children and adolescents will no longer receive additional rations. To make up for this severe retrenchment, the Government has at the same time doubled the weekly meat rations (250 to 500 grams) [8.8 to 17.6 ounces], the added 250 grams to be sold at an especially low price. Besides that, the weekly potato ration has been raised from 1750 to 2500 grams [3.85 to 5.5 pounds].

The population, anticipating the reduction in the bread rations, has shown noticeable agitation, spurred by fact that the yield of the last harvest was very satisfactory. It is argued that the present collapse must be attributed either to governmental mistakes or to the fact that the farmers are hoarding their products.

The public insists that there must be a culprit somewhere and that he must be punished. Different arguments are being advanced. In the cities and in the industrial districts the farmers are blamed. They are accused of having concealed their supplies and of having fed their cattle with breadstuffs .... The farmers themselves have, of course, a very different explanation to offer for the present crisis. A recent article in the *Deutsche Tageszeitung* is significant, as it demands the immediate cessation of all enforced measures regulating the work on the farms during the period of war on the ground that then only may agriculture reach its highest point of productivity.

The threatened general strike which was to have been called as a protest against the new bread-rationing was averted at the last moment by the appointment of delegates of the labor unions to assist in the distribution of the rations and by the written declaration of Dr. Michaelis, President of the War Grain Board that granted certain demands of the unions.

Scholars writing on the food situation generally agree that after the immediate food crisis had passed, conditions began to improve. The harvest of 1917 was better than expected. Although local shortages persisted, authorities had learned how to offset shortages in one food type with an increase in the ration for the other. However, local differences, as pointed out in Document 1.12, continued to cause concern among the laboring population.

1.12 MAJORITY SOCIAL DEMOCRAT HERMANN KRATZIG ON THE FOOD SHORTAGE, NOVEMBER 19, 1917[15]

Dr. Beckhaus, the District Commissioner in Bielefeld, has made the sensational announcement that the potato harvest must be regarded as a failure. The Berlin food authorities ought not to believe that there was a crop failure. They ought to assume for an absolute certainty that gigantic quantities of potatoes have been kept back to be utilized as fodder or to be sold illicitly at extortionate prices. No one need be surprised that the inhabitants of Berlin, thrown back on short rations, are furious when they hear of this sensational announcement. It practically amounts to denying the sun's presence in the sky at noon, if the attempt is made to suggest that we have had another failure of the potato crop this year, for the whole world knows that we have a magnificent crop.

Why don't the authorities immediately requisition the potato crop? Do they not realize that the people of Berlin, under-rationed as they are, have staked their last hope on getting an extra half-pound of potatoes a day? ... Do they have the least notion of the distress that exists among the people of Berlin? Have they the least notion of the effect that this announcement will produce on the spirit of the Berlin women working as laborers, artisans, and officials? It would be a crime against the nation not to exclaim, "Thus far and no farther!" It is high time that the food authorities stopped their official bungling.

We must immediately requisition the entire potato crop, and the immediate increase of the potato ration! The shameless farce that the profiteers have been playing for three years must be ended once for all.

The government had been able to maintain capacity, by squeezing its allies—shown in Document 1.10—and ruthlessly exploiting food resources in conquered nations, first in Romania and then in the Ukraine. In a desperate throw of the dice, the Supreme Command had requisitioned additional food so that the soldiers could be well fed and motivated for the great spring offensive of 1918 (Figure 1.2). By the spring, urban consumers were again feeling the pinch, as illustrated in Document 1.13.

FIGURE 1.2 *Dead horse butchered for food during December 1918 street fighting (Imperial War Museum).*

1.13 EDITORIAL IN *VORWÄRTS* ON THE DECREASE IN THE BREAD RATION, MAY 17, 1918[16]

The War Food Department officially announces:

The development of the grain importation from the Ukraine unfortunately does not permit our bread provisioning for the last months of the harvest year to be based upon this uncertain and not clearly determined source. Therefore, in order to be certain, we are chiefly dependent for the rest of the year upon the German domestic stocks. The small stores available for distribution require a cutting down of consumption. Accordingly, the daily flour ration ... will be reduced from 200 to 160 grams. A compensation will be granted by an increased ration of sugar; the distribution of victuals during the weeks of smaller bread rations will be increased.

With this publication the government announces a measure that cuts deep into the life of many millions. Potatoes and bread are the basic pillars of the war food economy. Both are distributed in such small portions that a further reduction is a serious danger. It is a more serious danger in the fourth war year than in the third or second, when the obtaining of substitute victuals was easier and the physical condition of the people was better. The physical and moral powers for the endurance of privations are considerably lower.

The War Food Department claims that the provision of food to the population has been more constant this war year than last, that the ration of 7 pounds of potatoes per head will extend until far into July, that large amounts of victuals were distributed, and that the shortage in fats was offset by distribution of great amounts of good marmalade or tolerable artificial honey. That is correct. But ... even the best marmalade is after all only a miserable substitute for fat, which in need might satisfy the palate but certainly cannot compete in nourishment with butter or lard.

It is shameful that the city population on Sundays has to beg potatoes in the country and drag them back to the city. It is nevertheless an absolute necessity. Sanity demands that these Sunday "hamsters" remain unmolested in so far as they cover only their own restricted needs.

Lastly, vigorous attention must be called to one thing. When bread prices mount, wages must not be reduced. From the most varied branches of industry complaints are coming in that the employers are systematically attempting to save on wages. The wages of the workers, which for a long time have been insufficient to secure a minimal existence, cannot be further lowered.

The Supreme Command's food gamble, like its offensive, failed. In preparation for the advance, the generals had positioned supply depots close to the front so that food could be more quickly distributed to the advancing troops. When the Allies began their own offensive, the German army lacked sufficient transport to remove most of their supplies while retreating, allowing them to fall into enemy hands. The situation in the urban centers, where people were already on short rations to support what was hoped to be the war winning push, had become dire indeed.

Conclusion

The *Reichstag* Subcommittee that later investigated the fraying of the *Burgfrieden* was correct in seeing the impact of the food crisis on the war effort. It replaced the consensus of "The Spirit of August 1914" with a virulent class conflict, intensified interest group competition, and spurred the military and its civilian allies into thinking that the solution to the country's nutritional crisis was the annexation of foreign territories and the expropriation of their resources.

Thought questions

1. Given the end result, would Germany's nutritional situation have been better if things were organized more fully or earlier?
2. Hermann Kratzig (Document 1.14) demands that the government confiscate the potato crop. Do you see this as an effective solution to the food crisis?
3. If you were confronted with the price data in Chart 1.2, how would you have changed your food consumption?
4. Based on the data in Chart 1.3, how effective were price controls and how did their impact vary by commodity?
5. What impression do you get from the location of food riots in 1916? Access http://www.dolchstosslegende.com/food-riots.html and view the map showing the location of the riots. Which parts of Germany were more prone to disturbances than others?

CHART 1.2 *Select food prices 1914–1915 in Berlin*

Product	Average price, December 1914	Average price, December 1915	Percent increase or decrease
Meat (M/lb.)			
Beef	1	1.5	+50
Pork	0.9	1.4	+56
Bacon	1.1	2.2	+100
Ham	1.7	3.0	+76
Veal	0.9	1.5	+50
Mutton	0.9	1.5	+67
Horse	0.9	1.6	+61.4
Grains (Pf/kg)			
White bread	61.2	67.6	+10.4
Wheat flour	46.1	51.6	+11.9
Rye flour	40.0	45.1	+12.7
Potatoes	9.7	8.5	−12.5
Fats (Pf/kg)			
Butter	305.6	495.6	+62.1
Lard	199.0	499.8	+151.1
Sugar	52.9	62.0	+17.2
Other			
Milk (Pf/lt)	21.4	27.5	+28.5
Eggs (Pf/egg)	13.1	20.7	+58.0

Source: Archibald C. Bell, *A History of the Blockade of Germany and the Countries Associated with Her in the Great War* (London: Her Majesty's Stationary Office, 1961), pp. 408–409.

CHART 1.3 *Impact of price controls calculated in shillings and pence per pound*

Product	November 1915		November 1916		Increase or decrease with controls	Increase since July 1914
	s.	d.	s.	d.	Percent	Percent
Rye bread	0	8.50	0	7.25	−14	21
Wheat	1	0.75	1	3	+16	49
Butter	2	3.25	2	4.75	+5	105
Lard	2	4.50	2	10.50	+20	315
Sugar	0	3.25	0	3.75	+14	36

Product	November 1915		November 1916		Increase or decrease with controls	Increase since July 1914
	s.	d.	s.	d.	Percent	Percent
Eggs/dozen	2	5.75	2	9.75	+52	357
Beef	1	2.50	2	0.75	+70	170
Mutton	1	4.50	2	5	+75	164
Veal	1	4.50	1	10.50	+36	106
Pork	1	3	1	8.75	+38	249

Source: Archibald C. Bell, *A History of the Blockade of Germany and the Countries Associated with Her in the Great War* (London: Her Majesty's Stationary Office, 1961), p. 570.

Further reading

Those wanting to know how individual Berliners (especially women) coped with the escalating food crisis and its political consequences should look at Belinda Davis, *Home Fires Burning: Food, Politics and Everyday Life in World War One Berlin* (Chapel Hill: University of North Carolina Press, 2000). George Yaney, *The World of the Manager: Food Administration in Berlin during World War I* (New York: Peter Lang, 1994), does an excellent job explaining how food was collected and distributed. The evidence he presents is an interesting corrective to the contemporary narrative of "price gouging" and "profiteering." Avner Offer, *The First World War: An Agrarian Interpretation* (Oxford: Oxford University Press, 1989), places the problem of war nutrition in a global perspective.

2

Blockade

Institutional context

For German nationalists, especially those living in the western third of the Empire, the High Seas Fleet was a source of national pride. Unlike the army, which was in fact a consolidation of pre-Unification federal state armies (see "Institutional context" in Chapter 5) led by a largely aristocratic officer corps, the navy was the one great imperial military institution. It enjoyed its own command (largely staffed by officers from bourgeois backgrounds) and a cabinet to advise the Kaiser on naval matters. Perhaps most importantly, it was supported by one of the most potent lobbying groups in the pre-war period—the Navy League—that had more than 3,000 local chapters that sponsored "learned" talks on naval matters and distributed pro-navy literature.[1]

For a variety of reasons, many of them linked to his personal vanity and unstable personality, Kaiser Wilhelm promoted a series of Navy Bills in the 1890s that resulted in an arms race with Great Britain, a nation that had hitherto acted in peaceful concord with a united Germany. The Anglo-German arms race soured this relationship and ultimately pushed Britain into an *entente* with its traditional enemies France and Russia.[2] When war did break out, the High Seas Fleet lacked the will and experience to challenge Britain for naval supremacy; after the indecisive Battle of Jutland, the fleet remained bottled up in its ports in Kiel and Wilhelmshaven for the duration of the war and morale within the ranks dwindled.

The one aspect of German naval operations that appeared to offer hope—submarine warfare—had a very checkered result. When the Allies declared a naval blockade of the Central Powers, cutting off the importation of both food and munitions, Germany responded with a blockade of the Allied powers enforced by its submarine fleet. The sinking of neutral and non-military shipping (among others the British-owned *Lusitania*) and the heated American response, forced the Germans to scale back unrestricted submarine warfare, much to the chagrin of those in the Supreme Command who demanded all-out total war. After the Hindenburg–Ludendorff duo assumed control of Germany's military effort, they forced the resignation of more moderate leaders such as Chancellor Theobold von Bethmann Hollweg and Foreign Minister Richard von Kühlmann and reinstituted unrestricted submarine warfare in 1917. The result was war with the United States and the circumvention of the German blockade through the convoy system.[3]

The Allied blockade of Germany

The German use of unrestricted submarine warfare was not without effect, although these were not what its promoters had planned. It created enormous ill will among the Allies and seemed to justify the British blockade as a tool of warfare. After the Collapse, the Allies were so convinced that their blockade had helped bring Germany to its knees that they continued it as a weapon in the diplomatic negotiations after the Armistice.

An American attempt to gauge the impact of the blockade

After the outbreak of war in August 1914, there was serious debate in British political and military circles as to how the war was to be conducted. One school of thought held that massed offensives against strongly prepared German defensive positions in Belgium and France was folly. Far better to strike at the German Achilles heel—their reliance on imports from the Western Hemisphere—as a means of weakening the fighting ability of the soldiers at the front and the strength of workers in war industries. When the United States entered the war in 1917, Americans quickly picked up this debate.

After the American declaration of war, the US Department of State continued to diligently collect information regarding the economic situation within Germany (particularly with regard to food supply) from a variety of sources. They gleaned information from the German press, but such reports were highly suspect. (From our reading of the German press, we noted that the local press tended to be accurate as to local circumstances, while the national press was worthless as a barometer of the true situation.) Consular officials in Norway, Denmark, the Netherlands, and Switzerland debriefed neutral businessmen who had traveled through Germany. Diplomats stationed in The Hague regularly sought information from Russian POWs and forced laborers who had escaped to Holland. All these sources were by nature impressionistic. The situation cried out for "trustworthy" personal confirmation.

Such confirmation was available from an interesting source: American citizens who left Germany after July 1917. The great majority of the approximately 1,200 American citizens resident in Germany left the country in the first three months after the declaration of war in April.[4] For a variety of reasons—often personal or familial—fifty holders of American passports left Germany between the middle of July and the beginning of December. This group of late leavers provided just the sort of "trustworthy" testimony on the situation within Germany that Washington was eager to obtain.

In mid-July, the US consul in Christiania (Oslo), Norway, developed a simple form that his deputies could use to collect information from the deportees. The consul was so proud of his work that he circulated it to US embassies in Copenhagen, The Hague, and Bern, who adopted it for their own use. It asked for the sources' name, occupation, and place of residence in Germany. The fourth and fifth questions sought to ascertain how long the source had lived in Germany and when he or she had left. Question number six was startling: how much weight did the respondent lose? The questionnaire goes on to inquire about scarcities, the labor situation, and the general health of the population. It then returned to the food question, asking the respondents about the weekly allowance of twelve food groups (plus soap) and how much each item cost. It then goes on to address a series of shortages (clothing, medicine, bandages). The respondents were asked if they saw any riots or heard any revolutionary talk. The first pages ended with two questions about the domestic transportation network. The second page began with a series of questions about the political/military situation. Only then did the questionnaire get down to a series of very specific questions of interest to military intelligence. A space remained blank on the bottom of the second page so that the interrogator could record his remarks as to the truthfulness or reliability of the witness.

Fifty such questionnaires have survived, providing an alternative analysis of the food situation in Germany in 1917, and by extension the efficacy of the Allied blockade. Document 2.1 presents some of the responses.

2.1 AMERICAN CONSULAR REPORTS ON FOOD SITUATION IN GERMANY[5]

Anne Ingold ... arrived here [Copenhagen] from Germany on July 2. She is a student of music in Berlin living in small apartment and is a woman of much intelligence. In order to obtain food it was necessary to go out among the poorer people. In the fall and winter there was practically nothing to eat except the very coarsest bread and not more than 2 potatoes a week. In April the conditions were so bad that the food strike for increased rations took place. However on June 1st there was no difficulty in buying all the meat wanted and some small quantity of vegetable but no butter, milk, cream or fats of any kind. People are complaining openly of the government and demanding more food. [Report taken July 23, 1917.]

Christoph Lang formerly weighed 175 pounds but he has lost between 50 and 60 pounds. Appearing very emaciated with an extremely bad color as if he had no red blood in his body. [Report taken July 31, 1917.]

Olga Epstein, art student, 4 years in Munich and Berlin, lost 15 pounds. "I lived in a pension where the proprietor's son was connected with the army supply department. The pension often had eggs, meat and other rationed food, which had been obtained by smuggling." [Report taken August 27, 1917.]

Ludwig Lasker, cigar salesman, 3½ years in Berlin. Lost 29 pounds. "I lived in a hotel since September 1916. I never got enough to eat. I never got eggs—only 250 grams of meat a week. The bread is horrible and has not improved since this year's harvest." [Report taken September 3, 1917.]

Helen Gilson Cooper, wife of dentist in Frankfurt for 20 years, lost no weight, "but it cost a lot to keep it." [Report taken September 4, 1917.]

Charles G. Hartley, dentist in Berlin for 11 years, lost no weight. "I had a housekeeper and did not pay much attention to the various [ration] cards. I was frequently able to get extra butter, eggs, etc., from the country and did not suffer from the food shortage." [Report taken September 6, 1917.]

Henry Liebermann, wholesale kid glove business in Berlin for 1 year and 2 months, lost 20 pounds. Claims that people are not so sick now as in peacetime. [Report taken September 12, 1917.]

August Henning, accountant for American Radiator Co. in Berlin for 1½ years, lost no weight, "through paying higher prices ... was able to get enough food." [Report taken September 22, 1917.]

Arthur Eberlein, patent medicine salesman in Frankfurt for 14 years, lost no weight. "I managed to procure enough food through connections and acquaintances and owing to that fact was able to pay any price asked." [Report taken September 28, 1917.]

Mrs Sophie Siemer, in Hamburg eight years, lost 46 pounds. "Everyone is thinner, but doctors claim that statistics show better health. Absolutely everyone, however, has an anxious worried look .... I think real old people suffer. More is being done for the children .... Everything is short but for money everything can be had. However one suffers from the want of fat." [Report taken October 8, 1917.]

Alice Luce, president of a girls' school in Berlin, lost no weight. "I lived in a flat and suffered little inconvenience from the food situation. Friends in the country sent me butter, eggs and meat. I also took meals in the 'war charity' restaurants where the food was remarkably good and cheap." [Report taken October 17, 1917.]

Agnes Kennedy, visitor in Dresden for 3 years, lost 25/30 pounds. "I lived in a pension ... where the food was plentiful—only shortages were bread, fats and sugar. Could always buy Danish milk in bottles—or Dutch condensed milk." [Report taken October 17, 1917.]

Oscar Nagel, U.S. citizen. "I know of and have seen but very few people, that is men in particular, who in the past two years have not lost 20–30 or even 50 pounds in weight. That is of the population in the cities. The country people have up to now been much better off, but since the summer restrictions have been increased and enforced that in the country district the people began to feel the lack of food also most decidedly." [Report taken October 31, 1917.]

Mrs. Nathalie Martin, widowed, lived in Berlin ½ year. "She claimed to have gained 50 pounds. She is notorious as the mistress of the Duke of Mecklenburg, who followed her here [to Copenhagen] when she left Germany." [Report taken December 4, 1917.]

The last report in the file (made on January 4, 1918) was from William Kent, US Consul in Bern. He recounted a conversation with a female acquaintance that had formerly living in Leipzig. "She had," he wrote, "for many months vainly attempted to secure permission to leave the country. I was shocked at her appearance." Although she was a woman of some means and accustomed to living in comfort, "her privations had been so great that she had lost 70 pounds of flesh through her inability to secure food, and her general appearance was that of one emaciated, ill, and broken spirited."

The largest number of respondents (eight) classified themselves as visitors—some in the homes of family members but others as long-term tourists. The second largest group of respondents (seven) classified themselves as housewives. Several of these had remained behind after their husbands had already left in order to tidy up their family's affairs. Dentists make up the third largest contingent of Americans leaving between July and December, followed by students, salespeople, and businessmen. The remaining number included the principal of a girls' school and a nurse.

The length of time all had spent in Germany varied. An equal number (eleven respondents or 12 percent of the total) had been in the country less than a year or from one to three years. The vast majority (33 persons or 66 percent) had been in Germany since before August 1914. The largest number of the respondents—23 or nearly one-half—lived in Berlin. Five lived in Dresden, four in Hamburg, and three each in Frankfurt and Munich. The rest were scattered around the country.

The amount of weight respondents lost presents a most interesting picture. Fully 70 percent of the respondents reported that they had lost weight. Of those who reported a weight loss, 61 percent lost 20 pounds

FIGURE 2.1 *Comparison of daily meal before (the front row) and during Great War (the rear row) (Imperial War Museum).*

or more. Forty-eight percent of all respondents were in this heavy loss category. Thirteen respondents—or 26 percent—reported that they had lost no weight, while two claimed to have actually gained.

Three important points emerge from an analysis of the State Department data: (1) individuals depended upon complex webs of personal or business relationships and social status; (2) official rations only provided approximately two-thirds of the needed nutrition, forcing most people onto the black market; (3) people in the large cities suffered more than those in smaller towns.

Recognizing the impact of the blockade after the war

Whatever role the blockade played in bringing Imperial Germany to its knees, Germans saw its continuation after the Armistice as an inhuman act of aggression and vindictiveness. Although the Supreme Command and those civilian officials compliant with its wishes during the war denied that the blockade impaired the country's ability to continue the war, after November 11 the new government changed tunes.[6] Officially sanctioned conferences were held and papers were published arguing that the blockade had a profound impact on public health. Documents 2.2 and 2.3 come from one such conference held in January 1919.

2.2 CONFERENCE REPORT OF GERMAN DOCTORS ON THE HEALTH EFFECTS OF THE BLOCKADE[7]

In a confidential inquiry started in 1917 by the Imperial Health Office on the condition of health in Germany, it received a report from an old folks home that laconically read, "Inmates have all died." The Entente may with due satisfaction take notice thereof, this being only a small particle of the result produced by the blockade imposed upon us with the avowed purpose not only of cutting off supplies for the army but of inflicting bodily harm on Germany's civilian population: women, children, old people, and all those unfit for military service. It is today possible to give our enemies a receipt for the grand total: 763,000 persons belonging to the civilian population in Germany have succumbed to the effects of the hunger blockade. The terrifying number of victims requires no comment.

This figure is irrefutable .... Whoever was in Germany through the years of 1914–1918 knows how much he missed and is still missing eggs, milk, butter, meat, bread, and potatoes .... For instance, it is impossible to maintain one's power of resistance in the long run with one-third of the accustomed fare; this decrease in resistance to diseases entails an acceleration and aggravation of certain complaints. The poor fodder for cattle is bound to reduce the amount of milk for babies, while without fat and albumen there is no possibility of bringing up children without grave harm to them. Further, as the livestock is used up and average slaughtered weight declines, meat rations are bound to become ever smaller; and if hospitals can no longer be granted any extra allowances of milk, biscuits, dough materials, butter, and the like, an adequate and competent feeding of patients entrusted to their care, let alone the strengthening so necessary after severe illness, is no longer be possible.

2.3 A STATISTICAL ANALYSIS OF INCREASED MORTALITY CAUSED BY THE BLOCKADE[8]

In order to ascertain the number of victims of the blockade, the cases of death in the civilian population during the war was compared with the cases of death in the last year of peace 1913. According to my statistical analysis, there was no significant increase in the death rate in 1914. Even in the years 1915 and 1916 the increase of mortality—9 percent and 14 percent, respectively—is not yet excessive. In the two subsequent years, however, the grave harm done by the blockade made itself felt. In 1917, there was an excess in the mortality of the civilian population amounting to about 32 percent, and in 1918 an excess of 37 percent, as compared with 1913. According to careful calculation, the blockade caused 260,000 excess deaths in 1917 and 294,000 excess deaths in 1918. This calculation excludes the cases of death produced by the influenza epidemic.

Among children and young women, the number of victims of underfeeding was very high. A classification of deaths according to ages for the year 1917 shows that at the ages of 1–5 years there was a surplus of about one-half, at the ages of 5–15 years a surplus of 55 percent as compared with deaths in the year of peace 1913, while with women between 15 and 30 years of age there was an increase of deaths amounting to about 45 percent. In 1917 alone, upwards of 50,000 children between 1 and 15 years of age and 15,000 girls and women between 15 and 30 years of age died as a result of the blockade. Regarding men and women over 60 years of age, the blockade in 1917 led to premature death in about 127,000 cases!

Conclusion

Germany was clearly not able to sustain its own population from the food that it could produce itself. Any policy that the government adopted to ameliorate the situation raised new problems. Rising wages in factories producing for the military acted as a magnet drawing men and women from the countryside. Soldiers might be furloughed from the front at planting and harvesting time, but that lowered the number of men available to generals to conduct operations. Prioritizing the use of cereals for bread production lowered meat production, a source of enormous discontent. Lack of fats hurt young people and drained the energy of workers. Allowing market forces to do the rationing (raising prices) was deeply unpopular and contrary to the sense of solidarity that the government needed to promote to sustain the war effort. The shortage of other consumer goods severely restricted by the blockade—fruits, coffee, and tobacco—added to a sense of malaise and deprivation.

The fact that the blockade was not lifted at the Armistice added to the generalized sense of betrayal that motivated Stab-in-the-Back thinking. More immediately, it impacted the actions of the new provisional government, the Council of People's Deputies. William Carl Mathews has argued that Gustav Noske's controversial actions to put down revolutionary unrest and reestablish order in alliance with volunteer forces provided by the military was predicated on the unfolding nutritional crisis.[9]

CHART 2.1 *Weight change for Americans leaving Germany, April 1917–January 1918*

Pounds gained or lost	Number of persons $N = 68$
Gained	2
Remained same	13
Lost	
1–9	5
10–19	6
20–29	12
30–39	4
40–49	2
50–59	3
60–69	2
70–79	1

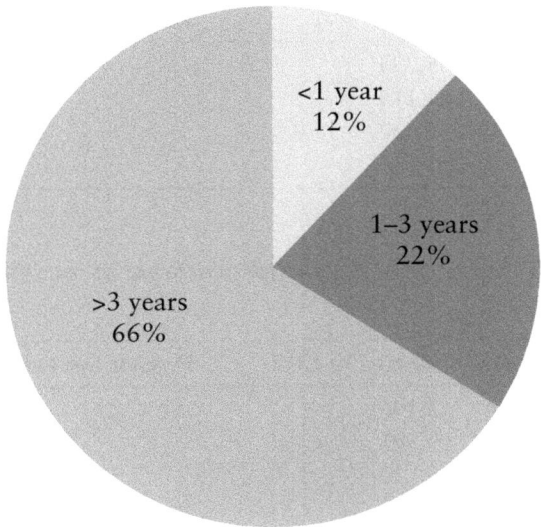

CHART 2.2 *Length of stay of Americans leaving Germany, April 1917–January 1918*

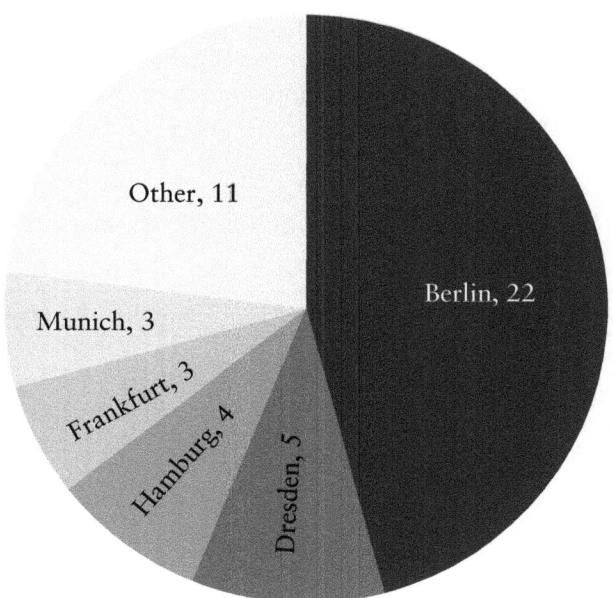

CHART 2.3 *Former residence of Americans leaving Germany, April 1917–January 1918*

CHART 2.4 *Number of deaths attributable to the blockade*

Year	Deaths	Percent increase over 1913 rate
1915	88,235	9.5
1916	121,114	14.3
1917	259,627	32.2
1918	293,760	37.0

CHART 2.5 *Number of deaths attributable to the blockade by age cohort, 1917*

Age	Number of deaths in 1917	Percent increase over 1913 rate
0–1	3,506	2.4
1–5	30,591	49.3
5–15	19,920	55.0
15–48	12,856	42.2
48–60	19,720	29.2
60–70	22,890	35.2

Thought questions

1 How did the experience of Americans in wartime Germany show that the ability to stay properly nourished depended upon access and money?
2 How might unequal access to food have heightened class and regional antagonisms among Germans?
3 Why might military leaders such as Ludendorff, who had promoted unrestricted submarine warfare, have been loath to recognize the impact of the blockade?
4 Looking at Chart 2.4, what conclusions might you draw about the growing weakness of the German population as the war progressed?
5 According to the data in Chart 2.5, which age cohorts suffered most from the malnutrition and which the least? Why do you think these age distinctions exist?
6 Note that Document 2.2 asserts that 260,000 persons died in 1917 as a result of the blockade while the analysis in Document 2.3 puts the figure of "excess deaths" at 127,000. How might you explain this discrepancy?

Further reading

Students seeking primary documents on the blockade have two excellent sources: Suda Lorena Bane and Ralph Haswell Lutz, eds, *The Blockade of Germany after the Armistice, 1918–1919; Selected Documents of the Supreme Economic Council, Superior Blockade Council, American Relief Administration, and Other Wartime Organizations* (Stanford: Stanford University Press, 1942) and Archibald C. Bell, *A History of the Blockade of Germany and the Countries Associated with Her in the Great War* (London: Her Majesty's Stationary Office, 1961). The Bell study was commissioned immediately after the Great War but the study report was not released until the later date.

The most recent monograph on the blockade is Eric W. Osborne, *Britain's Economic Blockade of Germany, 1914–1919* (New York: Frank Cass, 2004), but C. Paul Vincent, *The Politics of Hunger. The Allied Blockade of Germany, 1915–1919* (Athens: Ohio University Press, 1985) is still worth consulting. Using height and other body measurements, Mary Elisabeth Cox, "Hunger Games: Or How the Allied Blockade in the First World War Deprived German Children of Nutrition, and Allied Food Aid Subsequently Saved Them," *The Economic History Review*, 68, no. 2 (2015), pp. 600–631, has been able to show the profound impact malnourishment had on German children.

3

The Labor Question

FIGURE 3.1 *Wilhelm Groener (Bundesarchiv Bildarchiv)*.

Institutional context

German trade unions were closely linked to political parties. The dominant union federation was the Social Democratic General Confederation of Free Unions (*freie Gewerkshaften*). Although guided by a Marxist belief in class conflict, most of its officials were practical men committed to building up their unions and sustaining their members. The second largest union federation (the General Association of Christian Trade Unions) was affiliated with the Center, the political party of Catholics that grew out of Bismarck's assault on the autonomy of the Catholic Church in the 1870s (the *Kulturkampf*). While the Marxists of free unions based their actions on an ideology of class conflict, the Christian unions were grounded in Catholic social thought that promoted social solidarity and the harmonization of interests for the common good. Given Imperial Germany's sharp confessional cleavages, the free unions predominated in Protestant areas, while the Christian unions were strongest in Catholic majority areas. Given their ideology, Christian unions were loath to strike at any time and had promised not to do so during the war; the free unions agreed.

In the burgeoning war industries, which drew workers from the entire *Reich*, it was not unusual then to have multiple unions in the same enterprise. Despite their resolve, strikes did occur. The decision to strike was a negotiated affair. When strike committees were formed to enforce discipline and negotiate with management, these were frequently composed of an alliance of Socialist and Catholic groups.

Political context

The Socialist Workers' Party of Germany (which took the name Social Democratic Party in 1890) was founded in 1875 out to the merger of two earlier socialist groups. At its Erfurt Congress in 1891, the party aligned itself with Marxist ideology. Its first representatives in the *Reichstag* were August Bebel and Wilhelm Liebknecht. During the years of Bismarck's repressive anti-Socialist laws, the party developed a strong cell structure and active press. By 1912, it was the very model of a modern mass party, with regional and local chapters, a central newspaper—*Vorwärts*—a party school, and a cadre of party-paid functionaries. It also sponsored its own trade union organization, which acted as training and recruiting ground for the party leadership.

As it grew, different tendencies emerged within the party. There were the "intellectuals" at the party school and publications, the "ditch diggers" (*Kanalarbeiter*) who worked in the party's apparatus and there were union functionaries. Coincident with this, ideological tendencies developed ranging from revolutionaries who favored mass action to revisionists who thought socialism could come at the ballot box, with practical union representatives frequently holding a middle ground. The venerable August Bebel served as a unifying figure between the two wings of the party. With his death in 1913, Friedrich Ebert and Hugo Haase, representing the two wings of the party, were elected party leaders.

The party survived Bismarck's persecution and later harassment through a rigidly enforced culture of unity. Although there was a tradition of lively debate within the party, once a decision was made, all members were expected to comply. This was particularly true of the party caucus in the *Reichstag*. The party was opposed to imperialist war and in July 1914 organized rallies against the possibility of war; one demonstration in Berlin is estimated to have drawn 100,000 people. When events unfolded in such a way that it seemed that Germany had been attacked and was fighting a defensive war, attitudes within the *Reichstag* caucus swung in favor of war. When the government requested war credits, the party caucus debated the issue and the majority voted in favor. The minority accepted party discipline and voted with the majority. The war thus received unanimous support from the deputies and parties of the *Reichstag*.

United Social Democratic support for the war lasted less than fourteen months. In December 1915, some of the members of the caucus decided that they could not longer submit to discipline and voted against renewed war credits. These dissidents were expelled from the party in March 1916 and ultimately founded the Independent Social Democratic Party in April 1917, with Hugo Haase as its leader. The Spartacus League, founded the previous year by former SPD radicals Rosa Luxemburg and Karl Liebknecht (son of party cofounder Wilhelm), was accepted into the new party as an independent group. Although differing on strategies, both Spartacists and Independents supported the strike movement that broke out in the summer of 1917.

Deteriorating conditions

Germany's leaders had entered the war with the assumption that the military would triumph in short order. If the "short-war illusion," as scholars refer to it, had implications for Germany's ability to feed itself, it had an even stronger impact on the country's ability to produce the tools of war. When the mobilization order was issued, men were called up without regard for the essential work that they did in the war industries. This led to a critical shortage of skilled labor in factories and mines. After the front was stabilized in October 1914 and stalemate set in, those essential personnel who survived the offensive were recalled to their pre-war positions and the ranks in the army were filled out with a wave of young recruits not skilled in factory tasks.

Once hope for a swift victory faded, divisions began to emerge within the workers in the weapons and munitions factories. Social Democratic union functionaries, following the party line, supported the *Burgfrieden* and attempted to tamp down nascent shop-floor discontent. In the course of 1916, a group of anti-war radical socialists, taking the name of Revolutionary Shop Stewards (*revolutionäre Obleute*), was formed outside the union hierarchy. They staged their first strike in the summer of 1916 to protest the imprisonment of Spartacist leader Karl Liebknecht. This so-called "Liebknecht Strike" was limited to Greater Berlin and a few factories in Saxony. It was a political rather than an economic strike but it fed off the same popular discontent that had fueled the much more widespread and significant bread riots. The Majority Social Democratic Party (the Social Democrats who did not leave to join the Independents) and its affiliated labor union confederation (as well as the Catholic unions) were opposed to the strikes, as illustrated in Document 3.1.

3.1 STATEMENT OF THE MAJORITY SOCIAL DEMOCRATIC PARTY AND THE TRADE UNIONS ON "LIEBKNECHT" STRIKES, JULY 26, 1916[1]

Workers! The prolonged war weighs heavily on all nations and entails great sacrifices. It severely tests the endurance of those at home and at the front, and it is natural that ill feeling and discontent should develop. Irresponsible individuals who wish to mislead labor into resorting to measures that will make matters worse rather than better are unfortunately abusing this situation.

Anonymous leaflets that have been circulating for several months among members of the party and the trade unions, to sow hatred and distrust against the representatives ... chosen by the workmen themselves. We consider it our duty to warn workers about the machinations of the apostles of protest and a general strike, working in darkness and anonymity. The organization of wage protests and strikes rests with the competent union committees. They are doing everything to promote the reasoned demands of their members.

Just now, when our brothers in uniform at the front must withstand a mighty onslaught by the armies of our enemies and must make indescribable sacrifices (when just before the harvest, the food supply is most restricted), any thoughtless action may be fatal and harm the interests of workers ....

Our most important task is to hasten the coming of peace. The competent organizations in the labor movement are conscious of this great duty and are working untiringly to fulfill it. Workers remain loyal to your organizations and repulse all attempts to divide them!

With the support of the trade union leadership and the Majority Social Democratic Party—and promises of internal reform—the government succeeded in breaking these strikes.

FIGURE 3.2 *Volunteer strike breakers (Imperial War Museum).*

A second, and more far-reaching, set of strikes broke out in mid-April 1917. An official statement on these strikes by the Majority Social Democratic Party (Document 3.2) combines an understanding of the grievances striking workers felt with a warning toward the government that it would have to make good on its promises of reform.

3.2 *VORWÄRTS* ON THE SUMMER 1917 STRIKES, APRIL 17, 1917²

It has been known for some weeks that a comprehensive strike was planned for 16 April in Greater Berlin, the same day when the reduction of the bread ration, was to take effect. The workers, by staying away from their factories, wished to express their opposition to the new measures .... But this is not the sole problem that led to the strike. Undoubtedly the great world events of the last weeks had made a very strong impression upon the people of Greater Berlin. The great majority believes that the announced reforms of the way Germany is governed must not be postponed. The Easter Decree [in which the Emperor promised reforms

> after the war], undoubtedly, has exerted a calming effect, but doubt and uneasiness for the future cannot be allayed. The Constitutional Committee appointed by the *Reichstag* [to draw up the reforms promised in the Easter Decree] is an unknown entity. Based on experience, we have limited hope it will produce the promised reforms. As a third, and undoubtedly decisive factor, was the profound desire for peace .... Everybody should understand yesterday's strikes as the result of these motives .... Yesterday did not do any harm to the nation. It should, however, be considered a warning for both sides.

After the strike, many of the Shop Stewards (including their leader Richard Müller) were drafted into the army. The government, however, did not rely solely on coercion. The shortage of skilled hands combined with the need to drastically ramp up production had resulted in a permanent labor shortage in war critical industries. This dire situation was exacerbated as employers competed to attract the necessary skilled labor through offering higher wages and more attractive working conditions such as a forty-hour week.

The problems of worker discontent and supplying the army was already on the agenda when the strikes broke out. When Paul von Hindenburg and Erich Ludendorff took over the Supreme Command in 1916, their supporters instituted a far-reaching economic mobilization (the so-called Hindenburg Plan) that included a reorganization of industrial production. Reams of new regulations were issued and new boards were created. To their delight, unions were given a seat at the table, input into work rules and the responsibility for assisting in worker compliance. This was the Auxiliary Service Law (*Hilfsdienstgesetz*) at the center of Documents 3.3, 3.4, and 3.5.

A non-Prussian general, Wilhelm Groener, was assigned the important task of making the Auxiliary Service Law work. Groener was the son of a non-commissioned officer in the Württemberg army. He enlisted at age 17 and between 1893 and 1896 attended the War Academy. In 1898, his extraordinary logistical talents were recognized with an appointment to the General Staff, where he was assigned to the railway section, a vital center in the preparation and execution of the Schlieffen Plan. Groener's role in the efficient delivery of men and material to the front during the 1914 offensive was recognized by promotion to Major General. In May 1916, he became part of the leadership staff of the newly created War Food Ministry and in November 1916, was named deputy (Prussian) Minister of War. Although this is our first acquaintance with Wilhelm Groener, he will remain a central actor in this story to the end.

3.3 GROENER'S STATEMENT IN THE *REICHSTAG* ON THE MUNITIONS WORKERS STRIKE, APRIL 27, 1917[3]

I am glad that the last speaker [a Majority Social Democrat] condemned the strike, but he might have gone farther. Not only are long strikes bad. Every strike is bad, even if it lasts only three hours. We must use all means to increase our production, and so long as a worker has the least strength it is his moral duty to put it at the disposal of the Fatherland.

What then was the cause of last week's strike? With the long and hard winter behind us, I understand very well the depression felt by the workers and the anxiety caused by the sudden reduction of the bread ration. It was a very regrettable coincidence that at the very moment when workingmen could breathe again this measure had to be introduced.

But if we demand of the workers that they stay at work and that they utterly renounce strikes until the end of the war ... we must give them avenues through whom they can make known their wishes at the right time, in the right way, and in the right quarters. What are these avenues? I long ago advised the government to introduce representatives of the workers' organizations into the provincial and local organization of food supplies, in order that they may themselves cooperate and see how things stand, and in this way be able to restrain their comrades. I hope that this advice will be accepted to the fullest extent .... This is not, as some may present it, a political measure, a socializing of food policy. It is nothing less than an immensely practical measure of the sort we need in the present situation for the conduct of the war.

That is one avenue. Now for the second. We have the Auxiliary Service Law. This gives the workers definite rights, rights that the *Reichstag* has granted, and through this mechanism all complaints and questions of pay must be directed. Just as I have proceeded against the fomenters of strikes, I shall proceed with the same vigor against those who seek to restrict the rights that the workers have gained through the Auxiliary Service Law. For on this point there can be absolutely no doubt .... I direct an earnest but final appeal to the workers to content themselves with the rights conceded to them, and to co-operate unremittingly and loyally in carrying out the Auxiliary Service Law .... I have no doubt that our workers will stand loyally behind the army and deliver the arms and munitions that we urgently need. For this reason our motto must be, "Work, and again work, until the successful ending of the war."

3.4 GROENER'S PROCLAMATION TO THE MUNITIONS WORKERS, APRIL 27, 1917[4]

To The Munitions Workers!
In the West, near Arras, on the Aisne, and in Champagne, our brothers in field grey are engaged in the greatest and bloodiest battle in the history of the world. Our army needs arms and munitions. Have you not read Marshal von Hindenburg's letter? Whoever strikes at home instead of working takes upon himself unpardonable guilt. Our soldiers must bleed for your faults. Who dares defy Marshal von Hindenburg's call? He is a scoundrel who strikes as long as our armies face the enemy.

Read and re-read Marshal von Hindenburg's letter again and again! You will recognize where our worst enemies are. Not out there near Arras, on the Aisne, in Champagne—with them your soldier sons and brothers will settle accounts—not in London—with them our sailors on the U-boats will thoroughly settle accounts.

Our worst enemies are in our midst. They are the faint hearted and those who promote strikes. These people must be branded before the whole nation as traitors to the Fatherland and the army. Whoever listens to their words is a coward. Read in the Imperial Penal Code what paragraph 89 says about high treason. Who dares to refuse work when Marshal von Hindenburg demands it? Hindenburg's letter and this manifesto are to be posted in all munitions works in such a way that all workers may daily have them before their eyes as a permanent encouragement to overcome cowardice and to perform their duty toward our beloved German Fatherland. We are not far from the goal. The existence of our people is at stake. Good luck at your work!

3.5 LETTER FROM THE TRADE UNION LEADERSHIP TO GROENER, APRIL 27, 1917[5]

As the representatives of German workers' organizations, we declare our full agreement with the major arguments of Hindenburg's statement to the workers. Strikes at the present time must be avoided. The preservation and security of the Empire take priority. After all the pronouncements of the enemies, no intelligent person can doubt that only an increase of Germany's power of resistance that can bring us an early peace ....

> For a year past, England and France, supported by the United States of America, have piled up vast masses of shells and munitions on the French front to fire on our countrymen who are fighting there. Only a man without heart or conscience can refuse them the necessary means of defense.
>
> Workers represented by our organizations—we are absolutely convinced—share these views. For our part, we will do everything to strengthen them. Irresponsible people have attempted, fortunately with little success, to use strikes to serve political ends. The desire for a rapid ending of this bloody struggle of the nations is strong in the German people no less than in other belligerent countries; it is naturally explicable and intelligible. The desire to find a means for ending the war influences the working population, too. It is regrettable that some groups, however unimportant, try to accomplish this by refusing to produce the arms necessary for national defense.

Although he was successful in working with the unions to minimize strikes, Groener ultimately suffered a falling-out with the highly strung and dictatorial Erich Ludendorff and was exiled to the Eastern Front. He would reemerge in October 1918 as Ludendorff's replacement as Quartermaster-General and leading deputy to Hindenburg.

Conclusion

The conduct of modern warfare necessitates the full mobilization of the economy and the careful coordination of scarce resources. It is an intense, intricate business and requires the balancing of a multitude of competing interests, both between army and industry and competing interests therein. Reality-based efficiency experts such as Wilhelm Groener realized that the bluster preferred by the Ludendorff types was totally ineffectual and counter-productive. Through the Auxiliary Service Law and programs of its type, the government and military figures such as Groener promoted social harmony and the prospect of reform as a means of increasing productivity and ensuring labor peace. Despite mounting casualty lists and increasing material want, they were by and large successful.

Thought questions

1 In Document 3.4 paragraph 4, Wilhelm Groener expresses one of the main themes of the Stab-in-the-Back Myth—that Germany's greatest enemy is not its enemy in the field but treason at home. What actions is he describing as treasonous?

2 Notice Groener's injunction of Hindenburg as he chastises the strikers and tries to motivate the workers. What does this say about the Field Marshal's prestige? Is it interesting that the Emperor was not invoked?
3 Do you find it interesting that Groener assumes that a working class audience will be moved by Hindenburg's words?
4 The established unions and the workers that they represented supported the war effort and benefitted from working with the government. What sort of problems did this relationship present?

Further reading

The classic work on the issues discussed in this chapter is Gerald Feldman, *Army, Industry, and Labor in Germany, 1914–1918* (Princeton, NJ: Princeton University Press, 1966). One comes away from Feldman's work appalled by the bureaucratic chaos that existed (quite contrary to Anglo-American stereotypes of German efficiency) and amazed by the creativity of military planners in laying the foundation of "war socialism."

4

The January Strikes

Institutional context

Under Prussian law, the kingdom was divided into twenty-four military districts. Each was the province of a Deputy Commanding General, responsible for maintaining order. In extreme cases, the DCG could suspend newspapers, forbid public meetings, and declare martial law. As this system was in place long before the evolution of the various food boards, changed circumstances of the Hindenburg Program, and the Auxiliary Service Law, there was inevitable conflict between these generals and the leaders of the other responsible bodies. There was also minimal coordination. Some generals acted as little potentates (as was the case in Berlin); others worked well with the civilian authorities.

Historical significance

For the post-war propagators of the Stab-in-the-Back Myth, the strikes of January 1918 were tremendously important. This narrative ignores the bread riots of 1916, the strikes of the summer of 1917, and the naval mutinies that took place in Kiel and the North Sea ports. Why was this? Strikes during wartime, especially in vital support sectors, are bound to be controversial. The wildcat strikes conducted by workers in the arms industry in April 1917 and January 1918—complicated as they were with political issues and the split within the Social Democratic movement—were bound to be even more contentious. Was it appropriate for a socialist party and union leadership to *support* war and *oppose* striking workers? It was simply too much for ideologically committed Marxists to swallow; they cried betrayal of the working class. For many within the civilian government and the military, the strikes were nothing less than treason. The result was a confluence of interest on both the Left and the Right to highlight the strikes as a defining moment in the internal collapse of Imperial Germany.

Personal context

Friedrich Ebert was born in Heidelberg in 1871 to a modest tailor and his wife. He trained as a saddle maker and, as a traveling journeyman, was introduced to Social Democracy. What drew Ebert to the movement was less ideology (through his entire career he was not moved by ideological arguments) than the opportunity for practical work. He ultimately settled in Bremen, took an editorial job at a socialist newspaper (the *Bremer Bürgerzeitung*), and became a full-time party functionary in 1900. His success in hosting the Bremen party congress in 1904, his reputation as a non-ideological moderate, and his class origins, led to his elevation to party Secretary General the following year. He was elected to the *Reichstag* in 1912, and was elected co-chair of the party when August Bebel died in 1913.

Ebert was a staunch supporter of the war effort. Two of his sons died in the war; a third son, although severely wounded, returned to his unit after convalescence rather than accept a desk job. Ebert's support for the *Burgfrieden*, however, came at a price: the promise of domestic reforms. In the disintegration that followed the failure of the 1918 offensive, Ebert became more assertive in his demands for a full parliamentarization of the government.

FIGURE 4.1 *Frederich Ebert. Bundesarchiv Bildarchiv.*

Like Friedrich Ebert, Philipp Scheidemann was born into an artisanal family (his father was an upholsterer) and trained in a traditional craft (in his case, a typesetter).[1] He became a Social Democrat during his years traveling as an apprentice. While working in Marburg, he attended lectures at the university. In 1895, Scheidemann left typesetting and became an editorial assistant in a succession of socialist newspapers. Ultimately, he was appointed editor of the Social Democratic newspaper of his hometown, Kassel. He was first elected to the *Reichstag* in 1903 and in 1911 was made a member of the party's executive committee. After the Social Democrats emerged as the largest party in the election of 1912, he was named vice-president of the *Reichstag*, a largely honorific post that reflected the respect with which he was held within his party and across party lines. It was also a groundbreaking moment, as it was the first time that a Social Democrat held such a high public position. Scheidemann was a frequent spokesman for the SPD in parliament, where his humorous and refined style served to convey sharp points that a more fiery speaker could not have made. Like Ebert, Scheidemann was a party moderate with feet in multiple party constituencies. More popular than Ebert, he tried to reconcile the wings of the party before and during the schism of 1916. When the anti-war left created the Independent Social Democratic Party, Scheidemann was named co-chair of the Majority Social Democrats who followed Ebert's line.

FIGURE 4.2 *Philipp Scheidemann. Bundesarchiv Bildarchiv.*

The strike in Berlin

In the last week of January 1918, strikes broke out in the major industrial centers of Germany. While these were partially political and organized by the Independent Social Democrats, the Spartacist League and the Revolutionary Shop Stewards around political issues, they also reflected real shop-floor concerns with living and work conditions. Because of the heavy hand of military censorship—even *Vorwärts* was shut down although it opposed the strike—news of the strike is impossible to follow in the German press. In a similar vein, official government documents, released after the war to the Subcommittee investigating the collapse, were fragmented and problematic. Although newspapers in the Allied countries were surely biased to uncover the worst, in many ways they pieced together a convincing narrative. Documents 4.1–4.7 provide the story of the January Strike as it appeared to outside observers.

4.1 "MOBS, CRYING FOR PEACE, RIOT 2 DAYS IN BERLIN," JANUARY 26, 1918[2]

Severe rioting on Wednesday [1/23] and Thursday [1/24] in Berlin was reported in dispatches received [in Amsterdam] today. One report asserted that mobs were marching in the streets demanding peace. It is regarded as of great influence that the Thursday newspapers had not arrived today from Berlin as usual.

4.2 GOVERNMENT STATEMENT ON THE STRIKE, JANUARY 29, 1918[3]

In Berlin and in some other places in the Empire, workers have seized the present moment to attempt to bring political pressure on the government through a cessation of work. A committee formed by the strikers has put forward demands that, among other things, are concerned with domestic policy. To the extent that the strikes are an expression of doubt about the determination of the Government to follow through on promised domestic reforms, they are wrong.

Concerning the peace negotiations at Brest-Litovsk, likewise touched upon in the demands, it would seem that the workmen on strike do not clearly perceive that their behavior must lead to the opposite of that which they wish to obtain. Instead of assisting the peace negotiations, they impede their progress by supporting our enemies in the claims that they are making upon our negotiators. The government is negotiating in Brest-Litovsk to secure a peace that protects the vital interests of Germany. The government expects that the workers on strike, upon calm reflection, will realize the harm wrought by their behavior and return to their work. This is their sacred duty toward the Fatherland.

We are still in the midst of a hard struggle. Everyone at home who stops or neglects his work commits a sin against our brothers in the field, who with their blood and endurance are driving off the foe who is bent on defeating Germany, destroying our economy and impoverishing the German people. This includes the German working class. The overwhelming majority of our patriotic workers, who so far have rendered great service to the well being of the people, will do their part to bring the strike to a speedy end.

4.3 THE DEMANDS OF THE STRIKE DIRECTORATE IN BERLIN, JANUARY 29, 1918[4]

The workers themselves without any suggestion or instruction from any directing body have again initiated a strike. Yesterday's strike is similar to the spontaneous movement that erupted in April 1917, when the bread ration was reduced .... It was only after the workers had left the factories in great number that they elected a strike directorate consisting of delegates of the strikers and representatives of both Social Democratic parties .... The meeting formulated the following demands:

1. Accelerated conclusion of a general peace without indemnities or annexations.
2. Participation of workers' delegates from all countries in the peace conference.
3. Amelioration of the food situation by better distribution.
4. Immediate abolition of the state of siege and restoration of the right of public meeting, suspended by military authorities.
5. Abolition of militarization of war factories.
6. Immediate release of all political prisoners.
7. Fundamental democratization of state institutions.
8. The institution of equal electoral suffrage and direct secret ballot.

4.4 "ULTIMATUM IS ISSUED TO KAISER BY THE SOCIALISTS," JANUARY 29, 1918[5]

A dispatch to [a Geneva newspaper] reports that there have been clashes between soldiers and strikers in the suburbs of Berlin in which lives were lost. The dispatch adds that the troops in some instances refused to fire on strikers. The cessation of work in Hamburg now is virtually complete, according to a ... dispatch from Rotterdam. The strikers demand an immediate peace on the basis of no annexations and no indemnities.

4.5 "1,000,000 NOW OUT IN GERMAN PEACE TIE-UP," FEBRUARY 1, 1918[6]

The German strike has now spread to Munich, where the big Mauser armament works are involved ... according to dispatches received here tonight .... [a Cologne newspaper] reports that the military commander of Hamburg has ordered the strikers in that city to return to work .... The strike has been extended in districts near Berlin ... where 500,000 men have quit work. Similar number of workmen is on strike in the remainder of the empire .... Clergymen vainly exhorted the strikers in Hamburg yesterday to return to work. The workers proceeded to the trades union headquarters and adopted a resolution ... demanding immediate peace without annexations or indemnities, better labor conditions, and improvement in the food supply. A deputation waited on the general in command of the district and said the strikers would not resort to violence. The Berlin papers explained that the German authorities do not refuse to treat with proper labor leaders regarding the strike. The government takes the position, however, that on important political questions it cannot negotiate with the workers, and, in any case, with strikers .... The broad features of the news filtering in today from Berlin are, first, that the strike movement undoubtedly is extending and, second, that the German authorities are endeavoring to minimize its importance. Thus far there has been no news regarding the attitude the government will adopt.

In the Upper Silesian industrial region ... the strike has gained virtually no ground, and the news from the iron and steel districts of the Rhineland and Westphalia also is reassuring. In Spandau, work is in full swing in most of the government workshops, the trade unions refusing to have anything to do with the strike. A dispatch from Stockholm says the German strikes are largely due to scarcity of food. The people are indignant over the exportation of flour to Austria, and also over profiteering and the illegal procuring of foodstuffs, which flourishes despite the utmost effort of the authorities. The strikes in Hamburg and Kiel have resolved themselves into hunger demonstrations. The extent of food profiteering in Berlin alone is illustrated by a report in the *Berliner Tageblatt* that fines imposed in the ... criminal court in one day exceeded 100,000 marks.

Socialist leaders from all over Germany have been summoned to Berlin for a discussion of important home and foreign political questions. The strikers' committee, which was formed in Berlin with representative of the two wings of the Socialist party as members of it, has formulated certain demands. But generally speaking, an early peace without annexations seems to be the greatest desire of the workers, who threatened reprisal for the arrest of their leaders.

The German press generally condemns the strike and warns that strikers that have gone the wrong way about getting an early peace and are instead harming their own country. Some of the papers, however, blame the government.

4.6 "WORKERS ORDERED TO JOBS OR FACE LIFE IN THE TRENCHES," FEBRUARY 3, 1918[7]

Reports reaching Stockholm from Berlin indicate that the strike has reached its high water mark and is now beginning to recede. The Majority Socialists appear to have been half hearted in the movement from the beginning and strike has been opposed by the Catholic trade unions and the Hirsch Dunker union, which is the largest non-socialist trades union in Germany, as well as the non-socialist parties in the *Reichstag* majority bloc.

Geneva. Germany's workers are still in a restless mood, and, although the strike movement appears to be on the wane, largely through the adoption of drastic measures by the authorities, there are threats of further demonstrations and continuation of sporadic disorders. Berlin and its environs remain the center of the disturbance. The city is under military control, which finds a particular demonstration in a number of factories where strikes are in progress. These have been militarized, according to current dispatches, and the workers warned to report to work yesterday morning or undergo military discipline.

> The most serious disturbances appear to have occurred in Berlin on Thursday, when crowds got out of hand, overturned street cars, interfered with workers who were on their way to their employment, and frequently collided with the police. In one case, when a panic broke out after a shot had been fired, the police are declared to have charged with drawn sabers, thirty strikers and many onlookers being wounded. At Spandau ... there were similar disorders and a mob is reported to have attacked soldiers.

4.7 "TROOPS SAVE BAVARIAN KING FROM STRIKERS, FEBRUARY 3, 1918"[8]

[A Zurich newspaper] declares that, having decided that the strike must be crushed by vigorous measures, the German government is acting with speed and firmness. The rations of strikers have been cut down. From Hamburg, Leipzig, Bremen, Mannheim, and Cassel come reports that the generals commanding these localities are using the iron hand. An intensified state of siege now prevails throughout Germany. Local strike headquarters are being raided. Meetings have been prohibited and in some places the men have been told to return to work or be ready to leave for the trenches .... Seven Berlin factories have been placed under martial law and the strikers ordered to resume their work by 7 AM Monday morning at the latest. Their failure to return will be punished by military discipline.

[A Swedish newspaper reports] from a reliable source that the rioting in Berlin Thursday was precipitated by a shot fired when the police were trying to disperse a crowd which was proceeding towards Charlottenburg crying "Peace and bread"! A panic ensued when the shot was fired and the police charged the crowd with drawn sabers. The strikers sought to shelter behind overturned tram cars and ... hurled projectiles at the police, who were unable to keep the excited people under control. About thirty strikers were wounded and taken to a hospital .... The rioting, the newspaper states, covered all sections of Greater Berlin except *Unter den Linden* and the *Schlossplatz* where the Kaiser's palace is located. Many streetcars were overturned and derailed. Detachments of cavalry and machine gun corps have been collected in the neighborhoods of Berlin.

Yesterday's issue of *Vorwärts* ... reads: According to reports in the evening papers only isolated and insignificant excesses occurred today. These were more the acts of youths and of mobs than actual demonstrators. The prevailing opinion is that the strike has passed its zenith. In some factories the number of workers was increased by a thousand over yesterday. Most of the [bus] companies and streetcar lines were able to maintain traffic in an orderly manner. All the newspapers reappeared.

An important element in both the left- and right-wing Stab-in-the-Back Myths was the intervention of Majority Social Democratic leaders in the Berlin strikes. The party had not been involved in the planning of the strikes (Ebert will later claim to be surprised by them), but when they broke out individual party members and union leaders approached the Majority Social Democratic executive committee and asked them to join the strike committee as a way of curbing Independent control. The executive was uncertain whether to join the strike committee because they did not believe that the strike should have taken place at all. While Ebert argued against, it was decided that three Social Democratic representatives should join the strike committee with the goal of concluding the strike as quickly as possible. For the left *Dolchstoß* adherents, the SPD functioned as "strike breaker" and Ebert was a traitor to working-class interests. For many (but not all) nationalist Stab-in-the-Back theorists, the Majority Social Democrats committed treason against the Fatherland by joining the strike committee, despite their avowed intention to end it. Document 4.8 is Ebert's account of his activities in this disputed event.

4.8 EBERT ON THE JANUARY STRIKES, FEBRUARY 16, 1918[9]

The strike movement of the last week in January has left in its wake lively political discussions. Abroad, too, the movement has naturally aroused great interest. Reactionary newspapers that present every strike in the enemy countries as a sign of the collapse of the Entente now serve up with veritable delight press comments in enemy countries' newspapers against Social Democracy. The Annexationists and with them the entire reactionary gang have behaved as if they were enraged; they accuse us of treason and of prolonging of the war. That of course is miserable hypocrisy. This gang has, during the entire war, denounced every political movement as treasonous that was not in consonance with the Annexationist war religion.

The strike movement primarily directs itself against the dangerous actions of the imperialist politicians. Through their manipulation of the state of siege, the advocates of a Victor's Peace were able to behave in a boastful and misleading way. Even representatives of the Progressive People's Party and the Center repeatedly declared that foreign countries must conclude that the spirit of the Annexationists rules Germany. Indeed, nothing has inflamed the war spirit abroad—thereby prolonging the war—than the demands of our Annexationist politicians.

The *Reich* leadership most certainly could have prevented the strikes. In recent weeks, we have consistently (in both official and unofficial discussions) called their attention to the ever-growing bitterness of the laboring population and we have asked them to change their policies.

Whatever could still be done toward increasing the bitterness of the masses was done by the obstruction of suffrage reform in the Prussian *Landtag* and the impudent demands of the big industrialists for forcible measures against the Social Democrats. The laboring masses that are suffering the most from shortage of food are expected to calmly accept this. Anyone knowing anything at all about mass psychology had to tell himself that this was dangerous, but the *Reich* leadership completely lacked understanding of the situation. Instead of quieting the laboring class by the removal of the causes of bitterness, it took a hard line.

Doubtless the mass strikes in Austria and Hungary had a suggestive effect upon the German laborer. But had the masses of the people not been so enraged, those strikes would not have added fuel to the fire any more than the leaflets of the Spartacists and the Independents. Originally the strikes in Berlin were concentrated in only a handful of munitions factories. Soon, however, deputations of party members from other industries began to appear at party headquarters .... All declared that the anger within the laboring class was so strong that it could only be expressed by quitting work. The leadership of the strike ought not to be left to the Independents and the Spartacists.

The mediation of the dispute was a difficult task for our representatives. On one side were the Independents, who insisted that they would negotiate only if all strike representatives could participate; on the other side was the Chancellor, who wanted to talk to representatives of the strikers if they were functionaries of the trade unions. Our purpose was to bring the strike to an orderly conclusion as soon as possible, the more so because it had fulfilled its purpose as a demonstration ....

The negotiations with the Chancellor took place from Tuesday [29 January] through Sunday [3 February] without any results, although the strike originally was intended for only three days. Had it been possible ... to commence negotiations on Tuesday, and had the government shown an earnest will toward quieting the workers, work probably would have been resumed in Berlin on Thursday.

That was shown by the course of the strikes in other places. At Bielefeld, Brandenburg, Bremen, Breslau, Danzig, Dortmund, Kiel, etc.,

> the strikes were concluded in two or three days. The strikers were given the opportunity to meet and discussion their demands; the authorities negotiated with their representatives. At Cologne, after negotiations with the workers' delegates, the mayor went to the meeting of the strikers and spoke to them. The Premier of Bavaria, too, took the right position toward the strikers and addressed them, publicly thanking Majority Social Democracy for its good services. In all of these places the strikes soon subsided. If it happened differently in Berlin, this was because the *Reich* leadership completely mishandled the situation. It lacked the foresight and understanding of the situation that was so evident among the numerous district officials.
>
> Whether or not the *Reich* leadership has learned from the experience is questionable. At present it does not look so. If it wishes quiet to prevail among the masses, then it had better stop the persecution of the workers who participated in the strike and consider complaints that the state of siege is being manipulated. Further, it must repudiate the Annexationists and pursue a clear peace policy without open or veiled annexations and reparations. The promised equal suffrage law must be enacted as soon as possible. Finally, but not last, the scandalous smuggling of victuals must be prevented and food must be equitably and impartially distributed.
>
> At its meetings during the strike, the leadership of the party unanimously pledged to protect the country. The *Reichstag* Majority Social Democratic caucus unanimously agreed to that resolution. The central authorities of the trade unions expressed themselves similarly. It rests now with the government to do its share, in order that the war, into which our people went with the motto: "We are not motivated by lust for conquest" be soon concluded with the same motto.

As Ebert's statement suggests, the Majority Social Democrats were particularly sensitive to any intimations of treason. Since the outbreak of the war, they had supported war financing and had encouraged workers to contribute their utmost to the war effort. The fact that the party and its allied unions had not started the January Strike—and only assumed leadership to bring it to a speedy conclusion—was particularly galling. Both Ebert and Philipp Scheidemann attempted time and again to make this clear, Scheidemann most openly in the course of a parliamentary debate on the matter on February 26, 1918, recounted in Document 4.9. Wallraf, the minister of the interior, whose fiery attack on the strikers (in Document 4.10) included perhaps the earliest explicit reference to the German army being "Stabbed-in-the-Back," followed him to the *Reichstag* tribune.

4.9 SCHEIDEMANN'S SPEECH IN THE *REICHSTAG* ON THE STRIKE, FEBRUARY 26, 1918[10]

The government has celebrated its great triumph on the occasion of the last strike. It seems to me that we have experienced something similar to what we experience in foreign policy: the politicians are simply overruled by the military. Gentlemen, if you do not wish to make yourselves a laughingstock in the eyes of the whole world, never speak of foreign money having possibly played a part in the outbreak of this strike. It originated in the fact that the people did not think that the government had done all it might have done with regard to the food supplies .... The rich could have all they wanted, the poor lacked the necessities of life; the working and middle classes endured far more than anyone would ask of the landed proprietors. But this was only one contributory cause. The anger over what they thought was the unnecessary prolongation of the war and indignation at the delay in the franchise reform .... at a time when the people's blood was being shed in torrents also helped to bring about the strike .... It was a shameless lie to accuse the strikers of having intended to betray their country .... In addition to the Socialists, the other non-Socialist unions took part in the strike.

How foolish and how shortsighted it is to talk of treason on the part of 500,000 workmen in Berlin! ... The strikers did not think of betraying their country; they only wished to voice their dissatisfaction .... The strikes did no more harm than the work stoppages that occur when the factories lacked raw material and coal. Also, there were great reserves of munitions because the militarily experienced a quiet winter .... The strikers wished only to demonstrate for peace, liberty, and bread. After their newspapers had been confiscated there was no other way for them to raise their voice except by demonstrating .... I repeat, the notion of treason to the Fatherland on the part of the strikers was conjured up only in order to provide an excuse for persecuting the Majority Social Democratic Party.

4.10 MINISTER OF THE INTERIOR WALLRAF ON THE STRIKES, FEBRUARY 26, 1918[11]

My views on the question of how the strike originated and what action it compelled the government to take differ, of course, from those of Deputy Scheidemann. He regards the strike as the outcome of

> some justifiable discontent .... Herr Scheidemann waved aside, with an air of superiority, the idea that foreign influence helped bring about the strike. I am of a different opinion, and will give proof in support of it .... As early as last April the news came that there was unrest among the workers and that it would end in an uprising. Chancellor Bethmann Hollweg warned local governments about this .... The strike broke out, did not attain any great dimensions, and was soon put down. Toward the end of the summer it became evident to the government for the first time that international influences were at work. The first pamphlet was found in Dresden in August; it was printed in Zurich and advocated violent manifestations against the ruling system ....
>
> German labor ought also to know that the officers of the state, who administer law and justice, will fight against these criminal machinations. The criminal code threatens those who ... give support to hostile powers or injure the fighting powers of the German Empire or its allies, with heavy penalties for treason to their country! Anyone who dishonorably and disloyally *attacks our brave warriors from behind* as they carry out their sacred task, makes himself an outlaw, and must be punished with the extreme rigor of the law.

Conclusion

The two contradictory *Dolchstoß* schools both accentuated the January Strike. For Communists and left Social Democrats, Friedrich Ebert, Philipp Scheidemann, and their colleagues were "strike breakers." The union leadership acquiesced with attempts to break the strike and supported drafting strike leaders into frontline service. (This despite claims Ebert made in his Treptow speech that he was trying to get strikes reinstated in the factory workforce.) For nationalists, Ebert and Company were traitors for even engaging with the strikers. Joining the strike to end it—a claim of which in any case nationalists were skeptical—was still accounted treasonous activity. The January Strike achieved iconic stature for both left and right *Dolchstoß* schools not because of its impact on the war effort—it was quickly over and had as little impact of production as non-strike supply-chain problems—but because it allowed opponents of the Majority Social Democrats to label the party and its leadership as traitors from whichever perspective the accuser wished to argue.

Thought questions

1 What provoked the strikes? To what extent were the workers' demands political and to what extent were they economic?

2   What differences existed among the striking workers and within the two Social Democratic parties?
3   If the Left's response was chaotic, how would you describe the government's response?
4   How did Philipp Scheidemann seek to minimize the impact of the strike on the war effort?
5   How would you characterize strikes in a time of war? Are they treasonous if they impact the war effort?

Further reading

Students will find Philipp Scheidemann, *The New Germany* (New York: Appleton and Company, 1929) an eminently readable memoir that goes into considerable detail about the 1917 and 1918 strikes.

5

Military Collapse

Institutional context

Just as the *Reich* was composed of sovereign states, so the German military was a composite unit. In times of peace, each state recruited, trained, and equipped its own army. In time of war, each of these armies came under the control of a Greater General Staff dominated by Prussians. To facilitate this expected consolidation, select officers from the non-Prussian armies attended the Prussian War College. The brightest among these (such as Wilhelm Groener) were then seconded to work for a length of time with the General Staff. Each army, including the Prussian, was directed by a War Ministry, which was engaged in many of the same activities as those pursued by the General Staff, leading to conflict that became apparent in the course of the war.

The titular head of the German military in time of war was the Emperor, who as King of Prussia was Supreme Warlord. As Wilhelm II was ill suited for this role, command functions on the Western Front fell to the Supreme Command (*Oberste Heeresleitung* or OHL) at Spa, which after August 1916 was led by the heroes of the Battle of Tannenberg, Paul von Hindenburg and Erich Ludendorff.

Two structural realities in the organization of the war effort need to be clear. The first is the distinction in German military parlance between the front line, the staging area, and the Home Front. The concept of the front is obvious. The staging area was the sector behind the front, where food, munitions, and fresh troops were brought up and where units heading to the front or rotated off the front lines were retrained. As long as manpower was sufficient, units enjoyed a regimen where they served one-third time each in the trenches, in the staging area, and then in reserve. Military discipline was reputedly more relaxed in the staging areas, which had a high percentage of non-combat personnel. Each army corps had a home area (Home Front) in Germany from which it drew recruits and where it retained training and support units of men not fit for front service (the old and severely wounded or those who did not want to serve at the front who had influential connections) who performed corps administrative tasks, guarded prisoner-of-war camps, etc. In wartime and post-war discourse, it is sometimes unclear whether one was referring to the Home Front or the Homeland (the *Heimat*)—civilian Germany.

The second structural reality was the distinction between units that were given four grades—1st through 4th. These rankings were based on the age of the unit (whether it was based on pre-war or newly created regiments), the number of veterans in each unit as opposed to fresh recruits, the combat experience of the unit and its perceived élan. Higher-ranking units were given the newest uniforms and equipment, they underwent continual retraining and they were assigned the toughest places on the front line. Lower grade units were less quickly reequipped and were assigned to quieter areas of the front. By the eve of the offensive of 1918, almost all 3rd- and 4th-grade units were assigned to the East and the Balkans while the 2nd-grade troops were concentrated on the "quiet" southern sector in the Vosges. One problem the Supreme Command faced by the summer of 1918 was that many if not most of the 1st-grade units had been severely depleted in terms of manpower and their weapons and uniforms were deteriorating, although they usually displayed continued high morale.

Status of forces

As Germany entered the fourth year of war, her military situation was precarious. She had been able to hold off the Allied offensives of 1917, but at great cost. Substantial forces had to be detailed to prop up the Austro-Hungarian army in the Balkans and on the Italian front. Equally worrying was the American entry into the war and the certainty that at some future date a large, albeit unseasoned, American force would take up its position along the Western Front. On the positive side of the ledger, both the Tsarist regime and the Provisional Government that succeed it had been overthrown by Bolsheviks intent on peace at nearly any price. The harsh Treaty of Brest-Litovsk (March 1918) not only offered the hope that troops could be redeployed to the Western Front, it also held out the prospect of shipments of meat and grain that would quell domestic unrest.

The situation in 1918

Aware that the Americans would soon arrive in numbers on the continent, the Supreme Command planned a last great offensive to decide the war before that came to pass. A major concern was having sufficient troops to force a breakthrough. In Document 5.1, from September 10, 1917, Hindenburg wrote the Chancellor detailing his needs and grievances. In particular, he argues that there existed an insufficiency of quality draftees and that too many able-bodied men have been given exemptions and were needed in the service. Although the army leadership was concerned about "disintegrating influences"—by which they meant anti-war propaganda—they felt that these were containable as long as the domestic situation did not deteriorate. The second document discusses the potential available resources that might be released from the Eastern Front and whether those would be as large as some hoped.

5.1 CHIEF OF THE GENERAL STAFF TO THE CHANCELLOR CONCERNING REPLACEMENTS AND LABOR, SEPTEMBER 10, 1917[1]

Our opponents are making desperate efforts to win the war. They have at their disposal many more men than we do, which will be further increased by America's entry into the war. The situation is similar with regard to military stores, especially munitions. In this respect, we are fighting against the industry of the whole world. The power of the enemy's artillery is superior to ours. The submarine warfare doubtless affords some relief, but it is not but it yet possible to determine the time at which it will cause a decisive weakening of our opponents' strength. It is certain, however, that before that happens our opponents will endeavor to bring the war to an end through a military decision.

The supply of men to replace casualties in our field army is insufficient. In particular there is an alarming lack of trained men for all arms. The question of the replacement of casualties already cripples the freedom of military operations to a considerable extent. For next year, the question of the replacement of casualties appears even more serious, unless we succeed in releasing exempted men in large numbers. Unless we succeed in replacing the casualties in the army, a positive outcome of the war is doubtful.

With reference to the will to victory, the feeling in the whole country as a whole appears to have become somewhat better. Disintegrating influences are, however, present in the form of radical agitators and politicians who malevolently pursue their aims. The danger is not great at present, but it is constantly increasing and will at once assume large proportions when difficulties arise, for instance with regard to food.

Note the cautious language used in Document 5.1. If the casualties that the army had suffered were not replaced, "a positive outcome of the war is doubtful." "Dissent within the ranks was containable" but it will "assume large proportions when difficulties arise, for instance with regard to food." These are diplomatically crafted red flags that readers in Berlin must have recognized.

The issues raised in Document 5.1 were revisited after the war by the *Reichstag* Subcommittee charged with investigating the Collapse. The author of Documents 5.2 and 5.3 was retired general Hermann von Kuhl. Kuhl (1856–1958) came from a middle class family (his father was a school teacher in Koblenz). He earned his doctorate in 1878, after which he joined the army, attending the Prussian Military Academy from 1889 to 1892. After serving as a company commander in several garrison posts, he returned to the Academy in 1897 as an instructor and was a section chief in the German General Staff. There, he was taken under the wing of Alfred von Schlieffen (much like Wilhelm Groener). In his non-duty time, he wrote military history and analysis. Kuhl was rewarded for his accomplishments when he was knighted in 1912 (becoming *von* Kuhl). In the August 1914 offensive he served as chief of staff of Alexander von Kluck's 1st Army on the far right wing of the sweep across Belgium. He received Germany's highest military medal, the *Pour le Mérite* for his service at the Battle of the Somme, after which he was promoted to chief of staff of Prince Rupprecht of Bavaria's Army Group. Rupprecht's was a courtesy appointment, so as Ludendorff did for Hindenburg at Tannenberg, Kuhl effectively commanded the army group. When Rupprecht resigned his command on November 11, 1918, Kuhl took his place and marched the Army Group back to Germany. After he oversaw the Army Group's demobilization, Kuhl himself resigned. He accepted employment at the Military History section of the German Imperial Archives. As an acknowledged expert, Kuhl was seconded to work with the Subcommittee and provide his expertise.

5.2 KUHL ON THE RELATIVE STRENGTH OF THE FORCES[2]

The decisive question is whether the aims of our campaigns in the East were so extensive that they impeded our ability to concentrate all available troops on the Western front for the great offensive in 1918.

At the beginning of 1918, the chief concern of the Supreme Command was to reach a settlement with Russia as soon as possible and to transfer all forces that could possibly be dispensed with in the East to the West in good time for the offensive planned on 21 March. But Lenin and Trotsky dragged out the negotiations. They were more interested in making propaganda for Bolshevism and preparing a world revolution. It was absolutely necessary to put a stop to this dangerous procrastination. Lenin and Trotsky were already endeavoring to infect our army with the spirit of disintegration.

5.3 KUHL ON REINFORCEMENTS AND SUPPLIES FOR THE ARMY[3]

The Supreme Command was fully aware of the serious problem with regard to reinforcements before the beginning of the great offensive in 1918. It could be foreseen that a crisis would arise in summer with regard to the provision of men to replace casualties. The Supreme Command had taken all possible measures to economize in the use of reinforcements, to draw every man that could be spared from the lines of communication and from special formations for use at the front and, above all, to utilize to the utmost extent the forces available in the East.

What conclusions ought the Supreme Command to have drawn at the turn of the year 1917–18 concerning the impending difficulties with regard to the replacement of casualties? A decision to undertake only defensive actions could not be based on the replacement issue. The offensive is by no means the cause of greater losses than the defensive; as a rule the contrary is the case. The constantly increasing superiority of our opponents due to the arrival of the Americans rendered defensive action hopeless in the long run. Hence the position with regard to reinforcements necessitated an attack. This was the only possibility of shortening the war. If the attack failed, then the war would of course be lost.

The number of men retained for work in war industries seemed excessively high. The army was calling for reinforcements, munitions, and material, while the employers demanded labor. We were constantly bedeviled by this conflict of interests. The enormous requirements in the form of war material called for by the Hindenburg program could only be met by withholding considerable numbers of physically fit men from service at the front. When the enormous numbers of men called up for service in the course of four years of war are taken into consideration, one cannot be surprised that the supply of reinforcements finally failed and that it was impossible permanently to reconcile the demands of the Army with those of industry.

In spite of this, such difficulties would never have arisen in the course of 1918 if the strength of the fighting forces had not shrunk to an alarming extent—especially from summer onward—due to the constantly increasing number of deserters and shirkers. Behind the front, hundreds of thousands of shirkers collected at depots and railway junctions. The losses due to men taken prisoner increased enormously. The deserters from the colors wandered about the country in bands. The reasons for these distressing manifestations cannot be examined in more detail here.[4]

Kuhl chose not to elaborate on the question of shirking and desertion, but the German National chair of the Subcommittee, Albrecht Philipp was not reluctant to do so.[5] Among other points that Philipp brought up was the question of whether Jews shirked their responsibilities to the war effort, referencing the notorious Jewish Census of 1916.[6]

5.4 DR. PHILIPP ON SABOTAGE OF THE WAR EFFORT[7]

Shirking: This made itself felt both at home and in the field. At home it took the shape of applications for exemption. It is of course difficult to give the exact figures here. During the war the public frequently complained of the numbers of exemptions demanded by the Jews. While the war was actually going on, complaints on this matter were already loud and there is no doubt that this fact that it influenced the mentality of those at the front. It is well known that, at the urgent request of Jewish circles, statistics were compiled on the number of Jews in the field. The publication of the results of this survey was supposedly prohibited for political reasons .... It was widely believed that nothing unfavorable to the Jews was published lest this have an unfavorable effect on the War Loans. I know, for example, that one Army Command forbade the publication of letters from the front that contained summaries on this matter.

Desertion to the enemy: Desertion to the enemy seems to have become a serious problem only after the first failures in 1918. Here also no exact statistics can be given.

Mutiny: The first mutinies to break out occurred in the Fleet in July 1917. They did not occur in the Army until a later date .... Army mutinies on a large scale did not take place until the very last weeks of the war.

Strikes: Strikes *en masse* as a means of sabotaging the war must also be considered. According to Barth this means was resorted to from 1916, although the first large strike did not take place till April 1917. It appears that the Government paid considerable attention to this question but that the means adopted to meet the danger were not altogether uniform.

Turning from the question of internal subversion and manpower issues, numerous questions were raised after the war about whether the Supreme Command properly anticipated the impact that the arrival of the American Expeditionary Force would have on the battlefield. Might the German position have been better served by remaining on the defensive? In his deposition prepared for the Subcommittee, Kuhl argued (in Document 5.5) that the Command had spent considerable time thinking through how many Americans would be transported to the continent and how long it would take for them to train up to the level of combat.

5.5 KUHL ON THE ARRIVAL OF THE AMERICANS[8]

The arrival and utilization of American troops was of the greatest importance for the course of the fighting in 1918. The question of whether the entry of the United States into the war was caused by unrestricted submarine warfare ... cannot be considered here. Instead, we have to consider whether at the end of 1917 the arrival and the probable services of the Americans had been rightly taken into account when we decided to assume the offensive or whether we were mistaken and this was one of the causes of the failure of the offensive. As a matter of fact, regard for the probable intervention of the Americans was a major factor in the selection of the date for the beginning of the offensive.

In July 1917, the first, symbolic, division of American troops landed in France. We calculated that the organization, training, and equipment of the follow-on troops would require so much time that they would not be ready for transport to Europe in large numbers before the beginning of 1918 .... It was initially thought that while American weapons and equipment were good, their training was insufficient. The first troops sent to the front, however, did well on the occasion of a German attack. It was expected that, with more practice and war experience, the American soldier would become a redoubtable opponent.

In March 1918, at the beginning of our offensive, there were seven American divisions in France, but of these only one was really a fighting division. Three were sent to the front to learn fighting, and the others were still under training. On the day of the armistice there were forty-three divisions available, although only twenty-eight were fit for service. If we count 28,000 men to the division, the twenty-eight divisions fit for service ... would amount to 30,000 officers and 870,000 men.

There is no doubt that the rapid transport of American troops to Europe ... was a surprise to us. During the first months we underestimated the rate, but we soon succeeded in ascertaining exactly how long it took for the disembarked American divisions to reach the front. The numbers assumed by us in July and August correspond approximately to those of the divisions really available, and the total strength to be expected toward the end of 1918 was also estimated accurately.

The American troops played an important role in the French counter-attack that began on July 18, 1918 .... In addition to the employment of divisions on other fronts, the Americans took over an independent "American Front" on the Meuse with the 1st Army at the end of August. On September 12, the Americans attacked us with fourteen divisions near St. Mihiel, leading to the loss of our position there. During the general offensive that began on September 26, the front between the Meuse and the Argonne in the direction of Sedan was assigned to the Americans. Although the Americans suffered great losses in these battles, their actions were important for the course of the war.

The American soldier showed himself full of courage, even if he lacked experience. Fresh, well fed, and with strong nerves that had not yet known the strain of battle, he advanced against our army, which was exhausted by the efforts of four years of war. This—and the significant reinforcement that the Americans brought to our opponents at the decisive moment—is why America's intervention was so important.

Our hopes of winning the war through our offensive in 1918, before the Americans could intervene in large numbers, were not fulfilled. We did not foresee the possibility of their arriving as speedily as they actually did. We were mistaken with regard to the tonnage available for the transport of troops and the effect of our submarines on this transport. The Americans arrived punctually and in such force that this influenced to a great extent the unfavorable result of the war for us.

Lastly at issue was whether the German army could have continued fighting after November 9. On this score, Kuhl presented (in Document 5.6) an extremely nuanced answer. He answers "yes" of course, but note how conditional that "yes" is.

5.6 "COULD WE HAVE KEPT ON FIGHTING IN THE AUTUMN?"[9]

Could we have kept on fighting in the autumn of 1918 after victory was no longer possible in order to achieve an armistice and peace terms consistent with our honor?

In the autumn of 1918, 2,424,000 men exempted from military service were employed in war industries and business. Of this number 1,187,000 were fit for active service. In October 1918 the War Minister offered to place reinforcements numbering 600,000 men at the disposal of the army, although admittedly this would reduce the production. It would also have been possible for a limited time to withdraw a few hundred thousand men more from the war industries.

In spite of their exhausted state and in spite of constantly decreasing numbers, our troops fought heroically until the last day. The men who came from home who were infected by revolutionary propaganda or who were demoralized at the front fled before the enemy's artillery barrage. After the shirkers and the deserters were gone, there remained a healthy core capable of offering powerful resistance. The machine-gun detachments in particular fought heroically until the last moment. For their part, enemy soldiers were also exhausted and, according to the general opinion of our men, no longer attacked with vigor.

General Ludendorff made the possibility of continuing the war dependent on our being allowed a breathing space. This breathing space would really have occurred, as can now be proved. We should have had time in November to equip and organize the Antwerp-Meuse lines and we should have been able to continue our resistance farther to the rear. This would have confronted the enemy with the question of whether they were prepared to risk fierce fighting into 1919 or would decide to moderate their terms.

The Allies were no longer in a position to pursue us in November 1918, as we had destroyed the railroads in our retreat. On the day of the armistice, they had reached the extreme point to which they could move supplies forward .... Exact details of this, as regards the British Army, are available. The American supply service had also completely broken down owing to the faulty organization of its system of transport. As a matter of fact, the British were not able to move forward again until six days after the cessation of hostilities, and then only with less than one-third of their divisions.

The state of the Army was of decisive importance. The Army was very exhausted after four years of war, after the defensive actions of 1917, after the all-out offensive in the first half of 1918, and after the constant and hard-fought rear-guard actions in the summer of 1918. The trench divisions had been left too long in forward positions, were listless, and completely unfit to cope with the hostile assault when our opponents' offensive began in the summer of 1918 .... The heavy losses could no longer be replaced. Our reserves were almost exhausted. Ten divisions had to be reformed because of loss of manpower in August and twenty-two in October. The general situation with regard to the replacement of troops was decisive.

But it was not only inferiority in numbers that weakened the power of resistance of the German Army. The morale of the troops had also suffered. The breakdown of the offensive, which had been undertaken with every hope of victory, had a very depressing effect on the spirit of the troops. It has also been shown that the Independent Social Democrats had been carrying on political agitation in the Army that endangered the discipline. The number of men taken prisoner increased dramatically. Behind the front, hundreds of thousands of shirkers collected at the railway stations and in the larger towns. Men on leave who had been incited to rebellion at home tramped about in large numbers behind the front without rejoining their units. Thus hundreds of thousands of men were not at the front at the decisive moment. This, in addition to men killed in combat during the retreat, explains the dwindling numbers of our troops.

I by no means wish to assert that the war was lost solely owing to the agitation conducted in the Army. Many causes worked together to bring about Germany's downfall. But it has been proved, however, that pacifist, international, anti-militaristic endeavors and the revolutionary undermining of the Army conducted from the interior of the country were very considerably to blame for our collapse.

It was the realization of these difficulties that were already partly present and partly impending that caused Field Marshal Haig to advocate moderate armistice terms at the conference of the allied commanders on October 25. He stated that the victorious Allied armies were at the end of their strength and that Germany was not yet broken from a military point of view. "During the last few weeks the German Armies have retired, fighting bravely in the best of order." General Petain was in favor of stringent terms, but did not believe that they would be accepted by Germany. Marshal Foch was of opinion that if the war continued in this case, no one could say how long it would last—it might be three or perhaps even four or five months.

Thus the possibility of the continuation of the war by Germany cannot be disputed. It was prevented only by the revolution that broke the sword in the commander's hand, subverting all order and discipline in the Army—above all behind the front—and rendered all further resistance impossible. Those who witnessed the devastating effect of the revolution on the Army will never be able to overcome the unnerving impression they received. It was then that Field Marshal von Hindenburg had to agree to the conclusion of the armistice in his telegram of November 10, in spite of its terms.

The Majority Social Democratic and Communist members of the Subcommittee for the most part stayed silent on the army's capacities as they existed in 1918 and the reasons for the failure of the German offensive.[10] *Reichstag* deputy and Majority Social Democratic publicist Simon Katzenstein, in his deposition (Document 5.7), specifically attempted to refute the Nationalist narrative of desertion and shirking.

5.7 MAJORITY SOCIAL DEMOCRAT SIMON KATZENSTEIN REFUTES THE KUHL-PHILIPP THESIS[11]

Radical Socialist and Spartacist propaganda existed. The amount and impact of this propaganda is debatable. The conditions and events that allowed hostile revolutionary ideas to have a measure of success are more important. This success was inevitable after the tremendous, unprecedented tension and fatigue that our great nation had to endure .... Increasingly after the summer of 1918, due to the worsening situation and lax discipline, massive evasion of military service by civilians and among troops in the staging areas rose to a level never previously witnessed. Desertion and shirking could no longer be effectively controlled. It would require an intensive investigation that goes beyond superficial anecdotal evidence to determine how much shirking went on as the result of personal relationship and bribery. This is particularly true in the case of the superficial rumors that Jews shirked service more than other groups. The same could be said of similar accusations against civil servants, landowners, and some members of the officer corps.

One should, of course, be wary of German sources and their inherent biases. Document 5.8, an article written by *Washington Evening Star* correspondent Herbert Corey, suggests that already in the month after the Armistice the Supreme Command was telling troops and the public that the German army was not defeated in the field. Corey, who was present in Berlin when the Great War broke out in August 1914, feared that this might be an ominous development.

5.8 HERBERT COREY ON THE STATE OF THE GERMAN ARMY IN RETREAT, JANUARY 24, 1919[12]

We had read the terms of the armistice when it was signed and we saw what all the rest of the world saw. That was not an armistice at all. That was unconditional surrender. The German armies would not be fit to fight a cat if the conditions of that armistice were obeyed, and the information we began to get at army headquarters was that the conditions were being obeyed. We wanted to know what was going on in Germany, as did all the rest of the world .... "Let us go to Germany," said Lincoln Eyre of the *New York World* one day. He and Frederick A. Smith of the *Chicago Tribune* and myself decided to go .... On the way to Luxemburg we ran into the rear of the 5th German army, commanded by von Marwitz, just as we had planned. At first these were just stragglers, limping along the road under their packs. Some had thrown their guns away. By and by we came to the rear guard. These men were young, well set up, well clothed, well shod. Their horses were notably good. Some led stolen cattle. They looked sullenly at our army car but said nothing. Perhaps at that time, it was only ten days since these men had been shooting at us with animosity and accuracy. The only live Germans in uniform any of us had seen in four years were either wounded or in the prison pens.

But we could not turn back. We were on a one-way road, and to get along at all we had been forced to crowd the retreating soldiers into the ditch at the cost of much blusterous horn-blowing. We realized that as long as we kept on going the Germans would think we had business there, but if we turned around and started back—well, anything might happen. We kept on. Now and then we got into a traffic jam in the narrow road. In one of these a German under officer spoke to me: "English?" he asked. "American," I said. There was a perceptible increase in cordiality. Evidently the English are very bitterly hated, while for one and another reason—mostly founded in hope—the Americans were not. We rode under the triumphal arches erected across the narrow streets of tiny villages. "Welcome Home Heroes," was the inscription. Each inscription was like every other one. Evidently each had been dictated from the central authority. Women and children lined the road and waved their hands with fluttering fingers at the marching ranks. They may not have known that Germany had been beaten, but I doubt if they cared. They welcomed the peace.

The soldiers knew the truth. Sometimes a company sang a deep-throated marching song and most of them had thrust flowers in the muzzle of their rifles, just as I had seen them do when they marched out of Berlin to go to war four years ago. They were happy that the war was over and they did not disguise the fact. They wreathed the great cannon and even the steel-tired camions, pushing on in their clouds of black and greasy smoke, with greenery and flowers. But they knew the German army had been defeated.

Only now and then an under officer repeated the one tenet of that dangerous cult which is gaining ground in Germany—a cult that would have its promise in future wars if the autocracy were to remain—and which is the "the German armies have never been defeated." I do not doubt that this was dictated from the general staff just as so many

> German activities have been. But the very men who repeated it knew that it was essentially false.
>
> "Could the German armies have kept on fighting?" we asked, and they shook their heads. "We were finished." they said. "Kaput. We could do no more."

The army that Cory witnessed in retreat—von Marwitz's 5th—was considered one of the best. Once Corey and friends got beyond the stragglers, they noted that the men were well accoutered and presented a fair picture. After talking with the men, however, it was clear that the ranks and the NCOs realized that they were defeated, despite what their generals said and despite the clearly engineered "triumphal" greeting in the homeland. Perhaps the first victory of the post-war battle of memory was for the Supreme Command to convince a fair number of the men and their fellows back home that they were *im Felde unbesiegt*.

Conclusion

The proponents of the Stab-in-the-Back Myth fell into multiple camps. For those most oblivious to a military reality that even the Supreme Command recognized, the German army was still "victorious" in the autumn of 1918. Others were convinced that the army was undergoing a rough patch but was not beaten and could continue the war after a "breathing space." Unaddressed by this school is whether a future victory was in any way possible. More "realistic" proponents of the *Dolchstoß* Myth argued that if the army had successfully pulled back to the Antwerp-Meuse (Antwerpen-Maas) line, Germany could have demanded of the Allies better Armistice terms.

At the heart of the Stab-in-the-Back question is when is an army defeated? When it is surrounded on the field of battle and forced to capitulate? When it is no longer able to carry on its primary mission of defending the homeland? Was there a difference between undefeated and unconquered in the field? If an army was beaten but unconquered in the field, does it follow that it must have been defeated by non-battlefield conditions? When Ludendorff demanded that the civilian government arrange a ceasefire at the end of September, he indicated that the army was on the verge of collapse. At a minimum, it needed to withdraw to a shorter, more easily defensible line of defense. But hadn't the Allies just pushed through the strong Hindenburg Line that had been so carefully constructed when Germany had the men and resources to devote to a defense in depth? Was there a serious possibility that the army could stop the Allies short of the Rhine? The various proponents refused to admit defeat short of a Jena or Waterloo when clearly the majority of the troops were no longer willing or capable of continuing the war.

Thought questions

1 Based on the documents you have read, was the Ludendorff offensive a good idea? Was it a gamble that should not have been made?
2 How did the military leadership miscalculate the impact that American troops would have in the war?
3 Based on these documents, was it realistic to assume that Germany could have continued fighting in November 1918?
4 In Document 5.4, Dr. Philipp replicates lies about young Jewish men shirking military service, when exactly the opposite was true. Why would he do that? What use did this lie serve?

Further reading

The single best source on the military collapse is Scott Stephenson, *The Final Battle: Soldiers of the Western Front and the German Revolution of 1918* (Cambridge: Cambridge University Press, 2009). Students wishing to find more correspondent accounts such as that cited in Document 5.7 should visit the Library of Congress, Chronicling America, Historic American Newspapers website (http://chroniclingamerica.loc.gov). There they will find digitized newspapers up to 1922. The site will be updated as ninety-year copyrights expire, so articles published after 1922 will be progressively available. A good search strategy would be to type in the names of prominent correspondents such as Lincoln Eyre, Frederick A. Smith, or Herbert Corey. Conversely, one can type in a newspaper, a person, or an event and search from there.

6

Whose *Dolchstoß*?

Personal context

George Ledebour and Richard Müller were leading figures in the revolutionary events of 1918–19, but they are scarcely remembered in the English-language secondary literature, perhaps because they ended their lives as political outcasts. Ledebour belonged to the unification generation and served in the Franco-Prussian War. He pursued a journalistic career with progressive newspapers before joining the Social Democratic Party in 1891. His leftward migration continued, leading him into the more radical faction of the Party. He joined the editorial board of *Vorwärts* in 1900 and the party executive in 1913. In the party schism of 1916, he joined Hugo Haase in the Independent Social Democratic Party and consistently opposed any accommodation with his old comrades. Ledebour played a critical role in the November events as he was one of the few leaders of the Independents who regularly attended meetings of the Revolutionary Shop Stewards. In 1919, he left the Independents for the new Communist party. Ledebour remained an ideological lone wolf his entire long life, ultimately leaving the Communist Party for a variety of left communist splinter groups. He tended to be an overbearing and difficult colleague, as his scathing critique of all and everyone, fully on display in Document 6.2 makes abundantly clear.

Richard Müller was born into a large family in Thuringia and was orphaned early in childhood. He eventually made his way to Berlin, where he became a metalworker and union activist. Müller early on demonstrated his ability as a leader of men. An organizer of the Revolutionary Shop Stewards, he helped stage the Liebknecht Strike of 1916 and then the April Strike the following year. When the January 1918 strike broke out, he advocated adding Majority Social Democratic representatives to the strike committee, much to the horror of Georg Ledebour. When the strike collapsed, he was drafted into the army and more radical individuals took his place in the shop steward leadership. Returning to Berlin in November 1918, he favored establishing a council-based government on the Soviet Russian model. Like Ledebour, Müller joined the Communist Party and like Ledebour he consistently came into conflict with directives issued by the Moscow directed Communist International. In the mid-1920s, he withdrew from politics, wrote his memoirs, and became a leading theoretician of left unionism.

On the revolution

The purpose of this chapter is not to recount the course of the revolutionary events in Germany in the years 1918–19. (Readers should visit the Chronology link at http://www.dolchstosslegende.com for a complete timeline.) Our intent is rather to show how parties and individuals of both the Left and the Right interpreted the events of those turbulent years in such a way as to fit into their own Stab-in-the-Back narrative. The first two documents in this section are speeches delivered on 18 December at the opening session of the Congress of People's Deputies held in the *Reichstag* chamber. The initial speaker was Richard Müller, head of the Revolutionary Shop Stewards. He was followed by Independent Socialist George Ledebour. Taken together, the two documents provide a picture of the dynamic within Germany's revolutionary movement in the weeks before the abdication of the Emperor. The second set of three documents is from the report of the special investigative committee set up in 1919 to examine the causes of the

FIGURE 6.1 *Meeting of Congress of People's Deputies in the* Reichstag *chamber (Bundesarchiv Bildarchiv).*

internal collapse. The concluding two documents are speeches given by Friedrich Ebert to the troops sent to Berlin in December by Wilhelm Groener to support the new regime against the Independents and Spartacists.

Revolutionaries on the revolution

The Independent Social Democrats and the Spartacist League had been planning for a revolution for some time. Finally, in October 1918, it appeared that their preparations were starting to bear fruit. There was, however, reluctance to, in Georg Ledebour's words, "land the first blow."

6.1 RICHARD MÜLLER ON PREPARATIONS FOR THE REVOLUTION, DECEMBER 16, 1918[1]

Preparations for the revolution had already been made in July 1916. Even if the goal and the time at which it could be attained were not so very clear at that time, the persons who took part in it were convinced that the political and economic changes brought about in Germany by the war must result in a revolution. It is a fact that those who took a prominent part in the preparations also became members of the Executive Council.

The revolution broke out in other places a few days earlier than in Berlin, especially on the seacoast. We had, however, already laid down the date for the outbreak of the revolution before we could have an idea that it would break out in other parts of Germany. The insane plan of those formerly in power who wished to sacrifice the whole of our battle fleet and tens of thousands of our finest fellow citizens in a final desperate struggle with England ... was discovered in time and thwarted. This led to the outbreak of the revolution sooner than we in Berlin expected.

On the day before the revolution broke out in Berlin (9 November) enormous numbers of troops were hurried to Berlin and it looked as if the threatened rising was to be crushed by force of arms. The bourgeois press, even including *Vorwärts*, sought to prevent the outbreak of the rising with all the means at its disposal. Even on the morning of November 9, *Vorwärts* implored Berlin workers not to strike until the possibilities of negotiations were exhausted. But the revolution broke out anyway. The old rulers did not have the courage to fight for their old rights ... and everything was turned upside down on that day. We had not reckoned with the old rulers' yielding their places to us so soon. During this state of confusion, those who had made these preparations endeavored to maintain order, and it was they also who at once summoned a meeting of the delegates of the Workers' and Soldiers' Councils in Berlin on 10 November.

6.2 GEORG LEDEBOUR ON THE INDEPENDENT'S RELUCTANCE TO STRIKE, DECEMBER 17, 1918[2]

Comrade Müller in his introductory remarks has already informed us in detail that at least since the year 1916 the determination and hope existed among a number of the pioneers of the Independent Socialist Party, especially in labor circles, that this worthless criminal society which has ruined Germany would be overthrown by a violent revolution. And all of us who were among these pioneers have each in his place done our best to enlighten the masses, to make demands, and to accelerate the revolution ... After the strike in January 1918, the conviction grew in all those taking part in this movement that if trouble started again we should not be content with a strike but should take to arms. From that time preparations were made for this purpose and especially people who now are members of the leadership were the principal advocates of preparing for a revolution. They obtained the weapons, they enlisted recruits, and we others who cooperated with them to a certain extent influenced our workmen in the course of a year of long and intensive work in parliament, the press, and elsewhere.

Comrades! For us it was therefore only a question of when the time would come when we could strike the first blow. We were, as it were, sitting on the bank watching the water rise. For months we discussed the matter and when the collapse on the Western front came, we said to ourselves, "It is now high time and the final preparations must now be made." Besides, we had not only made preparations in Berlin but also in the provinces ... We worked upon the men at the front. After the January strike, the government was kind enough to send excellent agitators to revolutionize the front, as it picked out all those who were denounced as strike leaders and sent them to the trenches ... We knew that a large number of regiments would join us at once when the time came.

I now come to the last days, and here I am sorry to have to call my friend Dittmann to account. On Saturday, 2 November, a meeting of what I will call the Revolution Committee was summoned. Beside myself, Comrade Haase, who is also a member of the *Reichstag*, was summoned and also Comrade Liebknecht, who had just been released from a penitentiary and a few of his friends. In addition, there were Independent Social Democrats, Comrade Daumig, and others whom I have already mentioned, in all about a dozen people. We discussed the situation, and all but Haase and one other came to the conclusion that the first blow should be struck on Monday, November 4 since arms were available—I was told that arms were available for about 10,000 workmen—since we could count on the troops and could hope with a certain amount of confidence to make ourselves masters of Berlin, if not at once then at least after a short fight with the police. In the evening, a meeting of the leading comrades from the factories that were working with us was to be held in order to report about the feeling among the workmen in the munitions factories. The principal thing was the munitions factories; in addition there were other factories, but only a small number. The party leaders of the Independent Social Democrats were also present at this meeting, as well as comrades from the factories.

We were first given descriptions of the feeling in a number of smaller factories that did not seem to be very favorable. The large factories were for it. I will only mention that the overwhelming majority of the comrades, that is to say about 70,000, declared they were ready to strike the first blow. Then Comrades Haase and Dittmann got up one after the other and protested with the greatest firmness against striking the first blow. Comrade Dittmann stated, "The time is not ripe for it. We won't get the people to join us." ... We others (Barth, Daumig, Heckert, and myself)

FIGURE 6.2 *Karl Liebknecht speaking to a crowd in the Tiergarten, December 1918 (Bundesarchiv Bildarchiv).*

strenuously argued that the first blow must be struck on Monday or it would be too late. Liebknecht proposed an alternative course: not seizing power outright but fighting in the streets. We were firmly opposed to this idea, but because Haase, Dittmann, and Liebknecht opposed taking the initiative, we put it to a vote. It was decided by twenty-two votes against nineteen that we would not yet start the revolution. We also sent word to our comrades in the provinces that they also should not begin ... Later events demonstrated that those of us who wanted to act immediately were right ...

It unfortunately came about that the scheme was frustrated. I do not use this in itself as a reproach; it only proves that on this, as on earlier occasions you did not grasp the situation rightly at all and that you had not the proper confidence in the revolutionary energy of our workers. That is the calamity, that we have always been hindered at every step up to the last moment by the wet blankets.

How right we were was proved later. The first blow was to be struck on 11 November; on 8 November, Daumig and Liebknecht were arrested ... and we therefore decided to strike the first blow on the morning of 9 November. Barth had also decided to do this because he believed that he was to be arrested and thus it came about that the first blow was struck on 9 November.

But what was the difference in the situation between 5 November and 9 November? The difference was that in the meantime the Majority Social Democrats, the ministers, and the brand-new Chancellor, Ebert, could prepare for the situation. The authorities already knew on 7 November that matters had got beyond their control; they were better informed ... These people and *Vorwärts* fought against the revolution until the last moment. The revolution finally had to be victorious without them. On 9 November, Scheidemann was still the minister of Wilhelm II; when he got out of bed, and when the revolution had broken out, he rushed to the *Reichstag* and proclaimed the Republic. You were a minister until the last moment; do you want to deny that? [Scheidemann: "Why not?"] Certainly, that is characteristic of the times.

Nationalist and reactionary analysis of revolutionary agitation

Nationalists and reactionaries opposed to the overthrow of the imperial regime soon developed their own interpretation of events. In Documents 6.3 and 6.4, Albrecht Philipp presents the emergent (implicitly antisemitic) conservative consensus on the agitation that led to the revolution. Document 6.5, offers a brief but reasoned rebuttal of both revolutionary and reactionary narratives advanced by Social Democratic parliamentarian Julius Moses.

6.3 DR. PHILIPP ON THE AGITATION FOR COLLAPSE AND OVERTHROW[3]

The anti-war propaganda emanating from pacifists indisputably had a paralyzing effect on the front. It was only natural, owing to the gentle disposition of many Germans, that the ideas of international reconciliation should take root. Moreover, the Socialist and pacifist press fostered the erroneous belief that the international solidarity of labor would pave the way for an early peace. In my opinion, this combination of peace propaganda and anti-militarism was particularly dangerous. Though these influences may have been harmless at first, they nevertheless had a terribly disintegrating effect and clouded the relations between officers and men.

The propaganda in favor of a so-called peace by mutual agreement falls into this category. Although the man in the trenches did not advocate an annexationist peace, he nevertheless (as far as my observation went) repudiated on soldierly grounds any peace by agreement, so long as he saw daily from the attitude of the enemy that the latter desired no such agreement. It was not until news came from home concerning not the possibility of a peace by agreement but of its sabotage by Germany, i.e., agitation against our own government and against the army command, that the will of the troops to fight was paralyzed.

The phenomena that I have described thus far lead directly to another question: the role played by propaganda that aimed at bringing about a revolution … The intention to start a revolution during the war was already in the minds of certain Left Socialists from the beginning; the formal decision for revolution was taken in 1916. According to [Bavarian Independent Socialist leader Kurt] Eisner's secretary, the work, "which was pushed forward indefatigably in silence and darkness, began just at the time when Germany seemed to have the upper hand." According to Ledebour the only point that remained uncertain was the date for striking the first blow. According to my personal observations, certain units were already strongly infected with revolutionary ideas as early as the summer of 1917. The main work in the sense of the revolution did not, however, begin until 1918, when Bolshevist ideas from Russia were already beginning to spread among the troops.

Revolutionary ideas were communicated to the front from the rear; in any case they were not native to the front. The wire-pullers, well out of reach, were clever enough to respect certain soldierly feelings of the man at the front. For this reason their remarks about Hindenburg intended for the front were at first very carefully chosen while he was denounced as a "bloodhound" at home as early as 1917. Thus there were thousands of little "stabs in the back" administered by the German revolutionaries were ruthlessly taken advantage of by the enemy.

Russian influences deserve special mention in connection with the revolutionizing of the German army. The documents dealing with the Bolshevizing of the army on the Russian front are plentiful enough to prove how the poisoning was done from the East. Bolshevik revolutionary ideas spread rapidly in the interior of Germany as well, but I consider that it is hardly possible to speak of a Bolshevization of the army on the western front until the moment when the German revolution broke out … Dr. Oscar Cohn did thorough work in this respect with Russian money and did not need to take the trouble of revolutionizing the western army once the revolutionaries were at the helm in Berlin.

If the whole of these phenomena regarding the poisoning or disintegration of the front are taken together it can well be taken as proven that they had a fatal influence on the result of the war. The Supreme Command, which recognized these things clearly and tried to stop them, could not get the upper hand. In part it was probably not quite clear as to what means to employ to remove these evils, and had frequently to yield to political considerations.

But, even if we had succeeded in eliminating all these causes of weakness, this would hardly have been a guaranty of a victorious conclusion of the war for Germany, for the arrival of the Americans and the collapse of our allies would have forced us to conduct defensive operations on the frontiers of Germany which could no longer lead to a victory over the foe.

6.4 DR. PHILIPP ON THE REVOLUTION AS THE CAUSE OF MILITARY COLLAPSE[4]

The revolution deprived us of the last remains of our power of resistance and delivered us defenseless into the hands of the enemy at the very moment when Herr Scheidemann was announcing from the steps of the *Reichstag* that the German people had been victorious all along the line. In October and November, everything depended on adopting a firm attitude toward the enemy at the armistice negotiations; the fate of the German people was at stake. And it was at this moment that we broke with our own hands the sword that the army had bravely wielded for four and a half years. What had been systematically prepared and carefully organized beforehand by revolutionary agitation suddenly occurred with devastating effect.

The real fighting forces, although exhausted and beaten, in the hands of their commanders were ready to fight to the last. But the intelligence service, motor driver units, and flying formations which were farther to the rear, the staffs of the higher commands, the reserve units, and, above all, the lines of communication, threw off all ties of discipline and order from the moment the revolution began. Thousands of the "scattered," shirkers and deserters, joined them. Obedience was considered to be out of date. A terrible picture was presented behind the front that can only be recalled with horror by those who saw it with their own eyes. Drivers sold their cars and men their rifles and machine guns to the civil population of Belgium. They opened the prisons in the occupied territory, stormed the supply stores, plundered food trains and fought for their contents with the inhabitants, stormed the troop trains, and compelled the railway personnel by force of arms to transport them. Automobiles laden with spoils hastened in a wild flight for home.

The saddest and most foolish invention in the revolution was the Soldiers' Councils, which with ridiculous affectation tried to assume the power of command without having the slightest technical knowledge. They set up offices where discharge papers were arbitrarily prepared for the men, interfered with the forwarding of supplies, stopped trams, seized automobiles found on the roads, occupied the telephone offices and prevented the transmission of orders, seized stores and disposed of their contents. I could adduce numerous instances from my personal experience.

In the rear of the army, the effect of the revolution on the system of communications and transport was absolutely catastrophic. The bridges across the Rhine were closed and mutineers who had the entire transport system in their hands occupied the railway stations at Aachen, Cologne, Dusseldorf, and elsewhere. The forwarding of supplies, without which the army could not be fed, was blocked.

These facts are the only explanation for Hindenburg's telegram of 10 November in which he says that an armistice must be concluded. The revolution rendered all further resistance impossible; the only thing that could be done was to sign.

The army was stabbed in the back by the revolution, after prolonged efforts had been made to subvert it before-hand. The Stab-in-the-Back legend is no vague and dangerous myth, as has been claimed. It is a clear description of one of the saddest and most shameful facts in German history.

> ### 6.5 MAJORITY SOCIAL DEMOCRAT MOSES CONCERNING THE "STAB-IN-THE-BACK"[5]
>
> The collapse in 1918 (and not only the military collapse) was not the work of the revolutionaries and not the work of those who administered a "stab-in-the-back." Dozens of factors contributed to this collapse, and it was by no means least of all due to the complete exhaustion, both physical and psychical, of our whole nation. Future historians will have to recognize this. The German nation did not want to carry on because it was no longer able to continue.
>
> It may be hard for the advocates of the old system to have to listen to the summing up of the collapse in the following words by such a patriot as the German National Deputy Walter Lambach,
>
>> Anyone investigating the causes of the collapse must seek for evidence among the beginnings of the feeling of depression; otherwise he will not get at the root of the evil. All defects increased like an avalanche between the end of 1915 and the end of 1918. There might still have been time at the start to find the right way, but in 1918 it was too late. Those in authority cannot plead that they were not granted insight into the mind of the man in the street. On the contrary, the flagging of the army's moral power of resistance was pointed out to them with all seriousness. All political parties did this, but it was done in vain. The "ruling" classes in the "oligarchy" could not be taught ... Germany collapsed without the ruling classes even suspecting that they themselves had done the work of destruction or how they had done it. Even now they do not know it

"Im Felde unbesiegt?"

According to Wilhelm Groener's later statements, he decided during the revolutionary events of November to send nine "trustworthy" divisions to Berlin to shore up the provisional government. These divisions began to arrive in the first week of December. On December 10, massive parades were held along *Unter den Linden*, as one after another these divisions marched down the *via triumphalis* with bands playing, welcomed by ecstatic crowds. A reviewing stand was set up just beyond the *Pariser Platz*, with sufficient room for the commandant of the Berlin garrison, the mayor, and a rotating cast of members of the Council of People's Deputies. In one iconic moment, an excited Friedrich Ebert is photographed waving his hat at the passing troops, his face alight with joy.

FIGURE 6.3 *A Guard Corps marching down* Unter den Linden, *December 10, 1918 (Bundesarchiv Bildarchiv).*

FIGURE 6.4 *The Council of People's Deputies (Bundesarchiv Bildarchiv).*

FIGURE 6.5 *Friedrich Ebert welcoming troops as they pass through the Brandenburg Gate and down* Unter den Linden, *December 10, 1918 (Allmay).*

What was Ebert up to? Document 6.6 is an excerpt from an oath-taking ceremony for officers of the arrived divisions, where he called upon them to help in the rebuilding of a new, democratic Germany. Document 6.7 is the text of remarks he made on December 10.[6.] The second speech deserves to be read in full, as the actual words that Ebert spoke are not what entered popular memory. He never, for instance, said that the army was "unconquered in the field of battle" (*im Felde unbesiegt*). This "remark" by "one of the authors of the Stab-in-the-Back" is an important component in the nationalist *Dolchstoßlegende*. In its full text, one can see that it is full of memory for those who would not be returning and those who were still suffering the wounds of war. One can well imagine that his two fallen sons were chief on his mind.

6.6 EBERT AT OATH-TAKING CEREMONY OF THE RETURNING TROOPS, DECEMBER 8, 1918[7]

As you return from the turmoil of war, you will find that there have been huge changes at home. The old system is overthrown. The people are creating new constitutional forms to heal the deep wounds that our country suffered in the war. The people have charged us with the interim leadership of the government. Peace, freedom, and order are our guiding star. We hope that you will support us in our difficult task. Take the following vow: We pledge to the Council of Peoples' Deputies on behalf of the troops we represent to use all our strength for the German Republic and its provisional government.

6.7 EBERT TO THE RETURNING TROOPS, DECEMBER 10, 1918[8]

Comrades! Welcome to the German Republic! Welcome to the home that has been longing for you! Anxious concern for you has hovered over us constantly. At this moment, as we welcome you to your native hearth, our first thoughts are for the beloved dead. Alas, many will never again return. Hundreds of thousands rest in enemy territory in silent graves. Hundreds of thousands more returned before the end of the battle, torn and mutilated by enemy bullets. All of you who have sacrificed to protect our homeland have our indelible thanks. We cannot repay your sacrifice, and mere words are insufficient to thank them. What can we offer you is gratitude and promise to provide for you with fidelity. The aid of survivors of the terrible carnage and disabled veterans will be made as soon as possible. We are glad to welcome you home.

Welcome with all my heart, comrades and citizens. Your sacrifices and actions are unprecedented. No enemy has overcome you. (*Kein Feind hat Euch überwunden*). We only gave up the fight when the superiority of the enemy in men and equipment was unstoppable. And despite your heroic courage, it was our duty not to require useless sacrifice of you. You have resisted all sorts of terror manfully—both enlisted men and officers—whether in the chalk cliffs of Champagne, in the swamps of Flanders or in Alsace, whether in inhospitable Russia or in the hot south. You have endured endless suffering, accomplished immortal, almost superhuman deeds, displayed unmatched examples of your steadfast courage year after year. You have protected the homeland and kept your women, children and parents far from the murder and fire of war. You have kept German fields and workshops from devastation and destruction. For this, the homeland thanks you with overflowing passion. You may return with your heads held high. Never have men done and suffered more than yours. On behalf of the German people, profound thanks and once more, a warm welcome home.

> You will find our country is not the way you left it. A new day has dawned. German freedom is risen. The German people have shaken off the old ruling class, which was like a curse on all our activities. They have made themselves master of their own destiny. Above all, the hope for German freedom rests with you. You are the strongest bearer of the German future. No one has suffered more heavily than you under the injustice of the old regime. It was for you that we threw out the old system and fought for your freedom and your right to work. We cannot receive you with rich gifts nor offer comfort and prosperity. Our unhappy country has become poor ... But from the collapse, we want a new Germany, with the vigorous strength and unwavering courage.

Conclusion

In this chapter, we have presented seven documents that constitute important elements in both left and right Stab-in-the-Back narratives. As Documents 6.1 and 6.2 show, the revolutionaries—Independents, Revolutionary Shop Stewards, and Spartacists—differed between and among themselves over what steps to take in the first week of November 1918. Did their actions constitute a Stab-in-the-Back? Their clear intent was to overthrow the imperial regime and set up a council-based government of their own, feeling that they had sufficient support among workers in the major cities, the mutinous marines and the army. Historians still debate whether they were delusional about their chances of success or the potential durability of council-based governance.

That Friedrich Ebert and the Majority Social Democrats thought the revolutionaries were utopians willing to act without asking the German people for their support was clear. Just as they felt compelled to join the January Strike to end it, so the Majority Social Democrats felt forced to join with the Independents in the Council of People's Deputies. Unlike the Independents—who saw the Council as a new permanent form of government—Ebert and Scheidemann saw it as a stopgap *provisorium* until a National Assembly could decide on the proper form of the future German government. When they expelled the Independents from the Council and decided to use the army to suppress revolutionary upheaval in December 1918 and in January of the following year, were these acts a *Dolchstoß* against the revolution?

The true test of the legitimacy of any government is whether it can maintain law and order in its capital. On what forces, when pushed to the limit, could the new government rely? Since it was unwilling to work with revolutionary Red Guard units, this left the generals of the old army and whatever loyal troops they could muster. When Groener sent "reliable" forces to Berlin, would they follow the orders of the new regime? In Documents 6.6 and 6.7, Ebert was clearly trying to bring the ranks over to the side of his new government. Only when these efforts failed and the units "melted away" did a turning point arrive and a new strategy have to be crafted. When the Revolutionary Naval Division attempted to seize power at the end of December, followed the next month by a communist insurrection, Ebert and Scheidemann felt compelled to turn to extreme nationalist and frequently antisemitic volunteer divisions (*Freikorps*) enlisted by Groener and the generals to reestablish order.[9]

Thought questions

1. For their own purposes, Richard Müller and Georg Ledebour argue that the left's preparation was extensive and broadly based. To what extent do you think that this reflected reality?
2. Do you notice any differences between Müller and Ledebour's presentation of the sequence of events?
3. Dr. Albrecht Philipp, German National chair of the Subcommittee investigating the collapse, also argues that revolutionary agitation was extensive and preparation for the overthrow of the government was well advanced? Why might he make that argument and what weight would you give to his observations?
4. Read carefully the two speeches that Friedrich Ebert delivered to homecoming troops. What are his main topics? While he stated that the enemy did not overcome them, is that his main topic? How does he try to convince the troops to stand by the new government?
5. In your opinion, did Ebert's actions constitute a *Dolchstoß* against the revolution? Were they at odds with his respect for seeking the democratic wishes of the German people?

Further reading

Students might enjoy the reflections of a Communist participant in the revolution: Arthur Rosenberg, *A History of the German Republic*, translated by Ian F.D. Morrow and L. Marie Sieveking (New York: Russell & Russell, 1965) and *Birth of the German Republic*. Rosenberg was a Communist Party *Reichstag* deputy and sat on the Subcommittee investigating the collapse.

7

Did an English General Start the Myth?

FIGURE 7.1 *Sir Frederick Barton Maurice (National Portrait Gallery)*.

Biographical context

Nationalist proponents of the Stab-in-the-Back Myth were convinced that the notion of a *Dolchstoß* originated with "an English general." The "general" most frequently cited as the source of their belief was Major General Sir

Frederick Barton Maurice. Maurice was a career military officer, historian, and author. He had served in India and trained at the General Staff College. After service in the Battle of Mons in August 1914, he was recalled to London and made Director of Military Operations of the Imperial General Staff. In that position he was the indispensable protégé of the Chief of the General Staff, William Robertson. Most importantly for his German "champions," he knew the strengths and weaknesses of the contending armies and had unimpeachable status as someone who could declare that the German army was "undefeated in the field."

Maurice was alarmed in early 1918 when Prime Minister David Lloyd George in Parliament overstated the number of troops available to General Douglas Haig in Belgium. Maurice wrote to his superior and when his appeal went unanswered, wrote a letter to *The Times*. This sparked a political scandal, the matter was debated in the House of Commons, and Lloyd George pinned the "misunderstanding" on inaccurate numbers supplied by Maurice's office. As a result, Maurice was forced to resign, a martyr to political expediency. An accomplished writer, he was immediately employed by several newspapers as a military correspondent and analyst. It was in this capacity that Maurice wrote the two articles cited by the *Neue Zürcher Zeitung* in Documents 7.1 and 7.2.

Cultural context

A common trope within German culture is the "*deutsche Michel*," the plain, idealistic, trusting, touchingly naive Everyman who fails to see the world as it really is and is prone to letting others take advantage. This provided a cultural disposition to seek external validation of one's beliefs, even if from the outsiders who are responsible of Germany's misfortunes. How better to prove a Stab-in-the-Back than to hear it from the "Other" especially if that "Other" was a prominent, knowledgeable opponent? Who could be more knowledgeable than the general who had spent four years marshaling enemy forces? And who could be more pleasing than an opponent who wrote supportive things about the strength of the German army and the bravery of the German fighting man?

Coping with defeat

The German collapse stunned supporters of the old regime. Throughout the war, the military had censored newspapers and sought to project as rosy a picture of events as possible. Nationalists had wrapped themselves in a cocoon of positive thought and rejected all suggestions of difficulties as defeatist. When defeat came, they were shocked into absolute silence as the magnitude of the catastrophe was too great to process. The watchword for those few clear-headed monarchists like Hindenburg and select members of the civilian government was "to save what could be saved."[1]

But for the great mass of nationalists, coming to terms with defeat was impossible. The invincible army could not have failed. The stalwart columns of men marching in orderly fashion over the Rhine bridges and returning divisions parading down *Unter den Linden* the second week of December 1918 were *unbesiegt*. How could this disaster have unfolded?

A potent explanation began with a simple one-paragraph item in the reactionary *Deutsche Tageszeitung*. That newspaper maintained its own wire service (much in the manner of the Associated Press or Reuters), with stringers in various European cities. Other newspapers, especially regional and local papers with a conservative bent, subscribed to this news service and used all of the articles provided by it or edited bits as they saw fit, ensuring that the broadsheet's items received extensive circulation. On December 18, the *Tageszeitung* carried a laconic, one-paragraph notice in the middle left-hand column of its first page that gained notoriety far out of proportion to its humble language.

7.1. *DEUTSCHE TAGESZEITUNG* NOTICE: "THE STABBED-IN-THE-BACK GERMAN ARMY," DECEMBER 18, 1918[2]

Our correspondent reports: According to the *Neue Zürcher Zeitung*, General Maurice has written in the *Daily News*, "Before the war, the German Army was the strongest in Europe. At the time of the armistice, the ratio of Allied to German forces on the Western Front was five to three and a half. The civilian population stabbed the German army to death from behind. The behavior of the sailors of the German fleet was disreputable. They chose to surrender their ships to the enemy, rather than to defy death. They were the ones who saved Paris."

This simple notice received wide circulation and became an established part of *Dolchstoß* lore. An examination of public statements, letters, and diary entries demonstrates that it was repeated and uncritically accepted across a broad swath of nationalist opinion. Its motif—that an English general recognized the continued strength of the German army and states that it was stabbed in the back by the Home Front—became the foundation stone of the entire *Dolchstoßlegende*.

In fact, whether willfully or through ignorance, the *Tageszeitung* correspondent misinterpreted his source. The *Neue Zürcher Zeitung*, true to its role as the leading Swiss newspaper, maintained a correspondent in London. On December 17, that correspondent filed a report (see Document 7.2) on two articles written by General Sir Frederick Maurice that had recently appeared in London newspapers. A close reading of the article is revealing, especially the last paragraph.

7.2 *NEUE ZÜRCHER ZEITUNG* REPORT ON MAURICE'S ARTICLES, DECEMBER 17, 1918[3]

General Maurice has recently examined with remarkable acumen the causes of the catastrophic collapse of the military and maritime power of the German Empire in two newspapers—the *Daily News* and the *Star*—for whom he is the military correspondent ... The first article is dedicated to the Army, the second to the Navy. It should be remembered that Maurice from 1915 until his forced retirement was the head of military operations of the [Imperial] General Staff. This gives his judgment a very special value.

According to Napoleonic theory of war, Maurice accords the main role in wars to the "moral moment," although he acknowledges that it is difficult to implement in practice. So it was that the natural tendency of those who lack military experience to focus only on the materialist side, concerning themselves mainly with tangible measures of strength. The belief in the justice of their cause sustained many British soldiers in the gloomy days of the war. It is impossible to estimate the military value of this outlook. Thanks to this, the army stood fast when all seemed to be lost. Without it, the finest army cannot prevail.

I [the reporter] can testify from personal observation that this faith inspired the whole British army. It did so without ostentation or contempt for the enemy. This faith was shared and encouraged with an equal fervency by the civilian population in the army's ultimate success. Never, even in the darkest days such as last spring, when the British army in France "had her back to the wall" ... was this belief shaken. The people said nothing and just biting the teeth together [the German equivalent of keeping a stiff upper lip]. An Englishman is never to be more feared. This quality was demonstrated time and again ...

According to General Maurice, there exists in our time only a thin barrier between a system based on autocratic law and order and Bolshevism. The whole system of discipline that was built by William II [and his predecessors] was based on an uncertain foundation ... [After German unification, the army grew ever larger] and an entire military aristocracy was created, which became ever more alienated from the people and the regular soldiers. Discipline within the German army was servile. Such a slave-like discipline can never endure contingencies. While the gulf between officer and soldier increased, the caste of officers became extremely efficient. They held their ranks because they were good at their job. A generation of Germans was brought up in this system and knew nothing else ... As long as there were sufficient professional officers, their training and efficiency made the German army a terrible instrument of war.

As these officers died or collapsed from exhaustion, less able men sought to continue the old system. It began to crack and then collapsed with a roar that can still be heard. Free men had defeated slave-like authority. Discipline as practiced in the English army, is one of the strictest in the world, but it is tempered by personal relationships between officers and soldiers based on cooperation. In this way, the British Army possesses superior qualities of perseverance and determination.

In his second article, General Maurice reflected upon the German navy. He argues that, the British always thought that the German soldier was a brave and efficient enemy on the battlefield; our people have always shown him the respect that brave people accord courage. The collapse of the army was therefore a surprise. However, it is easier to understand why the collapse of the German navy came about. The fleet was recently created through a succession of Naval Laws, but you cannot build a navy with laws. The German fleet lacked the essential emotional attachments and traditions to cause human beings to defy death. The German army had a great tradition. Before the war, it was the finest in Europe. Its collapse, although not as dramatic as that of the fleet, was the more remarkable and without parallel in history. The German army occupied enemy territory and was not badly outnumbered.

General Maurice estimates that at the signing of the armistice, the armed forces of the Allies and the Germans on the Western Front were at a ratio of 5:3.5 ... This proves once again that an army cannot fight without having the people behind them. Because of the courage of the German people had been worn away, the army and navy both broke down.

Said in another form, *I found pretty much everywhere* the same views towards the German collapse as those expressed by General Maurice. As for the fleet, there is a real feeling of disapproval towards the sailors who preferred to rebel and deliver their ships to the enemy rather than to seek an honorable death as has happened so many times in the history of the British navy. As far as the German army is concerned, *the common view can be summed up in the phrase: the civilian population stabbed her in the back. (Sie wurde von der Zivilbevölkerung von Hinten erdolcht.)*

We have highlighted phrases from the first and the last sentences of the last paragraph. On such phrases the *Dolchstoßlegende* was built. The wording used by the unnamed *Neue Zürcher Zeitung* correspondent is nebulous. Did he mean that *Maurice* believed that the civilian population stabbed the army in the back or that it was a "*common view*" within the British populace and not necessarily shared by Maurice? One way to know what Maurice truly believed is to examine his original article in the *Daily News*.

7.3 MAURICE IN DAILY NEWS, "ARMY'S VICTORY FOR THE CAUSE OF RIGHT," NOVEMBER 17, 1918[4]

The war is over, for though it may be a long time before a formal peace is signed it is inconceivable that Germany should in any circumstances be able to renew hostilities.

The cardinal fact in the war is that we have been fighting the *Central* Powers. It has been the central position held by our enemies which has given them their military strength. This is a commonplace of military history.

As in her first scheme of conquest in the west, so in the last, Germany began with a well-conceived and bold plan which won her a great measure of success. A second time she failed because the skill of her generals in the field was not equal to the skill with which they drew up plans at the table.

A second time in her blind confidence she underrated the power of resistance of her enemies. She neglected to take the American Forces into account, just as she neglected in 1914 to take our little Army into account, and on almost identically the same ground as had seen her failure four years before her generals repeated the blunder they then made.

On July 18 Foch by his counter-stroke between the Marne and the Aisne defeated Germany's second plan of conquest in the west, just as by his counter stroke of September 9, 1914, he completed the defeat of her first.

The final phase with its dazzling succession of victories is but of yesterday. How, starting from July 18, Foch by a succession of blows wore down the enemy's power of resistance and exhausted his reserves, and so paved the way for his great effort, which began on September 26, and two days later set the whole front in a blaze from Dixmude to Verdun; how our own Army, starting from their success of August 8, won victory after victory in three months of more glorious fighting than is to be found in the history of war, how they burst clean through the Hindenburg defensive system, and in a final triumph drove in between the Scheldt and the Oise towards the battlefield of the Mons; how the Americans and Gouraud, after weeks of desperate fighting, carried the Kriemhilde lines, and at the end of the war were on the battlefield of Sedan; how the French armies pressed in the enemy's center while King Albert led his Belgians and their French and British comrades forward to Bruges and Ghent, it is all fresh in our minds.

From the time when Germany's failure became clear the moral bond which held her allies together snapped. It was victory in the west which prevented Germany from coming to the help of her friends and made their downfall certain, but in any case final victory was hastened and made more complete by a military triumph ... So in every field the Allied arms triumphed gloriously ...

In a short review of so vast a subject it is impossible even to touch upon all the causes that have led to final victory, but in this, as in every war, the moral forces have had greater influence than the physical. For us it has been a struggle of right against wrong, of freedom against oppression, of justice against tyranny. We have blundered often, we have been grievously punished for our backslidings and mistakes, but we have won through because our cause is just. We have proved that we are not a decadent people, and we can with pride hand on our sons the trust bequeathed to us by his fathers.

Maurice expanded upon these opinions in a book that he wrote the following year, *The Last Four Months*, parts of which are excerpted in Document 7.4. He argued that accepting an armistice with Germany in November 1918 was militarily justified, debunking those critics of British government policy who insisted that the Allies should have pursued the enemy on to German soil. All the Allied armies were at the end of their supply chains and it would have taken weeks if not months to build up the supplies necessary to sustain the offensive. German military analysts latched upon this comment—and the attendant notion that the German army might have attained Ludendorff's "breathing space"—if the Home Front had not broken.

7.4 EXCERPTS FROM MAURICE, THE LAST FOUR MONTHS[5]

The pursuit [in November 1918] was delayed mainly by the very complete destruction of the roads and railways by the Germans as they fell back, and by the consequent difficulty of getting up supplies to the troops. The enemy's difficulties in retreat were, however, much greater. Far into Belgium the roads were blocked with masses of transport and the railways with thousands of trucks, for the removal of which the Germans had not sufficient engines. Our aeroplanes, swooping down from the sky, attacked the German convoys and railway lines with machine-gun fire and with bombs, causing great destruction and frequent panics.

The opinion is widely held that the Armistice of November 11 was premature. It is argued that we had the German armies at our mercy, and that the foundations of peace would have been more sure if we had ended the war by forcing the surrender in the field of a great part of those armies, or, failing that, had driven our beaten enemy back across the Rhine and followed him into the heart of Germany. The reception of the German troops by the German people, their march into the German towns through triumphal arches and beflagged streets with their helmets crowned with laurels, and the insistent statements in Germany that the German armies had not been defeated, that the Armistice had been accepted to save bloodshed, and to put an end to the sufferings of the women and children aroused amazement and disgust in the victors. There was very real anxiety lest after all we had failed to convince Germany that war did not pay; it was felt that we ought to have brought the realization of what war means home to the German people in their own country, and that, had we done so, the long-drawn-out negotiations in Paris would have been concluded more speedily and more satisfactorily. It is worthwhile, therefore, examining the situation as it was at the time of the Armistice, and considering the case as it presented itself to the men who had to decide whether hostilities should cease or not.

There is no question that the German armies were completely and decisively beaten in the field. The German plenipotentiaries admitted it when they met Marshal Foch, and von Brockdorff-Rantzau admitted it at Versailles, when he said after the Allied peace terms had been presented to him: "We are under no illusions as to the extent of our defeat and the degree of our want of power. We know that the power of the German army is broken."

Every road was littered with broken-down motor trucks, guns, machine-guns and trench mortars. Great stacks of supplies and of military stores of all kinds were abandoned. Every railway line was blocked with loaded trucks that the Germans had been unable to remove. The sixty miles of railway in the valley of the Meuse between Dinant and Mezieres was filled from end to end with a continuous line of German freight trains carrying guns, ammunition, engineering equipment, and other paraphernalia. On the Belgian canals alone over eight hundred fully charged military barges were found. It is beyond dispute that on November 11 the lines of communication immediately behind the German armies had been thrown into complete disorder by the streams of traffic which were converging on the Meuse bridges, disorder greatly intensified by the attacks of the

Allied airmen. The German armies, unable to resist on the fighting front, could no longer retreat in good order, partly because of the congestion on the roads and railways behind them, which not only hampered the movements of the troops, but prevented the systematic supply to them of food and ammunition, partly owing to the fact that there were not horses left to draw the transport of the fighting troops. The following description of the condition of the German Army at the time when it began its march back to the Rhine in accordance with the Armistice terms has been recently published in Berlin:

Many of the units of the army were unable to move for lack of transport horses. Even those which were able to march had but little of their former mobility because the loss of horses had been so great. The majority of the troops were unaccustomed to long marches, the horses were in very poor condition, and the daily losses even during the retreat to the Antwerp-Meuse position had been very great. There was a deficiency of boots, winter clothing, hoof-pads, and frost nails, and winter weather might set in at any time. Almost all the casualty clearing stations, the ambulances and the hospitals were overcrowded owing to the continuous stream of wounded and sick, which poured in in consequence of the fighting, which continued right up to the Armistice.

Not less remarkable is a report from the headquarters of one of the divisions of the 17th German Army of the Crown Prince Rupprecht's group. The number of the division is obliterated on the report, which is dated November 8, 1918, and was found in a Belgian farmhouse. I have therefore been unable to identify the division: Almost all the machine-guns in the division have been lost or are out of repair, and half the guns of the artillery are deficient. Owing to lack of horses, less than half the transport of the division can be moved, and if the retreat continues, many guns and vehicles will have to be abandoned. Owing to lack of petrol, much of the motor transport of the division cannot be moved. The division has not received rations for two days, and the condition of the horses that remain is becoming very bad, because owing to constant movement there is no time to collect supplies from the country, and forage for them is not arriving.

If ever armies were in a state of hopeless rout, the German armies were in the second week of November 1918. The morale of the troops was gone; the organization of the services on which they depended for their needs had collapsed.

The criticism of the decision to stop fighting on November 11 has been due to the feeling that the German people do not recognize that their armies were beaten in the field, and the fear that this state of mind may sooner or later cause them to fight again. My own conviction is that the reception of the German troops in Germany and the statements made in the German press and by the German people that the Armistice

> was not the consequence of defeat were not unnatural, and can be explained. In November 1918, the German people could only get news of what was happening on the front through the newspapers, and the newspapers got their information through the military Press Bureau. The officials of that bureau, either because they were so inured to lying that they could not tell the truth, or in the hope of staving off revolution by continuing to deceive the people, announced, from the first days when things began to go wrong for them right up to the end, that German armies were fighting splendidly, that the front was everywhere intact, and that the troops were falling back, slowly and steadily, according to plan, to better and stronger positions. No inkling was given of the true state of affairs on the front, and the German people ascribed the surrender either to the revolution, if they were not in favor of it, or more generally to the desire of the new Government to get the blockade raised as quickly as possible. When the German troops came back to their homes and began to talk, the truth gradually became known, and the German people were able to see for themselves the state of the army which had once been their god. I do not think that there is to-day any intelligent German who does not know that the German armies were utterly beaten, though there may be many who would not admit as much to a foreigner.
>
> It has begun to dawn upon most Germans that it is more disgraceful to admit that they accepted defeat, ignominiously surrendered their navy, gave up the greater part of their artillery and aeroplanes, handed over large quantities of rolling stock and military stores, and permitted the armies of their enemies to occupy the Rhine unopposed, that they did all this when they still had the power to fight on, than to acknowledge that their armies were defeated in the field. I do not believe that we shall in the future hear much more of the unbeaten German armies, except perhaps from a few extremists like Bernhardi, nor do I believe that if we had not stopped fighting on November 11 it would have been possible to make Germany any less capable of resistance than she is today.

Maurice's opinion could not be clearer but so determined were nationalists that he had in fact stated that Germany was betrayed by the Home Front that they insisted that *The Last Four Months* was written to backtrack from his earlier—"true"—position. This was of course not the case, but low-information nationalists, if they in fact were aware of *The Last Four Years*—could at least find the argument plausible.

Erich Kuttner, a Social Democratic journalist and editor, wrote a scathing indictment of the nationalist determination to find external validation for their belief, especially through their reliance on Maurice's supposed opinion.[6]

Kuttner wrote, "One can look through Maurice's book and articles from A to Z and not find support for the idea that the German army lost because it was stabbed in the back." Document 7.5 is extracted from his sarcastically titled *Der Sieg War zum greifen Nahe!*—Victory was within Reach.

7.5 KUTTNER ON MAURICE AS ORIGINATOR OF THE STAB-IN-THE-BACK[7]

Nothing is more characteristic of the Stab-in-the-Back Legend than the fact that its existence is based on a forgery. After … the end of the war, there appeared in the right-wing press an alleged words of the English General Maurice, who was said to have written in the newspaper *Daily News*, "The German army was not defeated by the Allies but was stabbed-in-the-back the home front."

It was these alleged "words of the English General" that were cited by Hindenburg and Ludendorff before the Committee of the National Assembly. It is very significant that neither of those generals, who continued in public to rely on the "testimony" of their English counterpart, have ever cared about the reality of this alleged utterance. Indeed, the "words" of General Maurice were from A to Z an invention. Its distributors recklessly disseminated this injurious falsehood to the German people.

General Maurice explicitly wrote the following in July 1922:

> I have never at any point expressed the opinion that the outcome of the war was the result of the army being stabbed in the back by the German people. On the contrary, I have always taken the view that the German armies on the Western Front on November 11, 1918 were no longer capable of effective resistance based on purely military reasons. I have said that if we had given the German armies time to recover, they could then have probably prolonged their fight, but that their final defeat was inevitable. These views, which I discuss in my book *The Last Four Months*, I hold and have always held.

On this point, Colonel Schwertfeger, himself a prominent right-wing war writer says, "I have studied the words and work of General Maurice myself. It should no longer be claimed that the General was the originator of the phrase Stab-in-the-Back or believes in its existence."

The enormity of the giant swindle (driven by the name and person of General Maurice in the right-wing press) is clear when one actually reads Maurice's book. Of course reactionaries still insist that the content of the "utterance" itself is correct, although its origin has been exposed as a clumsy falsification of history. Lies all around!

Despite Kuttner's demolition of the "Maurice Myth," supporters of the English origin of the concept found it hard to back down. We can observe this in sequential responses (Documents 7.6 and 7.7) by Hermann von Kuhl in his depositions to the Subcommittee investigating the causes of the Collapse.

7.6 KUHL ON MAURICE, #1[8]

Whoever invented the phrase "the Stab-in-the-Back"—whether it comes from the British General Maurice or not—is immaterial. It is simply a question of examining the evidence that can be adduced for one or the other view. I have previously recorded my opinion based on the evidence available to me. I am currently reviewing new material, but I can only repeat the remarks made in my earlier work on most points.

7.7 KUHL ON MAURICE, #2[9]

During the days preceding the conclusion of the armistice, we were engaged in retiring to the Antwerp-Meuse line. Perhaps we delayed too long, for political reasons, to retire to large positions in the rear. We did not want to create an impression of weakness during the negotiations for the armistice, but the negotiations dragged on for a long time and the troops became exhausted in the constant fighting. There is no doubt that we could thereupon have halted at the Antwerp-Meuse position and put up fresh resistance. But for this a breathing space was necessary. Would the enemy have granted us this?

General Maurice of the British Army enlarges upon this in his book *The Last Four Months*. His representation of the situation is admittedly strongly influenced by the endeavor to represent our defeat as the result of the superior generalship of Marshal Foch. Consequently, in many cases he brushes aside the numerous other circumstances which had an effect on the course of events in 1918 and endeavors to represent the German defeat as having been brought about by force of arms and to make it as great as possible. His opinion is worth all the more, as he has to admit, nevertheless, that even the Allied Armies had reached the limit of their powers in October and November 1918.

According to Maurice, on November 11, the Allied troops engaged in advancing toward the Meuse had reached the utmost point to which supplies could follow them ... A further rapid advance across the Meuse that would have ended the war with a great battle like that of Sedan was consequently, according to Maurice, absolutely out of the question. If hostilities had been continued the Allies would have had to halt until the roads and railways in their rear had been repaired and the supply service was working regularly. They would therefore have had to give us a breathing space that would have permitted us to restore order and retire beyond the Meuse. We could have established ourselves there in a strong position on a much shorter front. A great battle that would have cost much life would have been necessary.

Field Marshal Haig confirms the statements made by General Maurice in his dispatches that were published in 1919. Even though he claims for the Allies the glory of having inflicted a decisive defeat on the Germans, he has to admit that a further advance in November would have been rendered considerably more difficult for the same reasons as those given by Maurice. As a matter of fact, divisions were finally dependent on railway stations from eighty to one hundred miles distant, from which only bad roads led to the front. "The advance would have been considerably delayed if it had had to be carried out in face of the resistance of even a defeated foe. The difficulties of supply would have been extraordinarily increased in many respects, especially by the necessity of sending forward large supplies of munitions."

But as Kuttner pointed out, advocates of the various nationalist versions of the *Dolchstoßlegende* did not need verifiable truth. Nor did they particularly need Maurice, as any "English General" would do. According to D. J. Goodspeed, Erich Ludendorff would at times claim a second general as the source of the legend.

7.8 EXCERPT FROM D. J. GOODSPEED, LUDENDORFF: GENIUS OF WORLD WAR I[10]

As soon as Ludendorff returned to Berlin, he and [his wife] were given a luxurious suite in the Adlon Hotel, the same building where the Allied Disarmament Commission had its headquarters. To avoid publicity he called himself "Karl Neumann" and ... [was provided] with a separate exit to the Wilhelmstrasse so that he would not be embarrassed by meeting Allied officers in uniform.

> As a matter of fact, Ludendorff had no objection to exchanging reminiscences with senior officers who had recently been his enemies. The French military representatives were scrupulous never to address a single unnecessary word to a German officer, but some British generals were curious to meet the man who had so long been their principal opponent. One day when General Sir Neill Malcolm, the head of the British Military Missions, was visiting Ludendorff, he was surprised to be told that the German Army would never have lost the war if it had not been for the vacillation and weakness of the German government and people. They had, Ludendorff said, proved themselves unworthy of their warrior ancestors. Ludendorff was none too coherent, and General Malcolm, in an attempt to pin down his argument asked: "Are you trying to tell me, general that you were stabbed-in-the-back?" Ludendorff's prominent blue eyes lit up at the phrase. "That's it!" he shouted triumphantly. "They stabbed me in the back!" This casual catchword was later to become notorious as Nazi propaganda.

Conclusion

Honest military intellectuals like Hermann von Kuhl might read Maurice and temper their understanding of his words and whether he originated the concept of the *Dolchstoß*; for lesser lights, their first hearing that "an English general has said" was enough to cement the idea in their brains forever. Kuttner's devastating demolition of the lie that Maurice originated the *Dolchstoßlegende* was simply passed off as socialist propaganda.

Thought questions

1. After a careful reading of the article in the *Neue Zürcher Zeitung* do you think the paper's correspondent actually ascribed the Stab-in-the-Back notion to Maurice?
2. Why might the *Deutsche Tageszeitung* have misconstrued the original Swiss article?
3. What is the power of first impressions? Does it strike you as odd that nationalists were so impervious to the reality of Maurice's true opinion about the end of the war?

Further reading

Maurice's *The Last Four Months* is actually extremely well written, accessible military history. The author betrayed no bitterness at his dismissal. His ire is aimed at the host of "armchair" generals who maintained that the Allies should have chased the German army across the Rhine. Students seeking the most recent treatment of the military collapse simply must read Scott Stephenson, *The Final Battle: Soldiers of the Western Front and the German Revolution of 1918* (Cambridge: Cambridge University Press, 2009).

8

The Hindenburg Testimony

Institutional context

The emergence of a cult based around Field Marshal Paul von Hindenburg is one of the strangest occurrences of the Great War, speaking to the need of the German people for a hero/savior and the Emperor's manifest unsuitability for that role. Kaiser Wilhelm II was totally inadequate as a war leader.[1] His difficult birth left him physically and mentally impaired: a crumpled shoulder and withered right arm detracted from the military bearing he so desired: anesthesia administered to his mother crossed through the placenta and probably was responsible for his violent mood swings, his clear attention deficit disorder and unthinking verbal bellicosity. By the outbreak of the Great War he was distrusted by parties and politicians across the political spectrum. While he was legally Supreme Warlord, the Kaiser spent most of the war at Supreme Command headquarters, where he was reduced to the role of incapable observer.

The Emperor's incapacity left a vacuum that Hindenburg eventually filled. Paul von Beneckendorff und von Hindenburg descended from a distinguished Prussian military family.[2] He served bravely in the Wars of Unification and was present at the proclamation of the new empire in the Hall of Mirrors in Versailles in 1871. In the peacetime army he rose to general rank and was chosen to lead the 3rd Guards division, created for aspiring officers of the newly incorporated western territories of Prussia. After a career that never quite fulfilled its early promise, he retired to the city of Hanover in 1911. In August 1914 he was summoned back into the army to help manage the crisis on the Eastern Front provoked by the unexpectedly early Russian attack on East Prussia. His position was understood to be mostly symbolic. The de facto commander of the eastern Eight Army was Erich Ludendorff, quartermaster-general of the army and hero of the Battle of Liége. (As a non-noble, the dynamic Ludendorff lacked the social status to command an Army Group.) Ludendorff and Hindenburg developed a strong working relationship in which Ludendorff won the victories and Hindenburg garnered the laurels. The victories at Tannenberg and the Masurian Lakes

FIGURE 8.1 *Celebration of Hindenburg's 70th birthday (Imperial War Museum).*

FIGURE 8.2 *Poster for the 7th War Loan featuring Hindenburg (Bundesarchiv Bildarchiv).*

raised the old man to the status of national hero. Hindenburg reveled in that role, and along with his assistant demanded ever-greater control over military and civilian mobilization. In 1916, the duo emerged victorious from an intra-service power struggle and established what some scholars think of as a virtual dictatorship.

After the war, Hindenburg, retired to Hanover, the scene of his last posting before he was recalled to the colors. An enterprising publicist commissioned him to "write" his (mostly ghost-written) autobiography. Inasmuch as most nationalists and monarchists were completely disinterested in restoring the abdicated Wilhelm II to the throne, Hindenburg became the focus of conservative attempts to roll back the revolution. His testimony before the *Reichstag* committee would be the first step in what was assumed would be a campaign for president of the new Republic.

Investigating the war

In 1919, the provisional German government was faced with an unpalatable demand from the Allies that leading figures in the imperial military and government be turned over for war crimes trials. Germany was powerless to resist this demand outright, but the cabinet came up with a solution. Citing issues of national sovereignty, the National Assembly, elected in January 1919, set up its own committee to investigate war guilt and potential war crimes. If any guilt were ascertained, the malefactors would be tried in German courts.

When the original charge was given, one large committee representing in rough proportion all the parties present in the Assembly was constructed. While the Allies were most interested in pre- and inter-war issues, the Germans were also interested in the *end* of the war. The "Weimar" parties—the Majority Social Democrats, the Center, and the Democrats—had all supported the Peace Resolution passed by the *Reichstag* in 1917 that favored the speediest possible conclusion of a defensive war without annexations and indemnities. They therefore assumed that they stood on the moral high ground. Government officials and military leaders whose advocacy of an expansionist program of territorial conquest would be called to testify and discredited. The best way to do this, clearly, was to call witnesses and publicly interrogate them. What could go wrong?

The stage is set

One individual was absolutely central to the first stage in the development of the *Dolchstoßlegende*: Karl Helfferich.[3] The son of a wealthy textile manufacturer, Helfferich studied law and received his advanced degree in economics. From 1901 to 1906 he served in the Foreign Office and in 1908 was made a director of the *Deutsche Bank*. In 1915 he became state secretary in the Treasury, where he was responsible for war financing, eventually rising to the position of Vice-Chancellor. An early opponent of unrestricted submarine warfare and supporter of internal reform, in the course of the war Helfferich moved to the right and became a vocal supporter of the Supreme Command. At the conclusion of the war, Helfferich raised funds for anti-Bolshevik causes, the *Freikorps* and groups linked to anti-republican death squads. When the events in this chapter took place, he was a major player in the German National People's Party.

There was considerable excitement on among German Nationals about the opening of the *Reichstag* hearings and the decision that Hindenburg would testify. Although the investigation had originated in dual desires to short-circuit an international war crimes tribunal and to fasten blame on those in the German government who had started the war and had led to the country's ignominious collapse, it also proved a tonic to the Right. Nationalists used the occasion to lambast the investigation—frequently in antisemitic terms—as evidenced by an article in the reactionary *Deutsche Tageszeitung*.

8.1 "UNDER THE JEWISH FLAG," NOVEMBER 11, 1919[4]

Hindenburg and Ludendorff will shortly be called as "witnesses" to appear before the so-called "Investigative Committee." They will be asked to respond to questions that can then be twisted around so that the two generals incriminate themselves and can be brought before a "State Court." The left wing press has already tried this several times in the current interrogations, remarking upon the witnesses "strikingly weak memory" and similar aspersions.

Some would have preferred for Ludendorff alone to be brought before the "Investigative Committee." This body was invented for the sole purpose of acting like the "State Court of Justice" in order to find Ludendorff guilty for the prolongation of the war and the resulting increase in casualties. [In this way] guilt and accusations can be deferred from the Majority Social Democrats …

Until now the Left has taken little joy in their "Investigative Committee" because the affair has been so badly managed … that their wickedness has emerged plain for all to see. We feel that this will become even more apparent if Mr. Cohn, Mr. Sinzheimer, and their comrades question Hindenburg and Ludendorff … The left-wing press will play the role of the "choir."

> Hindenburg and Ludendorff "interrogated" by Cohn, Sinzheimer, Bonn, Gothein, and whoever else comes along! The German people are to blame for letting this disgrace be foisted upon them. They have in their hands [the means] by which they can free themselves if they want. [At the moment] they have the black-red-gold "Jewish Flag" blowing over them.

Hindenburg's arrival in Berlin and the events leading up to his testimony were all carefully choreographed to have a maximum political impact. When he detrained, an honor guard escorted him through crowed streets to Helfferich's villa.[5] There, soldiers of a guards regiment were posted to "protect" the former Field Marshal, while demonstrations of well-wishers took place in the street outside. The following day, Erich Ludendorff joined Hindenburg and his host for a strategy session. Together, they decided that Hindenburg would ignore the text of the questions the Committee asked him to answer and instead read from a prepared statement. It is widely supposed that Hellfrerich crafted this statement, with substantial input from Ludendorff. Hindenburg would then turn the answering of questions over to the aggressive Ludendorff, who in any case was the detail man in the relationship. While the triumvirate plotted, Berlin stood on edge.

FIGURE 8.3 *Karl Helfferich, Paul von Hindenburg, and Erich Ludendorff at Helfferich's villa after the generals' testimony (Alamay).*

8.2 "POPULAR ANTICIPATION OF THE HINDENBURG TESTIMONY," NOVEMBER 17, 1919[6]

After yesterday's exciting Hindenburg demonstrations, it was widely expected that similar scenes would be enacted outside the *Reichstag* this morning. But the streets surrounding the *Reichstag* were deserted. Snow had fallen again during the night, so that the *Reichstag* building arose in solitary state out of the expanse of glistening whiteness. The government had issued a warning against demonstrations and had doubtless also intimated to the heads of Universities and schools that they were on no account to allow as they had apparently done previously, their students and scholars to participate in the public sitting of the Inquiry Commission. But beneath the surface there was, nevertheless, tension to a degree unreached since the sanguinary days of January and March. Everyone is asking whether serious disorders are imminent, a question which after the uneventful celebration of the anniversary of the Revolution last Sunday would have been answered in the negative before Marshal von Hindenburg's arrival set Berlin in a ferment. The reactionary elements seized on the occasion to emphasize their disapproval of the existing order of things. Noisy youths, mainly soldiers and students, declared they would not allow Marshal von Hindenburg to be cross-examined by the Committee.

The newspapers contain a message from Marshal von Hindenburg of thanks for his reception, and an appeal to his admirers to abstain from further demonstrations. The Socialists hold mass meetings on Sunday to protest against these reactionary activities. The government has forbidden street demonstrations and has urged parents to keep their children at home with a view to preventing them from running grave risks since military precautions are to be taken.

8.3 "GERMAN NATIONAL ATTEMPTS TO USE THE PRO-HINDENBURG DEMONSTRATIONS," NOVEMBER 17, 1919[7]

The German National People's Party, representing the extreme Right, seems to be identified with the movement for exalting Hindenburg for political reasons at the same moment as they incite to anti-Semitism ... All these symptoms are naturally creating grave uneasiness, which found expression today in a speech by Herr Hirsch, the Prussian Premier, who condemned excesses of the extremists on both sides and advocated the solidarity of the working classes. The reactionary demonstrations have aroused all Social Democrats to fury. Herr Haase's funeral on Thursday clearly demonstrated the following he possessed. The Majority Socialists, realizing the importance of a reunion of both wings of the Socialist which it had been hoped to effect through Herr Haase's influence, are now working feverishly to attain this end. Obviously anything like a reactionary demonstration is calculated to help them. Herr Scheidemann, quick to seize the opportunity, contributes a leading article to the *Vorwärts* tonight headed, "The enemy is on the Right." He points out that the Berlin streets, where the workers are forbidden to assemble or march in processions, have become the playground for Monarchist demonstrations. Marshal von Hindenburg was greeted with music, a guard of honour was posted to receive him, cheers were raised for the Kaiser, and Republicans attacked, naturally without the Reichswehr intervening. Marshal von Hindenburg, he adds, is staying at Herr Helffrich's house. Two guards are stationed at the front door in his honour. There is no end to the German National Party demonstrations before the house, and Herr Helfferich meanwhile is appearing before the Committee of Inquiry. At the same time Marshal von Hindenburg proceeds to the *Reichstag*. Why? He is not to be heard yet. Herr Scheidemann draws the obvious deductions from these proceedings and summons his party to be ready to assert themselves.

8.4 THE PARTIES AND THE PROJECTED TESTIMONY, NOVEMBER 19, 1919[8]

It would be too much to say that there is any widespread anxiety at present, and the military preparations made for tomorrow's proceedings have done much to reassure the public. Still, in times like these you never can tell whether a small fire will not burst into a blazing conflagration. There is plenty of combustible material in Berlin, and that it will take fire in some day nobody doubts. There is the Military Monarchist Party, which never for a moment acquiesced in the present situation. There is the Independent Socialist Party, which regards militarists and Monarchists as the cause of all Germany's misfortunes. There is the Communist Party, threatening death to every other party in the country. If one were to credit the utterances of the extremists one might assume that all these parties and one or two others unenumerated are thirsting for each other's blood. It is, however, dangerous to take the statements of extremists *au pied de la lettre.* That the militarists and Monarchists aspire to it upset the Republic is no secret at all; the only question that arises is whether they consider the time appropriate for their intended coup. Many judges believe that the wisest heads among them entertain grave doubts on this score, but the hotheads may prevail over more sober counselors; and there always exists the possibility that events may precipitate a crisis. Herein lies the real significance of the Hindenburg demonstrations. That the workers do not wish for trouble is clear from the fact that despite the Communist's efforts to fan the flame of discontent into a strike, the metalworkers' dispute, which for many weeks kept large numbers of Berlin operatives out of employment, has been abandoned by universal consent. Nor have the bourgeois parties any desire for trouble. "They are too cowardly to risk their carcasses in a revolution," said a well-known politician to me today in the lobby of the *Reichstag*. The Majority Socialists, with *Vorwärts* at their head, are sounding a note of alarm at the Hindenburg demonstrations, but they are accused by the Independents of employing demonstrations as a bogy to frighten the Independents into the reunion that Majority Socialists so ardently desire. If, however, the gauntlet should be thrown down by the Military party, there seems little doubt that the challenge will be taken up by the entire working class population, which by a general strike could immediately paralyze such economic activity as the country still possesses and make chaos complete. That matters would not rest there is obvious. Then, when it was too late, Conservative editors. Monarchist officers, and reactionary politicians, who are openly or covertly encouraging these demonstrations, would doubtless repent. "We do not shrink from a trial of strength," I overheard an extreme Radical on Saturday, "If it comes, all the trees in the *Tiergarten* will not suffice for the hanging of those we mean to deal with."

While the parties tried to position themselves, the government seriously worried that the testimony was a preliminary step in a monarchist coup. As mentioned in Document 8.4, Independent Socialist leader Hugo Haase (co-chair of the pre-war Social Democratic Party and leader with Friedrich Ebert of the Council of Peoples' Deputies) had been assassinated on October 8, so tempers on the left were already high. Was, Social Democrats feared, Haase's assassination (only the first of numerous prominent republican figures) been the prelude to a monarchist coup? Gustav Noske—the Defense Minister and the person in charge of security in the capital—took actions to preclude that possibility, all the while feigning solicitude for the Field Marshal. Police loyal to the regime were dispatched to quell any possible violence and units of the military were placed around the *Reichstag* and lined the streets of Hindenburg's route.

8.5 "THE MEANING OF THE BERLIN DEMONSTRATIONS," NOVEMBER 19, 1919[9]

Wherever two or three people meet in Berlin today they put the same question to each other, "What is the real meaning of the Hindenburg demonstrations?" Hindenburg is by far the most popular figure in Germany, and therefore it was only natural that when he came to Berlin that he should receive an enthusiastic welcome. By young soldiers, university students, and all those youthful elements of the population whose imagination has been touched by his achievements, in whose hearts the Hindenburg legend has taken root, his coming was eagerly seized upon as an occasion for demonstrating their admiration.

Obviously, with such material at hand to work upon, nothing was easier than to organize manifestations in his honour. That this was done is beyond question. Army officers, university professors, even in some instances teachers in elementary schools, have stimulated this movement. When crossing the Königsplatz this morning, while the crowd was waiting in expectation of Hindenburg's arrival, I came across a school of young children, mostly boys of about 12, trudging through the deep snow in high glee at having a holiday with the chance of seeing the national hero into the bargain. Almost without exception the crowds waiting to give Hindenburg an ovation consisted of young men and women. I overheard many jesting remarks passed by students on the impression their demonstration would make and on the comments which the Radical Press would publish, declaring it "a complete fiasco," "a miserable failure," and so forth.

8.6 "COUP FEARS," NOVEMBER 19, 1919[10]

At midday today no one, not even demonstrators, took a serious view of the situation. It was not until the Lützow Corps guard of honour visited Herr Helfferich's house, Hindenburg's temporary home, an indiscretion which created general surprise, that people began to look serious. When this incident became known through this evening papers heads were shaken and the tone of comments on the situation became graver. It was realized that perhaps after all there might be more behind the incidents of the last few days than had been generally assumed.

> ... Anti-Militarists are very indignant at the action of the Lützow Guard Corps in sending a guard of honour to Herr Helfferich's house this morning to salute von Hindenburg, whose inspection of this guard is contrasted with the wish expressed by him on Saturday that there should be no more demonstrations. Feeling, however, is somewhat quieter today, it being declared in what may be considered well-informed circles that the counterrevolution is postponed. It is said that Herr Noske spoke very plainly to von Hindenburg in his interview with the Marshal on Saturday, pointing out that the government intended to take the strongest measures for the maintenance of public order. The parties of the Right are believed to discountenance any serious revolutionary attempt at present, because, should such an attempt succeed in upsetting the existing government, the onus of conducting public business would devolve upon them, and this is a responsibility they are very unwilling to assume. Moreover, it is practically certain that any military coup would have only very short-lived success, while terrible retribution would be dealt out to its promoters
>
> Later reports tend to show that the authorities are very nervous lest the German National Party should create disturbances tomorrow when Marshal von Hindenburg goes to the *Reichstag*. At any rate, that party is credited with the preparation of great demonstrations which the government are determined to prevent. Herr Noske has ordered the *Reichstag* building to be shut off for a long distance, strong cordons of military are to be posted in the streets round the *Reichstag*; pickets will shut off the streets through which von Hindenburg passes on his way thither and reserve of troops have been brought to Berlin. Order given to the forces entrusted with the maintenance of order are very far reaching, since not only are demonstrations expected in front of the *Reichstag*, but also the German Nationals are believed to intend the organization of these through the streets. These are tense ... since they would provoke the workers to counter demonstrations and possible occasion street fighting. It is feared that soldiers free from duty may join the demonstrations.

Helfferich's testimony

While pro-Hindenburg demonstrators filled the streets of the government district, the future of the investigation was being decided within a stuffy, hot committee room. A belligerent Karl Helfferich took the stand and completely dominated the proceedings.

8.7 HELFFERICH'S CONTENTIOUS TESTIMONY, NOVEMBER 13, 1919[11]

Dr. Karl Helfferich, former [sic] German vice chancellor, who was on the witness stand before the war investigation committee all morning, began a long drawn out vilification of the United States, culminating with the declaration: "America maintained a mere paper neutrality; President Wilson was satisfied to make money out of European blood and suffering." This declaration was greeted with "Bravos!" from the spectators and many German newspapermen. It aroused Deputy Cohen, who demanded that Helfferich be forbidden to use such expressions. But Chairman Wermuth ruled that the method of expression by witnesses couldn't be controlled. Deputy Sinsheimer [sic] here interjected the question: "Was not German anger at America artificial?" Helfferich banged the table angrily, and replied: "It was genuine from the very bottom, chiefly because of the ammunition, barbed wire, poisonous gases and food which America delivered to the entente."

8.8 "BATTLE OF TALK CLOSES BERLIN'S INQUEST," NOVEMBER 16, 1919[12]

Dr. Karl Helfferich ... appearing as a witness again today ... was fined 300 marks for refusing to answer a question submitted by Deputy Cohen. Dr. Helfferich said he never had answered a direct question from Cohen and would not. The deputies imposed the fine. Herr Wermuth disagreed and relinquished his seat [on the Committee]. He was replaced by Deputy Gothein. Then the public session was suspended amid great excitement.

8.9 "SCENE IN COMMITTEE," NOVEMBER 17, 1919[13]

The sitting of the Committee of Inquiry culminated in a quarrel even angrier than yesterdays. At the opening the chairman, Herr Wermuth, reproved Dr. David for his reference to the peace action undertaken in the second half of December 1916, by a neutral Power. Dr. David had asserted this peace action should have been regarded as an extraordinarily promising one that must have led to the strengthening of President Wilson's efforts. The *Reichstag* knew nothing of it. Had it known the Centre Party would under no circumstance have consented that everything should be thwarted by the ruthless submarine war. The chairman ruled that it was still too early for the discussion of this question in public. Helfferich continued, at first quietly. Throughout his evidence he adopted an aggressive attitude towards the Committee as a whole. He now suddenly caused much indignation by refusing to answer any questions asked by the Independent Socialist member of the Committee, Herr Oscar Cohn. The Chairman protested, but Herr Helfferich retorted that the Committee was a strange mixture of a Parliamentary Committee and a law court, and he himself a strange mixture of witness and accused. [He declared],

> We do not want to bamboozle each other. From the very first I've felt myself to be the accused here, if this were a law Court. I should refuse Herr Cohn as [my] Judge. You know what I refer to, I ask you to be satisfied with this allusion in order to avoid hard words, but if you force me I shall give evidence on that point also.

The committee, after private deliberation, ruled that Herr Helfferich must answer, but he remained obdurate and was fined M.300 (£15).

A further surprise came immediately afterwards, when Herr Wermuth announced his resignation of the chairmanship. Herr Gothein, who replaced him, at once adopted a stern tone, forbidding remarks by the pressmen and demonstrations by the public. Herr Helfferich then gave his opinion that Cohn was partly, perhaps primarily, to blame for the collapse of the German front. He said he referred to a sum of money the Russian Bolshevists had given Herr Cohn to support the German revolution. Herr Cohn defended himself at some length, incidentally pointing out that on a previous occasion in the National Assembly he said that anyone in the National Assembly or government who again advanced such charges against him would be a liar. Intense excitement again prevailed when Herr Cohn at the end of his statement exclaimed, "For me, Herr Helfferich is not a witness, but the accused." On the Chairman's refusing to allow Herr Helfferich to continue the altercation, the latter collected his papers and exclaimed, "Then I shall cease to be a witness and leave the room." The sitting broke up in disorder. It was later decided to resume the inquiry on Monday, when Marshal von Hindenburg will give evidence.

8.10 "HELFFERICH ACCUSES DEPUTY COHN OF TREASON," NOVEMBER 17, 1919[14]

Dr. Karl Helfferich ... who was fined today 300 marks for refusing to answer a question at the inquiry ... counted out the money and placed it on the table.

Deputy Gothein replaced Herr Wermuth as Chairman, the latter having declared his disagreement with the committee's decision. The new Chairman became enraged at the ensuing demonstration by the spectators, and threatened to exclude the newspapermen and others if there was a repetition.

8.11 "MAY ADJOURN INVESTIGATION," NOVEMBER 18, 1919[15]

It is more than doubtful whether the National Convention Committee prying into peace responsibilities will resume its investigation Monday, and its failure to do so will mean a tactical victory for the reactionary element brought on by Dr. Karl Helfferich's refusal to continue his testimony yesterday afternoon.

It is clear Helfferich acted on a preconcerted plan when yesterday he provoked Minister David to use language casting doubt on German diplomacy's loyalty towards President Wilson, to which Bethmann Hollweg and Zimmermann replied in most exaggerated terms. Even then Helfferich threatened to leave the witness stand. His reactionary friends dissuaded him during the intermission, because they considered the occasion inopportune ... However the reactionary elements decided in any circumstances to prevent Hindenburg and Ludendorff from being subjected to what they considered an undignified examination and Helfferich used the first opportunity today for another provocation which led to a sudden termination of the session.

When Helfferich was finished, the committee was completely flummoxed. One chair resigned, another was on the brink. Accusations of treason had been thrown in the face of a member (Cohn) that even the Majority Social Democrats could not support. This set them up to be blind-sided by the Field Marshal. As a courtesy, Hindenburg had been given six questions drawn up by the Committee so that he could prepare his answers. After consulting with Helfferich and Ludendorff, however, Hindenburg launched a surprise attack, refusing to answer questions and going on the offensive.

The Hindenburg testimony

Hindenburg had already expressed himself laconically on the collapse in his hurriedly written (or rather ghost-written) autobiography, *Aus meinem Leben.*

8.12 HINDENBURG'S AUTOBIOGRAPHICAL REFERENCE TO THE COLLAPSE[16]

We were at the end! Like Siegfried under the deceitful javelin thrust of the grim Hagen, our weary front collapsed; in vain she had tried to drink fresh life out of the dried up spring of our homeland's strength. Our task now was to save the life of the remaining forces of our army for the reconstruction of the fatherland. That left much hope for the future.

8.13 HINDENBURG'S TESTIMONY[17]

History will judge what I say to you today … When we [meaning Ludendorff and himself] assumed leadership of the Supreme Command, we proposed that the government combine all forces at its disposal for the successful prosecution of the war. What became of these proposals is known … I wanted complete and willing cooperation. Instead, as a result of party competition, we encountered failure and defeatism … We were constantly concerned whether we would maintain the support of the Home Front until the war could be successfully concluded. At this time [Hindenburg does not indicate a date, seemingly the last year of the war] the intentional undermining of the army and navy began. Those troops who remained loyal had to carry the additional burden of those, inspired by revolutionary ideas, who did not … Ultimately, we could no longer expect that our commands would be executed. We asked that we be allowed to enforce strict discipline to counter this subversion but our appeals were fruitless. We were no longer able to control the forces at our disposal. The collapse was inevitable. The revolution was only the capstone.

An English general rightly said, "The German army was stabbed in the back." The solid core of the army remained true. Like the officer corps, it stood firm. Where the true guilt lay has been demonstrated. If you need any more proof, I need only refer you to the statement that I quoted earlier and our enemies amazement that they had won.

That is the general trajectory of the tragedy that befell Germany. We succeeded brilliantly on many fronts and achieved unsurpassed victories. The accomplishments of our army and people deserve nothing but the highest praise.

FIGURE 8.4 *German Everyman washing his dirty laundry in public*, Kladderadatsch, *November 23, 1919, "Öffentliche Wäsche" (University of Heidelberg Digital Newspaper Collection).*

A dutiful *deutsche Michel* is shown washing his dirty linen during the *Reichstag* investigation while the sneering victors (John Bull, Marianne, and Uncle Sam) look on. John Bull says to Marianne, "He is and remains stupid Michel."

FIGURE 8.5 *An antisemitic interpretation of Hindenburg's testimony,* Kladderadatsch, *November 30, 1919, "An die Kurzsichtigen" (University of Heidelberg Digital Newspaper Collection). "For the short-sighted. You seek the truth? When it appears, you will wish it went to the devil!"*

An elegant, slender Hindenburg pulls back the curtain on the Stab-in-the-Back during his *Reichstag* testimony. An heroically drawn German infantryman is pierced by a lance wielded by a harshly drawn, Medusa-headed female with Jewish features wearing a Social Democratic hat. The antisemitic and anti-feminist features of the cartoon are clear, as is its disconnect from Hindenburg's refusal to go into the specifics of "the true guilt" for the *Dolchstoß*.

The cartoonist, Werner Hahmann, began to draw political caricatures for *Kladderadatsch* in 1914. His work frequently featured nationalistic and anti-Social Democratic themes, sharing the pre-war liberal perspective (nationalistic, anti-clerical, anti-Prussian, and mildly antisemitic) that was characteristic of *Kladderadatsch*.

With his testimony finished, Hindenburg settled back in his chair and let Ludendorf answer the questions of the committee. By the time that the day was over and the trio returned to Helfferich's home—where Figure 8.3 was taken—they had good reason to be satisfied. Not only had they turned the tables on their enemies, they had also gone a long way toward establishing the Stab-in-the-Back Myth in nationalist consciousness. This consciousness, to be sure, was not uniform. Some—represented by Figure 8.5 from the satirical weekly *Kladderadatsch*—attributed an antisemitic meaning to Hindenburg's words. Others found other points to highlight, either from their reading of the actual testimony or—like the *Kladderadatsch* cartoonist—imputing words that they wanted to hear. In any case, Hindenburg had achieved his goal of deflecting defeat from the shoulders of the military for a considerable swathe of the population.

All observers did not necessarily see the testimony as a triumph, perhaps because they could not appreciate what it was meant to accomplish. *The Times* correspondent in Berlin was quite sure that it was a defeat for Hindenburg and Ludendorff.

8.14 OBSERVATIONS ON THE BEARING OF HINDENBURG AND LUDENDORFF, NOVEMBER 20, 1919[18]

During to-day's proceedings some heated moments occurred. The two war lords consistently endeavoured to transfer the responsibility for Germany's misfortune from the shoulders of the military leaders to those of the political Government and revolutionary agitators. They were both somewhat surprised at the firm hand of the chairman, Herr Gothein, who throughout kept the witnesses to the point, refusing to all them to digress into convenient but irrelevant by-paths. Hindenburg was calm, massive, and impassive, making his observations without excitement. Even when he expressed indignation he did not do it indignantly. Ludendorff, on the other hand, was excited, and raised his voice to a shout when he declared that a certain article put in evidence by the Commission was an infamous lie. He repudiated part of Count Bernstorff's testimony, declaring it to be an insult to his honour—in short, making scenes generally that raised the temperature, if not to fever heat, at least to a pitch which made both Press and public declare that the proceedings for once were really interesting. Count Bernstorff was cool and collected. In a brush between him and Ludendorff the latter declared that "he was the defender of his own honour." The chairman retorted that it was his duty as chairman to protect the honour of the

> witnesses. The war lords did not capture the Committee and failed to intimidate it, though whether they contributed much to the utility of its labours is open to doubt.

The readers of *The Times* were not the only people interested in the testimony. The Allied governments were deeply concerned about the threat of a monarchist coup and followed the events of November 1919 closely. Document 8.15 is a memorandum written by political officer Charles Dyar at the US embassy in Berlin on the situation.

8.15 "MEMORANDUM ON THE POLITICAL SITUATION IN GERMANY," UNDATED[19]

The pause in the hearings of the Parliamentary Investigation Committee has been utilized for deliberations regarding powers, forms of procedure, etc. The Committee decided that witnesses were under obligation to answer all questions put to them by members of the Committee. New hearings will not be held until the beginning of 1920, and witnesses will be asked to submit written replies to questions of the Committee before they are asked to appear. The suggestion was made that questions be submitted to the ex-Kaiser, but no action will be taken on this until all other witnesses have been examined. The proceedings of the Committee were subjected to severe criticisms by Rudolph Breitscheid, the Independent Socialist leader, in a recent public meeting … Breitscheid particularly criticized the obsequiousness of the Committee in the examination of Hindenburg and Ludendorff and its failure to deal with reactionaries like Helfferich and Zimmermann as they deserve.

Conclusion

The Hindenburg testimony—and the carnival-like atmosphere surrounding it—was significant in itself. His statement solidified the boundaries of debate. One either believed Germany's hero that the army was stabbed in the back or one didn't. Opinions might differ as to the means, timing, and extent of the betrayal, but the nationalist position was now set in concrete.

The November hearings were also an important step in the development of the German National People's Party as a coalition of monarchists, Annexationists, Antisemites, the old German Conservative Party, and pre-war liberals (such as Karl Helfferich) who could not accept the downfall of the imperial regime. Welding together such disparate elements was a gargantuan task, especially in the dark months after the Armistice. It was not made any easier by the presence of belligerent and unlikable personalities such as Ludendorff. By focusing the new party's attention on the *Dolchstoß* and recruiting the "above party" Hindenburg as a symbol, Helfferich was able to create a coherent public profile for the German Nationals in the run-up to the elections for the first Weimar *Reichstag* in 1920.

Helfferich's intervention and Hindenburg's forceful testimony forced the Weimar parties and the Assembly majority to change the process. It was decided that the work of the committee was too large and four separate subcommittees were created. (These subcommittees would continue to jostle over competencies throughout the life of the National Assembly and into the first sessions of the new *Reichstag* elected in June 1920.) It was also decided that there would be no more public testimony. The subcommittees commissioned depositions, heard expert testimony, and debated in confidential sessions. The 4th Subcommittee—charged with examining the military and internal collapse—finally completed its work in 1927 and published its proceedings in 1928. By then, attitudes had hardened as the result of the two high-profile trials described in Chapters 9 and 10. The *Reichstag*'s work had become superfluous except for the historical record.

Thought questions

1   The newspaper sources that you read seem to indicate that there were real fears of a monarchist or nationalist coup. Was this all for show? What sorts of evidence do they cite?
2   Why did Hindenburg's testimony matter?
3   By changing its *modus operandi* from one of public testimony to one of private reports, did the Committee succeed in cementing the handful of original testimonies—especially Hindenburg's—in the public imagination?

Further reading

Like so many of the important figures of the Weimar era, Karl Helfferich is largely unstudied today. His life and especially his role in the *Dolchstoßlegende* is clearly put forward in John G. Williamson, *Karl Helfferich, 1872–1924: Economist, Financier, Politician* (Princeton: Princeton University Press, 1971).

9

The Ebert Libel Trial

Institutional context

The German legal system consisted of four levels of courts. The lowest is the Petty Court, followed by the *Amtsgericht*, the County Court *Landgericht*, and the *Oberlandgericht* or Court of Appeals. The *Amtsgericht* had jurisdiction over minor civil and criminal matters, while more serious matters were tried before the *Landgericht*. Plaintiffs or defendants who want to appeal petitioned the *Oberlandgericht*. The highest court in this system was the *Reichsgericht*, or "Supreme Court." The two trials considered in this volume were held before the County Courts in Magdeburg and Munich, respectively.

Cases heard before a *Landgericht* were conducted by a professional judge who was assisted by two lay judges. These lay judges, who served for long (although differing) periods of time, were chosen from the local citizenry for their supposed "judicious" nature. As a practical matter, they were usually well-to-do members of the business or professional classes, the very groups most attached to the imperial system and mind-set. After hearing the case at hand, the three would deliberate together and reach a consensual verdict that the professional judge would then cast into proper legal form. (The result of this deliberation can sometimes produce in somewhat convoluted judgments, as can be seen in the two cases at hand.)

In libel cases, the plaintiff (in the case of the Ebert Libel Trial both the plaintiff and the state's attorney) presents a file to the bench and makes opening arguments, after which the defendant is called to respond. The judge questions each party about the documents submitted and questions the witnesses that both call. The judges may decide to call witnesses on their own to further elucidate the matter in dispute. The parties are only allowed to call additional witnesses with the agreement of the judge. (This allows for enormous judicial latitude in the creation of the record upon which judgment will be based.) After all arguments are heard, the attorneys make a closing statement. Since the argument is made before a trained legal professional and his assistants, these statements are legally grounded and lack the emotional fireworks common in closing arguments presented in American courtrooms.

Libeling the president

Before the war, Germany had strict laws against libeling the head of state. If a journalist or public figure wrote or spoke something untoward about the Emperor, they were immediately charged by the state prosecutor, tried and not infrequently sentenced to jail. Friedrich Ebert was less fortunate.[1] For whatever reason, the state prosecutor was less diligent where Ebert's reputation was concerned and the president felt forced to begin legal proceedings himself. Between 1922 and his death in 1925, it is estimated that Ebert instituted between 150 and 200 proceedings against people who libeled him. Each time charges were filed, an official investigation took place and evidence was collected. The result of this process was always in his favor; once this happened, Ebert would declare himself satisfied and drop the suit.

It soon became of a sport on the extreme right to provoke libel charges. Emil Gansser, a Swiss-born chemist and inventor, made of a career trying to provoke Ebert to sue him. Gansser held several important industrial patents and was well known throughout Swiss industrial circles. He was also an early and aggressive supporter of the Nazi movement, using his commercial connections to raise money for the party. When Ebert visited Munich in June 1922, Gansser was in the crowd to meet him at the train station. He made quite a scene by shouting that the president was a traitor and was arrested. The matter was not pursued vigorously, but finally in February 1924, he was formally charged with libel. After the official collection of pre-trial testimony, which was in his favor, Ebert—as was his usual practice—declined to pursue the matter further. Gansser, however, refused to relent and demanded his day in court. He pressed his case by sending open letters to small right-wing newspapers across Bavaria. Every time the letter was published, Ebert sued the publisher. Bernhard Fulda, who has written substantively on the case, estimates that this occurred at least five times in 1924 alone.[2]

The *Mitteldeutsche Zeitung*

Erwin Rothardt, the editor of an insignificant antisemitic newspaper published in a small town near Magdeburg, also published Gansser's letter. Getting creative, he prefaced it with a challenge to the president. The headline introducing the letter read, "A Bitter Pill for Fritze Ebert." Baiting the president, Rothardt wrote, "Will Ebert swallow this pill, or will he … appear in court in Munich after all? Go on, Herr Ebert, and prove that you are not a traitor."[3] This went too far. Not only did the president successfully force the state to prosecute, he had his own lawyer file for libel.

The trial caused a sensation in the German press. In his excellent description of the trial, Fulda recounts how the news was collected, disseminated and then rewritten to suit political slant of the newspaper publishing the story.[4] Although students would benefit by seeing side-by-side examples of how one bit of testimony could be reported in nationalist newspapers as damning and in socialist newspapers as exculpatory, the articles are fairly inaccessible to readers without a deep knowledge of Weimar politics and rhetoric. We have therefore linked translations of some of the newspaper articles, particularly those of the reactionary *Deutsche Tageszeitung* which sent a special correspondent to Magdeburg to cover the trial and produce text for distribution on its wire service on our website.

The trial begins

The clearest and most sophisticated English-language coverage of the trial was provided by *The Times*, whose Berlin correspondent went to Magdeburg to cover the trial. Documents 9.1 through 9.4 set the stage. Document 9.5 is Ebert's testimony regarding the origins of the strike and his participation in it. In Document 9.6, Phillip Scheidemann corroborates Ebert's testimony.

9.1 "ALLEGED LIBEL OF PRESIDENT EBERT," DECEMBER 11, 1924[5]

The former editor of the *Mitteldeutsche Zeitung*, Herr Rothardt, appeared before the Magdeburg Court yesterday on the charge of libeling President Ebert. He had published in his newspaper an open letter from a Bavarian fascist named Emil Ganßer in which President Ebert was accused of treason in that he had taken part in the conduct of the great German munitions workers' strike at the end of January, 1918. Herr Rothardt added a footnote to the letter challenging the President to prove that he had not been a traitor and also made reference to a well-known photograph of the President in bathing costume.

The case which on the surface looks as simple as any of the few dozen President Ebert has brought against his traducers, is really much more, complicated. The alleged libel was deliberately made and the alleged libeler is not a professional journalist. The political background to the case is apparently the German Munitions Strike of January 28, 1918, but actually the pressing question of Monarchy or Republic, and not less actually the approaching Presidential Election. The result is a political struggle of first class magnitude, fought out as political struggles are so often fought out, in the atmosphere of a Law Court. The witnesses who have been summoned include many of the Majority Socialists, Independent Socialists, and Sparticists who were prominent in the Revolution.

In view of the material under examination it is not surprising that the Court should have reproduced something very akin to the atmosphere of the year 1918. Reading the accounts of the evidence one might easily believe that the Kaiser was still on the Throne and that it was President Ebert who was standing his trial. Yet through it all the strictest legal objectivity is observed. There is no sign of the case being treated outside the Court as *sub judice*, the Press comments being quite without any trammels of party reticence.

9.2 "THE STORY OF THE STRIKE," DECEMBER 11, 1924[6]

The defense, to give it its proper technical term, attempts to justify the alleged libel on the grounds that President Ebert was a member of the Strike Committee which took control of the German munitions workers' strike that broke out in Berlin, Leipzig, and other industrial centers on January 28, 1918, and in that capacity advised men to refuse military service. Since then most of the prominent actors in the strike have written their memoirs, and details of the occurrences are public property. In particular, Herr Scheidemann in his book "*Der Zusammenbruch*" ("The Collapse") gives a very full account of the strike and of the part played by President Ebert, among others.

He says in the book that the conditions then prevailing among the working population in 1918 had become absolutely intolerable ... Berlin was then under a state of siege which was very strictly administered. Workmen's meetings were prohibited; the Labour Press was under a severe censorship, and the newspaper *Vorwärts* was constantly being suspended. Yet during this period the Fatherland Party of Admiral von Tirpitz, which to-day would be little different from the Fascists, was freely advocating its policy of conquests throughout the country. Herr Scheidemann refers in his book to its tactless attitude towards the masses who wanted peace.

The more advanced workers' organizations had seized upon the principle laid down by the Russians at Petrograd and afterwards at Brest Litovsk of a peace without annexations or indemnities on the basis of national self-determination. Though Trotsky propagated this theory he did not apply it in Bolshevist practice, as General Hoffmann very plainly pointed out to him at Brest Litovsk, but the German workers caught it up and the Majority Socialists, Ebert and Scheidemann, who knew how events were tending, had already warned the German government that it must make a clear statement on the basis of the *Reichstag* peace resolution of 1917 at least.

The more extreme workers' leaders were, meanwhile, hastening on preparations for a general strike and were doing their best, as their leaflets now prove, to keep the trade union leaders, Majority Socialists, and all such "bitter enders" out of the Strike Committee.

The strike had already begun and the political demands of the strikers had already been formulated, when various factories sent delegates to the Majority Socialists and urged the Party Executive to be represented on the Strike Committee. The Executive, however, refused, unless invited by the Committee itself, and on this being done it nominated Herr Ebert, Herr Braun, and Herr Scheidemann to represent it. Its avowed purpose, as laid down in a resolution passed at the time, was to steer the movement into more peaceful channels and bring it to a close as early as possible.

The Committee consisted of 14 workmen, three Independent Socialists, and three Majority Socialists, of whom Herr Ebert was one. Their first effort was to negotiate with the government, and a sub-committee was appointed, which included besides Herr Ebert and Herr Scheidemann, two Independent Socialists and two workmen. Herr Wallraf, then Secretary of State for the Interior, flatly and persistently refused to receive a deputation that included workmen, while General Kessel prohibited the Committee from holding meetings. It was some time before Herr Wallraf could be brought to see that thereby he had destroyed the machinery for bringing the strike to an end.

9.3 "THE MYSTERY DEEPENS," DECEMBER 11, 1924[7]

A mass meeting of workers was held in Treptow Park—in the working-class quarter of Berlin—at which the workmen required to know what attitude they should adopt if the military authorities applied their usual method and drafted them off to the trenches. It is upon the events at this meeting that the present trial will turn.

On behalf of President Ebert a statement was read in Court yesterday saying that he had been on the side of national defense throughout the war and had spoken against the munition workers' strike, with the outbreak of which he had not been concerned. On January 28, 1918, the Majority Socialists had been requested to take control of the strike in order to avoid the worst. Herr Ledebour (the Independent Socialist) had told the strikers that the strike would be lost if the Majority Socialists came on the strike committee, and at that point he (Herr Ebert) had joined with it, with Herr Braun and Herr Scheidemann, in order to restore the balance. He had several times addressed the strikers and had told them that it was absurd to strike at a time when the British munition workers were even going without holidays. He declared that he had entered the strike committee to bring the strike to an end as soon as possible.

Evidence was given by Herr Dittmann, an Independent Socialist member of the *Reichstag*, who was one of the speakers at the Treptow Park meeting, at the close of which he was arrested and sentenced to five years' confinement in a fortress. He was asked whether a written question had been handed to Herr Ebert, who on that occasion stood behind him, and whether Herr Ebert had replied that the men should refuse to obey an enlistment order. Herr Dittmann's reply was that it was impossible, or he would have seen it take place, and in any case they would have known it was a trap. A subsequent witness named Syrib, one of the workmen who attended the meeting, declared on oath that Herr Ebert had advised him to disobey the enlistment order.

The unusual course was taken to-day of confronting President Ebert with a witness, and this witness was Syrib. The "confrontation" took place at the President's official residence in the Wilhelmstrasse. Under the Constitution the President is exempted from appearing in a court of law. The Socialist Press remarks, somewhat caustically, upon the fact that the witness had been brought into the case through the medium of German National Deputies, to whose Party he apparently belongs.

9.4 "SYRIB, THE CROWN WITNESS," DECEMBER 12, 1924[8]

The witness had asserted that Herr Ebert ... had declared at a strike meeting in January, 1918, that the workmen must refuse to obey an enlistment order. He admitted that he was 30 yards away and that he did not see the written question handed up to the platform, but he insisted that Herr Ebert had said: "Strikes can only shorten the war and anyone who gets an order to join up must refuse to obey it." Herr Ebert, he said, had made this statement while continuing his speech and had not changed his tone.

President Ebert in the presence of this witness yesterday said that now that he had heard the description of the incident by the witness he regarded it as quite impossible. "If such a paper had been handed up to me at the meeting, and if I had read it, I should have had to stop

FIGURE 9.1 Ulk, *January 9, 1925, "Vergiftete Waffen" (University of Heidelberg, University Library digitized historical literature collection).*

"Poisonous Weapons." The leadership of the German National People's Party are show as firing poison gas shells labeled "lies," "slander," "empty promises" and "distortions" provided by their allied media (the *Deutsche Tagszeitung,* the *Lokal-Anzeiger, Der Tag,* and the *Neue preußische Zeitung*) at the Prussian parliament building.

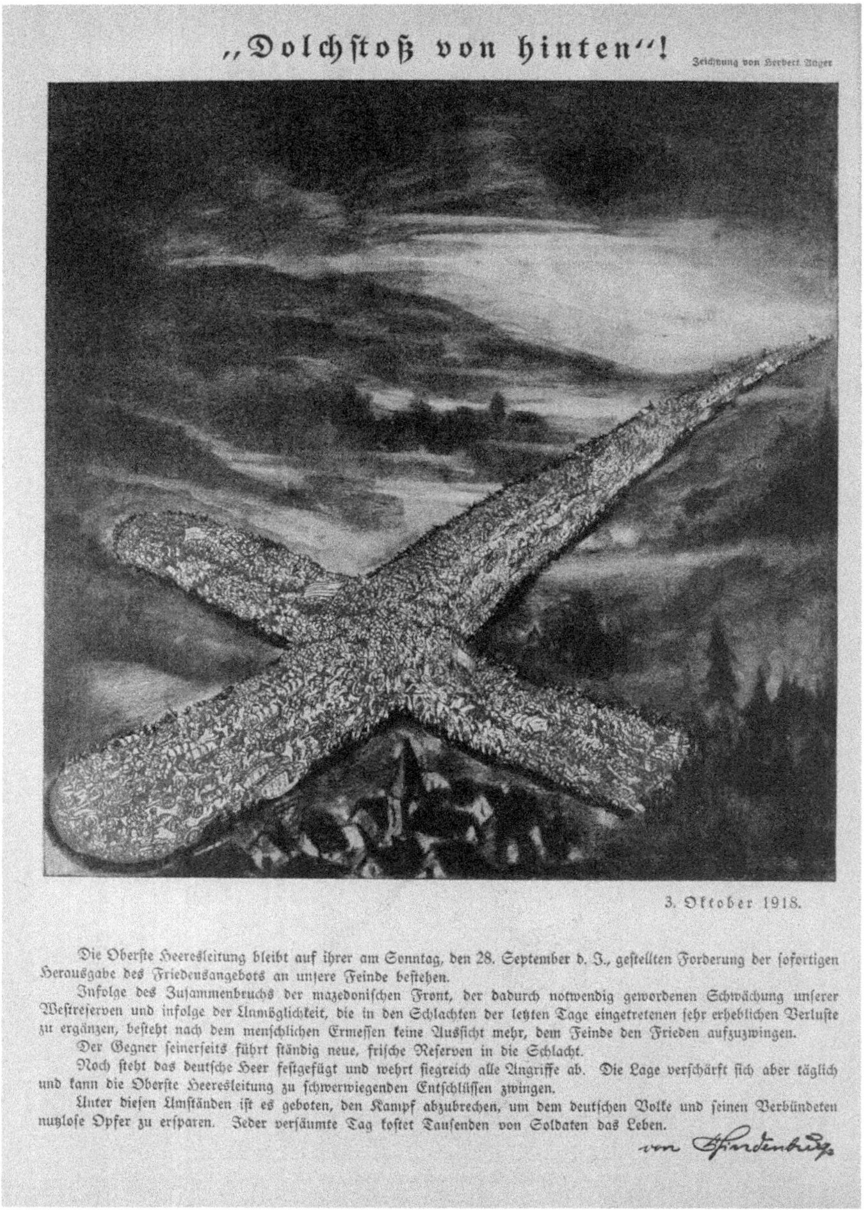

FIGURE 9.2 Lachen Links, *November 7, 1924, "Dolchstoß von Hinten" (University of Heidelberg, University Library digitized historical literature collection).*

An interesting Social Democratic take on the notion of the Stab-in-the-Back as a mass rebellion of a united, faceless people against militarism and the continuation of the war.

in my speech, which I made without notes, and put on my spectacles, because I was unable to read without them." He went on to say that he had never believed that strikes could shorten the war, and he had never, even privately, advised any man not to obey an order to join up. After two of his sons had been killed, his eldest son had rejoined the Army at the front. It was, however, possible that in his speech he might have said that if orders to join up were issued to strikers as a punishment the Socialist Party would try to get them reversed.

The witness Syrib admitted that he had been selected by Pastor Koch, a German National Deputy, to be a witness in the case, and had been set to collect other witnesses. The Court decided that these witnesses must be heard. Meanwhile, it took the evidence of a number of workmen and officers from Kiel on the influence the strike had at the time. The witnesses were asked whether the strike had interfered with the movements of German warships and submarines, whether it had hindered mine-sweeping, and whether it had occasioned loss of life. In spite of the objection that President Ebert could hardly be held responsible for all the consequences of the strike, the Court decided that these matters were relevant to the hearing.

In this mass of discursive reminiscence the original libel proceedings have almost been lost sight of. Investigation of the circumstances with which the libel was concerned seems, indeed, hardly to have been the main purpose of the real promoters of the affair. One of the German National newspapers observes somewhat unfeelingly that it does not matter if the accused is fined or sent to prison, since the aim of getting the promoters of the Revolution into the witness-box [sic] will have been achieved.

9.5 EBERT'S TESTIMONY[9]

From the beginning of the war to its end I put myself unreservedly on the side of national defense and acted in this sense. I expressed this through various speeches in and outside parliament. During the entire war, I was an opponent of strikes by workers in the war industries. I spoke very sharply against such strikes in my speech at the national conference of the Majority Social Democratic Party of Germany in 1916.

The strike of the munitions workers of Berlin in 1918 started without the assistance or consultation with the Majority Social Democratic Party. I knew nothing directly or indirectly related to the preparation of the strike. I was completely surprised by it. In fact, I was criticized in one of the pamphlets promoting the strike, which declared, "See that the union leaders, the government socialists and other bitter-enders are under no circumstances to be chosen as your representatives. Out with the boys from the union halls! These henchmen and voluntary government agents, these mortal enemies of the mass strike, have no place among the fighting workers."

On the morning of January 28, 1918, delegations of workers from various Berlin factories appeared at party headquarters and requested that we send representatives to the strike committee in order to prevent the worst from happening. I argued that we should not do so since the strike was started without consulting the party. The strikers had already chosen a strike committee and established certain requirements. The delegates then asked if we would send a delegation if the workers requested it. After a long debate, we agreed that we would. The deciding factor was the interests of the nation would be harmed if the strike continued ... Over the objection of the Independents, we were asked to join and we did ... Otto Braun, Scheidemann, and I were chosen by the party to represent it in this matter.

...On the same day, 29 January, all meetings, including those of the representatives of the striking workers, were prohibited. This even included the members of the strike committee under penalty of law. On the next day, *Vorwärts* was shut down as were all the offices of the unions. It was thus impossible to engage the striking workers and reach an understanding that would end the strike.

On 31 January, masses of striking workers gathered in the streets and public parks. On one such occasion I spoke to the strikers and urged calm and prudence. At the same time, I was negotiating with the government over ways to end the strike. The government, for its part, created all sorts of formalistic difficulties over the composition of our delegation that made local negotiations impossible. The strike was settled after about a week. I am still of the opinion that it could have been resolved in a few days if the national government had not engaged in formalisms but offered substantive negotiations, as occurred in Danzig, Cologne and Munich ...

I spoke to the strikers in Treptow Park, in the immediate vicinity of where I lived. In the speech [in question]—as far as I remember—I reported on the attempted negotiations with the government and I entreated the workers to act peacefully and prudently. I did not demand that they return to work; the excitement that prevailed among the strikers made that impossible. Had I done so, I would have only poured oil on to the fire.

... I joined the strike committee with the specific intent of bringing the strike to the fastest possible completion.

9.6 "SCHEIDEMANN ON THE CONTEXT OF THE STRIKE," DECEMBER 13, 1924[10]

We were in the middle of "turnip time," there was no longer any soap, and everything pointed to a continuance of the war. All families had suffered heavy losses, though fortunately not all of them had Ebert's misfortune to losing two sons. The strike broke out without our [the Majority Socialists'] knowledge. When our own people asked us—and not before—we joined the Strike Committee with the firm intention of putting a speedy end to the strike by negotiating with the government. There was a great deal of opposition against us in the Strike Committee: we were known as the "strike stranglers." The publication of *Vorwärts* was prohibited by the government—a piece of great stupidity. Herr Wallraf (the then Secretary of State) refused to confer with the workers, although he was advised of the serious consequences of his refusal. I put myself at the disposal of the workers, although I knew that I might be sent to prison at any minute. How necessary this was I soon found out ...

Herr Gustav Bauer, the next witness, was asked whether Herr Ebert had spoken to him about the attitude the workers should adopt towards orders to join up. He replied that the strike was a very unfortunate incident, and he joined the committee in order to put an end to it as soon as possible. The strikers were of the opinion that the enlistment order should be disobeyed, but Herr Ebert was convinced that it would be an absolute crime to encourage them in this view, although he declared at a meeting that the party would do everything in order to get any enlistment orders issued as a punishment to strikers reversed.

In the examination of Herr Hermann Müller, now leader of the (reunited) Social Democratic party, counsel for the defense, which is attempting to justify the alleged libel, essayed to draw from him an admission that the Majority Socialists, by joining the Strike Committee, had encouraged the strike by giving it the appearance of their support. Herr Müller stated, however, that all the Majority Socialist members of the committee were of the opinion that the strike could not possibly shorten the war and must be brought to an end as soon as possible.

Unexpected testimony

The trial brought a number of surprises, among them a letter from Hindenburg sent to Ebert immediately after the abdication of the Emperor promising his support and that of the army in containing anarchy and "rebuilding" the Fatherland. The nationalist press—for whom Hindenburg was the great hope—passed over this inclusion, while Social Democratic and liberal newspaper gave it great play. A second revelation came from Wilhelm Groener, who revealed that he had worked with Ebert in November to restore order in the capital. All sides overlooked this bit of news, as it did not seem to fit anyone's narrative. It would arise again at the Munich *Dolchstoß* Trial (the next chapter) where it received a great deal of attention. A last, humanizing element was added when the prosecution entered into evidence a letter that Ebert had written one of his sons regarding the strike.

9.7 HINDENBURG'S LETTER TO EBERT[11]

Dear Mr. Ebert! I am writing these lines to appeal to you, because I am told that you too are a loyal German man and your homeland means more to you than anything else even if this means disregarding your personal opinions and wishes. This is what the Fatherland needs in the present emergency. In this sense, I am your ally to save our people from imminent collapse … In your hands the fate of the German people has been laid. Whether the German *Reich* will rise again depends upon your decisions. I am ready—and with me the whole army—to wholeheartedly support you in this. We all know that because of the unfortunate outcome of the war the reconstruction of the *Reich* can only be made on new foundations and new forms. What we want is the recovery of the state that has existed throughout the age of mankind before delusion and folly completely destroy every pillar of our economic and social life.

9.8 EBERT'S LETTER TO HIS SON, DECEMBER 15, 1924[12]

A somewhat pathetic incident was the production in Court of a letter sent by Herr Ebert to his son Georg during an early period of the munitions strike. It had been returned with a postal notice to say that it could not be delivered because the addressee had been killed in action. In this letter, Herr Ebert had written to his son: "Our troops have earned the everlasting gratitude of the nation. During the last few days some senseless strikes have broken out here in consequence of the reduction of the bread ration. Such fools' tricks do not serve the cause of peace, but only strengthen the fighting spirit of the enemy."

The conduct of the trial

For most fair-minded observers, the conduct of the trial was a travesty. When the Syrib testimony fell apart, the presiding judge gave the defense time to find other witnesses who would make claims similar to those Syrib had made.

9.9 "THE CONDUCT OF THE TRIAL," DECEMBER 18, 1924[13]

The last stages were remarkable for the sharp brush between Herr Landsberg, President Ebert's counsel, and the presiding Judge. Herr Landsberg complained that the Court had repeatedly refused him permission to summon witnesses while giving every facility to the other side, and had also shown discrimination in refusing to allow him to put questions to witnesses in the interests of his clients. The Judge repudiated the accusation of partiality, and subsequently allowed Herr Landsberg to put his questions in a modified form.

The original witness Syrib, on whom the defense relied for discrediting President Ebert, proved, under the searching cross-examination of Herr Landsberg and his junior counsel, to have manufactured his own evidence and to have induced other witnesses to give false testimony, one of whom informed the Court that Syrib told him the exact words in which he was to describe the meeting at which President Ebert was alleged to have made his treasonable speech in the Treptow Park. But he also added that, as a matter of fact, he had never been in the Treptow Park and did not even know where it was.

The defense thereupon produced another witness, a cheesemonger from Dortmund, who had worked in the Spandau arsenal during the war. This witness said he had read the reports of the case in the Press, and had come forward to say that he himself was really the man who had handed to President Ebert the written question whether the workmen were to obey the summons to join up. He stated on oath that Herr Ebert had quite definitely replied that they were to refuse to do so. But a single question served to put this evidence in quite another light. The witness was asked whether he himself was one of those who had been called up, and he replied that he was not, as he had already been excused military service. Thereupon he was asked why he had put the question to Herr Ebert at all, and he replied that he had done so on political grounds.

The witness further said he had stood only a yard or two away from the platform, and could remember the incident perfectly. Herr Ebert had held the paper in his hand, read out the question and forthwith replied to it. But when counsel asked him whether Herr Ebert (who was even then notoriously shortsighted) had stopped to put on his glasses the memory of the witness was found to be at fault.

This proved to be the case also with other witnesses. A police official who had served during the war with the German "Flying Corps, Counter-sabotage department," and whom the defense had expected to deliver vital evidence failed in the witness-box to remember a single incident except that it all happened seven years ago.

The verdict is announced

The verdict truly came as a shock to the president's German supporters and foreign correspondents covering the trial. They were so sure that Rothardt would be found guilty and Ebert exonerated that, like *The Times* correspondent in Document 9.10, they had difficulty interpreting it.

9.10 "A DOUBLE-EDGED JUDGMENT," DECEMBER 24, 1924[14]

Judgment was given this morning at Magdeburg in the case against Herr Rothardt for libeling President Ebert by accusing him of treason during the war. Herr Rothardt was found guilty and was sentenced to two month's imprisonment and costs. The Court ordered the destruction of all copies of the newspaper in which the libel appeared and the publication of the verdict in two Magdeburg newspapers and the Berlin *Vorwärts*

As thus presented, the end of the case had all the appearance of a judgment in President Ebert's favour. Actually, it was the reverse and the Public Prosecutor and President Ebert's counsel have appealed on the grounds of misdirection. The summing-up was, indeed, of a piece with the rest of the case, and while the nationalist Press this evening appears with flaming headlines, "Ebert the Traitor!" and so forth, *Germania* suggests that there is something wrong about the procedure of political trials in Germany that urgently needs revision.

The actual finding of the Judge was that the libel was proved only in the technical sense, that it was so intended, and that President Ebert had been guilty of treason in taking any part at all in the big German munitions workers' strike of 1918. He rejected the evidence of the main witnesses of the prosecution as undeserving of any credit. But he distinguished between the moral, political, and historical aspect of the case and its criminal aspect. The former, he ruled, had no bearing on the case. The latter he held to be proved.

It was a no importance that President Ebert had joined the strike in order to prevent the extreme revolutionaries from securing control. That was a matter for history. The facts that weighed with the Court were that he had taken part in the affairs of the Strike Committee, that he had not prevented the issue of a handbill ... urging the strikers to hold out, and that he had said at a meeting on the evidence of a reporter who was present: "Your demands are just. Hold out calmly. Your comrades in other cities are standing by you." Although the reporter who had ascribed these words to President Ebert had taken no notes, written no report, and never adverted to the subject in the subsequent years, the Court held his evidence to be trustworthy. In these circumstances, the Court found Herr Ebert had been guilty of treason in the criminal sense and the motives which had inspired his action were of no importance.

The verdict and the implication that goes with it are hailed in nationalist circles with unbounded delight. The nationalist press considers that, whatever else may ensue, Herr Ebert is finished. More moderate opinion is left in amazement that a trial of this character, conducted in an atmosphere where, in effect, the plaintiff, and Head of State, was put upon his trial for a criminal offence, should be possible in the German Republic. It is not for an outsider to comment upon this new demonstration of justice as between Germans, but the verdict will, no doubt, find an honoured place in the strange collection of legal decisions now associated with German treason trials.

The verdict also came as a shock to the president himself. He tried to be philosophical. The cabinet resolution of support and their official visit the following day was clearly support that he appreciated. Even more so, if his diary was any indication, was a visit from Count Gerhard von Kanitz, the son of a famous pre-war Agrarian politician who had clashed with Ebert numerous times in the *Reichstag*. That such a political opponent should value his patriotism and service to the country was deeply meaningful.

9.11 EBERT'S DIARY ON HIS REACTION TO THE VERDICT[15]

Minister Count Kanitz came to see me in the afternoon to express his indignation and regret over the intrigues that led to Magdeburg trial and about the way that the trial was conducted. Even people on the political Right are sickened by these intrigues.

> In the evening, I attended a banquet hosted by the Central Association of German Bankers. The Chairman of the People's Party, Kiloser (who is also a member of parliament) twice expressed his indignation over the agitation that took place in connection with the Magdeburg trial.

The US ambassador, Alanson B. Houghton, considered the trial and its shocking conclusion to be so significant that he wrote the entire affair up in a long dispatch to Washington.

9.12 REPORT ON THE EBERT TRIAL BY THE US AMBASSADOR ALANSON B. HOUGHTON, DECEMBER 27, 1924[16]

In view of the political significance of the libel suit brought by the States Attorney on behalf of President Ebert recently against a newspaper editor, I have the honor to report the case in some detail.

The basis of the libel alleged by President Ebert in his suit was open letter written by [an Antisemitc] journalist, Dr. Gansser, to President Ebert, and printed sometime ago in the *Mitteldeutsche Zeitung* at Strassfurt. In this letter the writer used personal expressions, which President Ebert alleged were libelous and accused the President, in particular, of having instigated the munitions strike in Berlin in January 1918. In accordance with German law, the suit was brought against the responsible editor of the paper, a man named Erwin Rothardt. The trial, which began on December, was held in the local court at Magdeburg. The testimony of President Ebert was taken originally by deposition but, during the course of the trial, the Court decided that this evidence was not sufficient and therefore the judges and some of the witnesses held a session in Berlin in the house occupied by President Ebert for the purpose of taking his further testimony.

The case for the defense was based largely on the statements of one witness, named Syrib, who claimed that he was present at an open air meeting held in Berlin in January 1918, at which Ebert made a speech. This witness alleged that just before the conclusion of the speech Ebert was handed a note containing a question as to whether the strikers should obey orders calling them to active military service, and that after reading the note Ebert concluded his speech by declaring that conscription orders need not be obeyed. The course of the trial, however, the prosecution was able to demonstrate that the above named witness was untrustworthy. Just before the taking of testimony was concluded the defense brought forward another witness, named Gobert, that he was the person who given Ebert the note referred to above. This witness, too, proved to be unreliable, for the prosecution was able to show that he had already been arrested and convicted eleven times for various minor offenses and that the police authorities in Dortmund, his residence, considered him untrustworthy.

The case for the prosecution was conducted by the Socialist attorney, Dr. Landsberg, who was formerly German minister at Brussels. A number of prominent witnesses were called by the prosecution with a view to proving that both Ebert and the Majority Socialist Party had been guided throughout the war by motives of patriotism. The contention of the prosecution was that the munitions strike in question had been started without the approval of the Majority Socialist Party, and that Majority Socialist representatives had subsequently entered the Committee in charge of the strike merely in to keep the movement from spreading ... An interesting feature of the prosecution was the introduction of testimony by General Groener, successor to Ludendorff as Quartermaster General of the Army and, later, Minister of Transportation. General Groener read in court a letter written to Ebert shortly after the Armistice by Field Marshal von Hindenburg.

The prosecution read also a letter written by President Ebert to his son in the field, which was returned undelivered, the son had meanwhile been killed. In this letter, which was written about the time of the strike in question, President Ebert characterized munitions strikes as criminal.

The trial ended on December 23, when the Court announced its verdict. The Court found that the defendant editor was libel and sentenced him to three months imprisonment. In its statement giving the reasons for the verdict, however, the Court made a number of extraordinary statements. It declared that Article 185 of the Criminal Statutes code that any deliberate injury to the reputation of a person is to be regarded as a formal insult.

From this point of view, the defendant had been guilty, for he had used expressions concerning the plaintiff which he was aware were deliberately offensive.

So far as it concerned his assertion that President Ebert had committed treasonable acts, the situation was different. Article 186 of the Criminal Statutes provided that a person making such an assertion could be punished only in case the truth of the assertion could not be proved. Therefore, the Court had to examine the statements of the defendant to the effect that the plaintiff had committed acts of treason by (1) participating in the Berlin strike; (2) extending the strike to Kiel; (3) attempting to start a strike in Chemnitz; and (4) obstructing measures of the Supreme Military command. With regard to the last three points, the court stated no proof had been furnished that the assertions contained therein were true. With regard to the first point, however, the situation was different. In the meeting of striking workmen held at Berlin-Treptow—January 1918, Ebert had declared that it was the duty of German workmen to support their brothers in trenches. He also said that the workmen's demands were just and that they should avoid conflicts with the police. It had not been proved that the plaintiff had advised them to refuse conscription orders. The Court had, therefore, to examine the facts purely from the point of view of criminal law. It could not consider the case from a moral, historical or political point of view, for an action which might be justifiable in these respects might, nevertheless, be a criminal act.

Article 89 of the Criminal Statutes provided that any person who deliberately assisted an enemy during time of war, or who hampered the work of the Military Command, was guilty of treason. Not only the strikers, but all those who instigated, organized and supported the movement were guilty. During the trial it had been shown that the plaintiff personally and the Majority Socialist Party as a whole did participate in the conduct of the strike, although they had not organized it. Therefore, he had deliberately acted in the sense of Article 89 of the criminal statutes and had thus committed an act of treason. The point of view of the plaintiff's defense could not be considered.

The trial has been exploited by the nationalist campaign to discredit President Ebert himself and the Majority Socialist Party as a whole. Throughout the proceedings at Magdeburg the nationalist press has consistently misrepresented the facts, maintaining the infallibility of such unreliable witnesses as Syrib and Gobert and suppressing much of the evidence submitted by the prosecution. The verdict has naturally given the nationalists great satisfaction, while Liberals and Socialists have been made most angry in spite of all their statements to the contrary, it is evident that the judges were guided chiefly by political considerations in arriving at their conclusions. The reasons for their verdict, as summarized above, are of course pure sophistry. In effect, the Court expresses the opinion that Ebert and the Majority Socialist Party committed deliberately certain treasonable acts; and the conclusion is furthermore suggested that, if these acts had not been committed, Germany might have won the war. Thus, the time-worn legend of the "stab in the back" dealt the German armies by the Socialists is revived. The wisdom of President Ebert in bringing the suit may be questioned, but that the head of the government should not be subjected to the treatment he has received during the trial. It is not uncommon for German politicians to abuse their opponents in terms and by methods which are unusual in western democracies. It does not speak well for the German judicial profession as a whole, however, if judges cannot abstain from partisanship in deciding cases where political controversies are involved. The Socialists have often demanded that the reactionary members of the bench should be removed. Perhaps the trial of the present case may lead them to press more vigorously for action in this regard. In any event, the prosecution is meanwhile appealing the case in an attempt to obtain a revision of the verdict.

Upon the announcement of the verdict, the Marx Cabinet held a meeting and unanimously adopted a resolution, which they then presented to the president, affirming their belief in his loyalty and unselfishness. Similar action has been taken by the Prussian government and by the Democratic Party. It is particularly interesting, in this connection, to note that the People's Party joined in the resolution of the Cabinet.

Reaction to the verdict in the German press

Matthew Hanna, first secretary at the US embassy, supplemented Houghton's report in his own weekly review of the German press. As was normally the case, he clipped and translated representative articles from a broad spectrum of the press to send to Washington.[17] Included in his report were the reactionary *Neue preußische Zeitung* (known as the *Kreuzzeitung* from the large Prussian cross on its masthead) and the official party newspapers of Gustav Stresemann's People's Party's (*Die Zeit*), the Catholic Center Party (*Germania*), *Vorwärts*, and the Communist Party paper *Die Rote Fahne*. He added a scathing, long editorial written by Democratic Party founder Theodor Wolff in the left liberal *Berliner Tageblatt* that is reproduced here in abridged form.

9.13 WEEKLY REPORT ON THE GERMAN PRESS, DECEMBER 27, 1924[18]

The decision of the Magdeburg Court has been interpreted by the German press to suit the political convictions of the various papers. From the very beginning of the trial the political aspects of the case have thrust to the forefront. The reasons given by the Court for refusing to exonerate President Ebert from the charge of treason have been received with acclamation by the nationalist press which intimated that the decision of the Court will have political consequences. The extreme reactionary *Deutsches Tageblatt*, the Berlin organ of the Hitler-Ludendorff *Voelkische* movement, openly demanded Ebert's resignation. The German National *Kreuzzeitung* interpreted the decision not so much against the person of Ebert as against the whole Socialist party which it claimed was the central point of the trial.

FIGURE 9.3 Ulk, *January 1, 1925, "Ansaubere Hände" (University of Heidelberg, University Library digitized historical literature collection).*

"Unclean hands." The center person in the cartoon is Pastor Koch, the Berlin German National party official who found the witnesses (Syrib and Gobert) who testified against Ebert. Pastor Koch says to his plutocratic and aristocratic helpers, "With Syrib and Gobert we were unlucky. Perhaps if we keep digging, we can find yet another witness against Ebert." In the background, two vagrants volunteer. (Were they meant to be Syrib and Gobert?) This cartoon reflects press reports that Koch was looking for further witnesses to provide evidence for Rothardt's defense.

9.14 *NEUE PREUSSISCHE ZEITUNG (KREUZZEITUNG)*[19]

We have always looked upon our glorious army and fleet as the foundation of German greatness and freedom; the Socialists saw in "Prussian militarism" a terrible monster. We regarded the war which was forced upon us as a struggle in the field of honor which after a victorious conclusion was to bear fruit for the Fatherland; the Socialists at that time denied the Fatherland and the field of honor, they looked upon the war a "murder" and regarded the generals as "Wholesale butchers." In November 1918, the collapse of the army and throne, of greatness and freedom of happiness and splendor, filled us with pain and horror; the Socialists rejoiced with happiness and satisfaction over the victory of the people on the whole front. Now they also describe as treason actions

FIGURE 9.4 Lachen Links, *November 7, 1924, "Regimentsfeier"* (University of Heidelberg, University Library digitized historical literature collection).

"Regimental Feast." At a party of old officers, the standing officer says, "Gentlemen, just among ourselves, we own the discoverer of the Stab-in-the-Back Myth a thunderous 'hurrah!'" The cartoonist suggests that that Stab-in-the-Back got the officer corps off the hook for losing the war.

that we have always regarded as treasonous. During the trial they refused to admit their "patriotic" actions before the revolution. They drew a sharp and hostile line between the Majority Socialists and the Spartacist members in the executive committee of the strikers. But in our opinion they were the same as the others with one exception: the Spartacists and the Independent Socialists were not afraid of any personal danger whereas the Majority Socialists, at each step, thought of the threatening penitentiary. These international revolutionaries now parade as the patriots of 1918, it suits their political interests.

9.15 *DIE ZEIT*[20]

For years, we have suffered because of the objective political principles of opposing sides assumed the form of a personal struggle, and because for a long time Germany was a country of political assassinations. Each time that it seemed that Germany was at last on the way to recovery, the party contrasts reappeared in sharpest forms. It is a matter of regret that this trial took place at all. The role played by Ebert when a deputy may be subject for discussion. But whoever lived through that period, knows well that Ebert was the leader of the conservative wing of the Socialist party which was bitterly opposed to the radical elements. This caused a split in the Socialist party and resulted in the formation of the Communist party. No man has been attacked in the *Rote Fahne* as much as Ebert. More than one Socialist organization recommended his exclusion from the party after he became President. If Ebert should desire to become a candidate for reelection, which we have good reason to doubt, he would meet with a very strong opposition of the radical wing of the party. In the late summer of 1918 deputy Ebert, at a conference of party leaders, urgently demanded that steps be taken to combat the lack of discipline in the army.

In this trial it was not a question of politics but of system. We must break away from the idea that our political opponent is a villain who may be vilified at will. Such methods will never bring us to a national community of interest, but will tear us asunder hopelessly. We must break away from the habit of looking upon the men higher up as dishonest persons who are there merely to swell their own pocket-books. The unanimous resolution of the Cabinet is a political and human act. It is a protest against the theory that a political opponent is an enemy against whom everything is permitted. We hope that the resolution of the Cabinet will convince those who often speak of a united national front that we will never accomplish this if, to the delight of our enemies in foreign countries, we present the spectacle of vilification of the highest official of the *Reich*. It is to be expected that when the case comes up for retrial its political and moral phase will be given more consideration and that more significance will be attached to the motives which impelled the deputy Ebert during the strike. The sooner we learn that we must desist from such methods the better it will be for the German people.

9.16 *GERMANIA*[21]

It was clearly difficult for the judge to arrive at conclusions without being influenced by his own political convictions. It was the duty of the State's attorney, as it is in other countries and as it was once in Germany, to prosecute the slanderer and not leave it to the President to seek justice as co-plaintiff. If a Socialist had similarly slandered the Kaiser before the war, and if such a trial had taken place at all, it is hardly imaginable that the defendant would have gotten off with a couple of months imprisonment, that the Kaiser would have been forced to ask the State's attorney to prosecute the case or that the court would have suffered the debate to extend way back in the princely past. The spectacle is grotesque.

9.17 *VORWÄRTS*[22]

The Magdeburg Court conducted the trial as if not Rothardt but the President was the accused. It reached its decision with the help of the cunning differentiation between "political, moral and historical" grounds and legal grounds. The court claimed that Ebert's actions were deliberate but under the word deliberate we usually understand more than negligence; it means more than merely letting things go. The word means that a definite will, through certain actions in the direction of this will, is expressed therein. Yet the court admits that Ebert joined the striker' committee against his own will, having been forced to do so by his party friends in the factories. It even admitted that in the Treptow meeting Ebert spoke of the necessity of furnishing the best arms available to the soldiers in the field and also said that the French and British workmen did not waste a single hour in producing ammunition for their soldiers. The imperial government at that time thanked the Majority Socialists for their patriotic action; the Magdeburg court brands it as treason. But the final decision will not be based on the political opinion of a judge. It will be based on the "moral, political and historical view-point." It will take into consideration the events of 1918, and German justice of today, which made the decision, with such reasons as given by the Magdeburg Court possible.

9.18 THEODORE WOLFF IN THE *BERLINER TAGEBLATT*[23]

For almost a week the emissaries of a German National and Antisemitic General Staff, which itself remains in the background, have been trying to show proof before the court that President Ebert promoted a strike in January 1918, that he said at a meeting that conscription orders should not be obeyed, and that he is traitor. A quiet and sensible spectator sees through the conspiracy and realizes that the German Nationals, who prepared the atmosphere that caused the murder of Rathenau, Erzberger and other troublesome personalities, now want to remove, by means of poisonous calumny, the President whom they find so disagreeable. We have never contested, and there is no need even of emphasizing the fact, that there are many decent and honorable persons in the German National Party, even though their intelligence leaves something to be desired. But the shady characters … are also very numerous. Any methods to attain their ends, even the lowest, are welcome to the leading party demagogues and the decent and childish members have no ideas as to what is going on in their proximity. Who can forget that in the spheres of the men who in Germany call themselves patriotic nationalists, in the circles of German reaction, the art of slander, forgery and perjury has for such enterprises in Latin countries only? Who can forget that there is a German National, formerly Conservative, tradition of calumny?

Somewhat weak of character—not to use the word "cowardly"—are all those German National politicians—who, in private conferences in the house of the German President and elsewhere, recognize the patriotism and the statesmanship of Ebert and then do not dare to whistle back their pack and put a stop to the unclean practice. If men like Ebert, men having his patriotic sense of duty and his statesmanlike gifts; his cool head and his quietly deliberating mind, had been called to lead the *Reich* [before the war], Germany would not have slid into the most fearful of catastrophes. Is it necessary to refer always to all the books of memoirs which show how the gold lace clique of hungry office hunters, who

FIGURE 9.5 Lachen Links, *November 7, 1924, "Die Folgen der Dolchstoßlegende"* *(University of Heidelberg, University Library digitized historical literature collection).*

"The results of the Stab-in-the-Back Myth." The text: "Stab-in-the-Back delirium, a contagious disease, that for the most part has broken out in rightwing circles." A crazed Ludendorff is restrained by a straightjacket and confined to a padded cell while he imagines the knives of traitors piercing his body. By this point in his post-war political career, Ludendorff had divorced his devoted first wife, married a racist theosophist healer, participated in the Beer Hall Putsch, and was generally regarded as beyond the pale by even nationalist figures. He was to become the center of an antisemitic hero cult that competed with the Nazis.

would now again like to get to the top, fought for every particle of power, intrigued, bowed, flattered and bit their fellows in the calf? Does one have to be reminded that on every page of these memoirs reference is made only to incompetency, narrowness of mind and lack of character? Even now the German National newspapers like to tell that Germany was not sufficiently armed at the outbreak of the war, for which, of course, the blame is being thrust upon the Majority Socialists, the Liberals and the Center Party. The book of the deceased Secretary of State, Clemens v. Delbrück, an honest conservative, reminds us that the gentlemen of the right were very enthusiastic for an enlarged army, but that each time when a tax on wealth or an inheritance tax was proposed, refused to dig into their pockets and that their patriotic enthusiasm chilled as soon as it came to paying.

Ebert no patriot? Two of his sons succumbed to enemy bullets and the third, having secured his father's consent, returned to the front as late as 1918, although he had been severely wounded and was offered an assignment at home or behind the lines. Whereas the list of sacrifices of the nationalist parties in France and England was rather large, it is remarkable that no one of our conservative and now German National deputies fell. The God whom they so often mention did not save the Fatherland, but did, indeed, remarkably well protect the parliamentarians as well as the other satellites of the right parties. When the Kaiser and his paladins had fled and when after the military collapse, in consequence of this collapse, the revolution overran still barely existing barriers, it was above all Ebert, who, with calm determination, clearness of vision and indifference to all danger, energetically led Germany out of the chaos, blocked the way to the surging Bolshevism and tore the power out of the hands of excited radicals. Thus acted this patriot, at a time when many trimmers concealed themselves or asked for his protection, and when there was no army to protect a man in his position. To have acted thus is his unextinguishable historical merit. Konrad Hausmann wrote, "In his external bearing also he is constantly growing up to his station in life. Yes, indeed, his superior intellect, his tact, his character quickly secured him an extraordinary authority. So much the greater is the hatred bestowed upon him by all the enemies of the state and of its peaceful development, by the instigators and the brawlers, by all the obscene abusers."

And just as the left radicals sneeringly call him "the Socialist patriot" so do the representatives of the right call him—"traitor." It is not surprising that Maximilian Harden also pelts him with his offal in American and Dutch newspapers. Since all this did not help and could not besmirch the name and the achievement of the first President of the *Reich*, Ebert was forced to go before the Magdeburg jury court through an artfully, persistently continued campaign of calumny. Entirely in keeping with the Conservative nationalist tradition ... The jurors court in Magdeburg is to examine world history and make world history; it is to put itself back into the atmosphere of wartime, pick out single incidents from the confusing muddle of a strike meeting in Treptow, and on the strength of that decide whether the leaders of the Majority Social Democratic acted in the interest of the country or—against it, in not permitting the wild strike to spread like lightning without leadership ... The presiding judge of the Magdeburg court and the attorneys for both parties have rightly demanded that the press postpone all criticism and satisfy itself with objective reports. It is our duty to comply with this demand. In contrast to the instigating nationalist gallery-gods, we shall speak about the trial only after the examination of the constantly increasing number of witnesses has been concluded, after the speeches of the state's attorney and the attorneys for the defense have been made, after sentence has been pronounced.

It will then be time to deal with the witnesses discovered somewhere or other by a pastor or a former army captain; witnesses who after seven eventful years can still glibly repeat every word which they heard in the excitement of the meeting on the Treptow meadow. It will then be time enough to discourse on the former naval and present business manager of the German National Party, who states in court, of course fully convinced—a typical case of lesion of the brain—that if it were not for the strike submarine warfare could have been extended to the remotest parts of the world by February 1919, and who even now does not seem to know anything about the failure of Ludendorff's strategy, of American intervention, of the collapse of Austria-Hungary, Bulgaria and Turkey, and of a few other little things. Not a word about the Magdeburg trial. But it is permissible to entertain an opinion of the first officer of the *Reich*, and here one can only repeat: Ebert no patriot? He, who permitted Liebknecht's followers to slander him because he and his party voted for war credits, wanted to make Germany defenseless by means of a strike? After two of his sons had been killed by enemy grenades, was the third son who was once wounded already and with this third son the whole German army, the whole of Germany, to be destroyed by lack of ammunition? What a fury against the Fatherland and against his own flesh and blood! What a gruesome, satanical perversity! We have a right, without improper interference with court procedure, to place the patriotism of the President, manifested by deed and sacrifice, high above the mendacious mouthings of others.

American interest in the trial

The trial was followed with interest in the American Midwest, where German-Americans made up a significant portion of the population. While not of the daily high quality of *The Times*, these articles indicate that American newspapers were eager to provide material for their readers.

9.19 "PRESIDENT OF GERMANY DENIES CHARGE OF TREASON, DECEMBER 12, 1924"[24]

President Ebert ... is under fire of fascists and nationalists who are seeking to discredit him and force him from office. A scene in a case unparalleled in German history took place at the president's palace where Ebert confronted a witness in a libel suit brought against an editor, Herr Rothardt at Magdeburg. Rothardt called Ebert a traitor. The president was not required to testify because of his office, but feeling that the affair was a fascisti plot he offered to confront the editor's chief witness.

This man proved to be a carpenter named Syrib, a warped, bent little man, whose limbs were horribly twisted from wounds sustained in the world war. Syrib charged that Ebert, during the famous 1918 munitions strike, advised strikers to refuse service at the front if the Kaiser tried to break the strike by sending them there.

Ebert's protocol was read at Magdeburg court this morning. It declared that while the president did not remember all details of the story of the strike of 1918, the event as pictured by Syrib was "quite out of the question." The president maintained his patriotism equaled any one.

9.20 "GERMAN FASCISTI AND REPUBLICANS STAGE FIGHTING IN STREETS, MARCH 3, 1925"[25]

A street fight between the Fascisti and the members of the Reichsbanner, the republican organization, occurred in the Potsdamer Platz today after the Fascists had refused to stop selling anti-Ebert pamphlets containing vile caricatures of the late president ... A section of the Monarchist and Communist press today contained attacks on the dead President. The Communist party ... issued a proclamation opening its Presidential campaign despite efforts of the government to relegate

> politics to the background pending Ebert's funeral. The proclamation was largely given over to a fiery denunciation of the late President ... "Ebert is dead," the proclamation read. "Down with the Ebert party ... Ebert's mass terror caused thousands of proletarians to be murdered and tens of thousands to be hurled into jail."

Afterwards

The story of the trial has a strange postscript. During one of his rambling evening monologues at his eastern field headquarters in 1942, Adolf Hitler told his listeners that he did not believe that Ebert was guilty of treason.

> Ebert's goal at the meeting in Treptow Park was to speak against the munitions workers strike. However, in order to get the crowd to listen, he had to tell them something that placated them and was then carried away by their applause. This made him appear an advocate of strikes. In such an atmosphere, there is the same risk for every political speaker.[26]

Conclusion

Ebert's political enemies in the German National People's Party were frustrated by their attempt to begin the public phase of the trial before the December 7 election, believing that it would provide them with amply material to attack the Social Democrats. At Ebert's request, the trial was delayed until after the election but the nationalists did well in the election without it. During the course of the proceedings, Ebert developed severe stomach pains; a physical examination revealed that he was suffering from appendicitis. He delayed surgery until after the trial because he did not want people to think that he was trying to garner sympathy through ill health. His condition did not improve and he died on February 28, 1925, as the result of peritonitis.

Thought questions

1 The prosecution argued that the defendant (Erwin Rothardt) libeled Ebert. The court agreed that he had in a technical sense. What do you find in the documentation that would agree with this opinion?
2 While the court found Rothardt guilty of libel in one sense, on what grounds did it hold that Ebert was not libeled?

3 Ebert and his defenders agreed that the January strike was wrong but argued that since he joined the strike committee with the avowed intention of ending it; he was working to support the war effort. His critics claimed that by joining in a "treasonous" activity—whatever his intentions—he was then a party to treason. Which side would you agree with and why?

4 Was it ever shown that the January Strike hurt the war effort? Would the outcome have been different if the deputy commanding general in Berlin had acted in a less belligerent fashion?

5 What is your opinion about the conduct of the trial? As each of the defense's witnesses proved unreliable, was it fair that they continued to search for new evidence in the hope that something would stick? Was it an indication of the presiding judge's prejudice that he allowed and in fact encouraged this to happen?

10

The Munich *Dolchstoß* Trial

Personal context

Paul Nicholas Cossmann was born in 1869, the son of a famous Jewish cellist. After completing his university studies in Berlin he moved to Munich, where he found employment as a private tutor. Cossmann participated fully in the vibrant cultural scene of the Bavarian capital, in 1904 helping found the cultural monthly *Süddeutsche Monatshefte*. The following year, at the age of 36, he converted to Catholicism. A convinced nationalist, Cossmann willingly became a mouthpiece for the most radical Annexationist elements and the Supreme Command. Like Karl Helfferich, Cossmann moved sharply to the right in the course of the war so that by the time of the collapse he had completely abandoned his earlier liberal worldview. It was a natural extension of this conversion for Cossmann to put his monthly exclusively at the service of fellow nationalists who believed that the Collapse and revolution was the result of a secret Jewish-Socialist conspiracy.[1]

In April and May 1924, in the run-up to the scheduled national elections, Cossmann commissioned and published a collection of articles expounding upon different aspects of the *Dolchstoß*. Many, although not all, of these articles were very radical and had been chosen to rally voters to the Nationalist cause. The articles received wide national attention and circulation. When the anti-Republican parties emerged with 26 percent of the votes and 127 seats in the *Reichstag* (a swing of 10.9 percent in the popular vote from the June 1920 election), Cossmann's primary object had been achieved. His second objective—to prompt one of the objects of his hatred to file a libel suit—remained unfulfilled. To that end, he had the April and May volumes bound together, sold them at a concessionary price, and trumpeted their "findings" as the final truth on the matter. It wasn't until the following year that the Martin Gruber, the editor of the Social Democratic *Münchener Post*, took the bait. He wrote that the *Dolchtosßhefte* were a historical falsification and libeled Cossmann in a very personal and savage way. This provided Cossmann the opportunity that he desired—he could bring a lawsuit against Gruber for libel and use the trial to "prove" the reality of the Stab-in-the-Back.

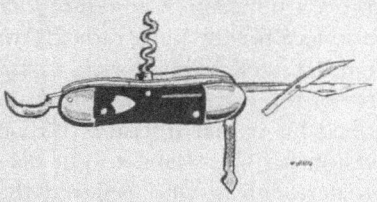

FIGURE 10.1 Lachen Links, *November 7, 1924, "der Dolchstoß bewiesen" (University of Heidelberg, University Library digitized historical literature collection).*

"Professor Cossmann's intensive six year search for evidence of a Dolchstoß, Professor Cossmann has finally resorted to with a search through the garbage of an officer's club."

FIGURE 10.2 Ulk, *November 20, 1925, "Der 'letzte' Kronzeuge" (University of Heidelberg, University Library digitized historical literature collection).*

The angel of peace is presented as "the last star witness" in the Munich *Dolchstoß* Trial. She demonstrates that she had been stabbed in the back by the rejection of the 1916 peace initiative and unrestricted submarine warfare.

In his October 1924 report on political conditions in Bavaria, the US consul mentioned the upcoming trial.

10.1 REPORT ON BAVARIAN POLITICAL CONDITIONS, OCTOBER 1924[2]

On October 19, there began in Munich hearings on the libel suit brought by Professor Cossmann, editor of the *Süddeutsche Monatshefte*, against Martin Gruber, editor of the *Münchener Post*, the Social Democratic organ. The dispute arose from the publication in the former periodical of a series of general articles under the general title of *Der Dolchstoß*, charging the socialists with having caused the loss of the war and from the very vehement and allegedly libelous replies of the latter. By the end of the month, the plaintiff had brought forward as witnesses Vice Admiral von Trotha, Admiral Heinrich, Admiral von Levetzow and other officers and civilians and the defense had called Messrs. Scheidemann and Noske among others. The plaintiff endeavored to prove that Germany's military breakdown was due to the propaganda of the German socialists, while the defendant is seeking to prove that it was due to the shortcomings of the government and its military leaders

Each of the principal local newspapers has devoted several pages daily to transcripts of the testimony, the *Münchener Post* also frequently calling attention to omissions on the part of the more conservative journals. *The Times* describes the scene in Documents 10.2 and 10.3.

10.2 THE TIMES SETS UP THE TRIAL, OCTOBER 20, 1925[3]

The hearing of a libel case which opened at the County Court here today will no doubt throw light on a much-debated Socialist and Nationalist Press controversy on the responsibility for the collapse of the German Army in 1918. The case involves statements contained in articles edited by Professor Cossmann in his periodical, the *Süddeutsche Monatschrift* [sic], accusing leaders and former officials of the Socialist Party of helping in Germany's downfall. The *Münchener Post*, the Socialist organ in Bavaria, retaliated and reproached Professor Cossmann for his attitude, making personal attacks upon his character and antecedents which are now construed as libelous. Martin Gruber, as editor of the *Münchener Post*, accepted the responsibility for these when addressing the Court this morning. After further discussion, the Court adjourned until tomorrow. The case will probably occupy the Court for at least three weeks. Thirty-eight witnesses have been called by the Court, including naval officers of Admiral von Scheer's Intelligence; General Groener, previously Minister of Communications; Wels, the Social Democratic leader; Herr Scheidemann, Dr. Landsberg, and Herr Gerhard Auer. Many others will be called by the respective parties, among whom are General von Stein, the former Minister for War and Quartermaster General of the Army, and Major Anker, of the German Crown Prince's staff. General von Hohn, Chief of Staff to the Crown Prince Rupprecht, is among the experts who will give evidence. It will be the duty of the Court to investigate, through the witnesses and material at its disposal, the various phases which led up to the disastrous collapse of the German forces, beginning with the policy followed by Bethmann Hollweg. Certain newspapers contemplate results which will affect Germany's political and economic future.

10.3 "CAUSES OF THE GERMAN DEFEAT," OCTOBER 22, 1925[4]

The third day's hearing of what is known here as the *Dolchstoß* (Stab-in-the-Back) because it is a tenet of the German Nationals that the German Army was defeated, not in the field, but by the defection of the working classes. The suit developed into a discussion of the personal impressions of two witnesses of the reasons for the collapse of the German forces in 1918.

It appears that the object of both parties is to bring a series of witnesses in an endeavour to prove, on the one side, that the breakdown of the German armed defence was due to poor food, inaction, and the hopeless, economic conditions in 1918, and, on the other, to the supposed revolutionary ideas instilled into the troops by Allied agents or traitorous Germans. Apparently this issue must be decided before the question of personal libel can be approached.

Today, the judge, having stated that he was not connected with any Parliamentary Commission, heard the evidence, lasting three hours, of Vice-Admiral von Trotha, formerly of the naval staff, whose testimony [focused] on the achievements of the German Navy during the war, in the course of which he admitted that the monotonous daily routine was responsible for discontent amongst the sailors, who, in 1918, were ripe for any form of disobedience. Under cross examination [he] denied that shooting [range of British naval guns] was superior to anything possessed

> by the German Navy or likely to have a demoralizing effect upon the crews. This statement provoked applause in Court.
>
> Quoting a statement attributed to Mr. Churchill, to the effect that only by internal cohesion were the Germans able to withstand the military pressure of the Allies, he inferred that this was not the case in 1917, when news of political agitation had begun to filter through and undermine the discipline of the ratings. If a repetition of today's proceedings becomes regular, it is likely that the case will continue until December.

While both the US consul and *The Times* correspondent accurately recounted the circumstances of the trial, they failed to comprehend the very personal (and ugly) nature of Gruber's libel. In his 1973 dissertation, George Botjer describes the "frenzied invective" with which Gruber attacked Cossmann.

10.4 GEORGE BOTJER ON GRUBER'S LIBEL[5]

> [Gruber's] front page campaign against the *Süddeutsche Monatshefte* concentrated mainly on the military situation, which was of course also debated at the trial. Aside from this, Gruber launched an *ad hominem* attack on Dr. Cossmann, which was characterized by what may fairly be called frenzied invective. His charge that Cossmann's "seemingly objective method is a journalistic counterfeit," was a mild opener. [*Münchener Post*, April 29, 1924, p. 1] The offending editions were consistently described, in headline and text, as "the lying *Dolchstoß* editions." Cossmann was called "a literary profiteer," a "political Shylock," a "moneybag patriot," and "a falsifier of history." [*Münchener Post*, May 3, p. 1] A statement by General von Vietinghoff in one *Süddeutsche Monatshefte* article, blaming the *Dolchstoß* on the Jews, occasioned this front page banner headline in the Post: "The Jew Cossmann as Jew Baiter!" In the story ... Cossmann was facetiously described as an agent of the Elders of Zion. The contents of the two *Hefte* were summarized as "the fanatical raging of the Jewish busybody Cossmann."

It is deeply ironic that the Social Democrat Gruber engaged in the sort of antisemitic demagoguery common to the Stab-in-the-Back proponents. As we will see in Document 10.11, little distinguished Gruber's libel from the characterizations of Cossmann that appeared in the National Socialist *Völkische Beobachter*.

In a change from its coverage of the Ebert Libel Trial, the *New York Times* reported on the Munich proceedings with fullness similar to *The Times*. Hoping to beef up its European presence, the newspaper had hired one of the leading American journalists on the Continent, Lincoln Eyre, to report on the trial.[6] Eyre's reports, reproduced in Document 10.5, recounts the stunning testimony that he tried to convince the Emperor to seek death at the front in the final days of the war. His subsequent report, Document 10.6, describes Hans Delbrück's denial of the Stab-in-the-Back.

10.5 "GROENER TELLS AT MUNICH TRIAL OF VAIN EFFORTS TO ENLIVEN WANING MORALE," OCTOBER 30, 1925[7]

A picture of the Kaiser steadfastly refusing the pleas of his army commanders to go into the frontline trenches as a boost to the waning moral of the troops, of the late President Ebert a short time later so earnestly fighting the Spartacists in the streets of Berlin that once he became their prisoner, was drawn by General Groener, Ludendorff's successor near the close of the war, in the "stab-in-the-back" trial here today. The case being tried is that of a reactionary magazine's libel charges against the editor of the Munich Post.

It was also brought out that Marshal Hindenburg entrusted the suppressing of the revolutionary activities of Red radicals to Ebert, whom he supplied with ten divisions, and in order to keep in constant touch with him a private secret wire between them was established. General Groener stated that Ebert insisted towards the end of the war on the Kaiser's abdication as the only means of preventing a revolution and suggested the Crown Prince's oldest son as successor to the throne. General Groener said he begged the Kaiser's aids to persuade the monarch to go to the front, not to review parades, nor distribute Iron Crosses, but to go into the trenches like a doughboy and take his chances of stopping a bullet.

"In case he fell it would be a glorious end. If wounded, the people would become sentimental and change their [patriotic] attitude," General Groener said. "The Kaiser refused to brave shot and shell, in which he was supported by Hindenburg, who also disapproved Ebert's suggestions about the Kaiser's abdication."

General Groener expressed regret at being unable to follow Ebert's plan and in court said: "Perhaps I should have told Ebert I would see that the Kaiser left the throne and told him to prevent revolution."

According to General Groener, the German soldiers had fixed the same date as the Americans for seeing the end of the war, using the slogan, "Home for Christmas!"

Ludendorff also told Groener on September 18, 1918, that peace must come by Christmas. That this slogan was taken to heart by the soldiers was shown by the fact that of ten divisions sent by Ebert to maintain order in Berlin, all absented themselves except 1,800 men a few days before that holiday.

Groener said that all members of the Nationalist Party also were absent from Berlin and that the reins of government had been entrusted to the Socialists. That the Socialists had no intention of overthrowing the monarchy, even a few days before the Armistice was brought out in the trial, the task of preventing the revolution having been given into the hands of Ebert and the other Socialists whose efforts at loyalty could not be criticized.

Groener said he entrusted Haase, the [Independent] Socialist leader later assassinated, with preventing the strikes, which service he well performed, though Haase requested that his promise to Groener must not be revealed on account of probable objections from the unions, and the secret was kept inviolate until today.

The attitude of the Socialists was summed up by General Groener by quoting Prince Max of Baden, then Chancellor, who said he wanted to save the monarchy, but the monarchy would not let itself be saved.

10.6 "DELBRÜCK REJECTS 'STAB-IN-BACK THEORY'," NOVEMBER 3, 1925[8]

That Germany lost the war because of the Ludendorff offensive of March 21, 1918, though gloriously carried out, was a strategic failure, and that Germany should have made peace long before, was the substance of the testimony of Professor Hans Delbrück, well-known German historian and political economist in today's session of the "Stab-in-the-Back" case.

Professor Delbrück denied there had been any successful stab on the part of the Socialists in breaking down the morale of the troops, that the revolution resulted from Socialist propaganda, or that the collapse of the monarchy was caused by Socialists' alleged desire to close the conflict. He testified he did not wish Germany to have a "Ludendorff victory," that is to say, a victory meaning annexation of the Flanders coast, Aix-la-Chapelle or other parts of Belgium, but desired to conquer in the sense of Frederick the Great, that is to say, the triumph of the German army without the annexation of territory.

> "I hang with all the fibers of my heart to the olden Germany, but in political cooperation of the head and heart, the head must have diplomacy." Professor Delbrück told the Court. "I have reached the conclusion that Germany can exist in only one form, a democratic republic."

The topics Eyre covered for the *New York Times* were sure to appeal to an American audience, but to gain an appreciation of the political dynamite exploded on the German domestic scene, it is essential to read the German press. The Social Democratic *Vorwärts* is most reliable in this case, without regard to how it made the party appear.

10.7 HERMANN VON KUHL'S TESTIMONY, OCTOBER 27, 1925[9]

In the *Dolchstoß* trial the last witness for the plaintiff Cossmann was questioned on Monday. His testimony was likewise intermingled with his report as an expert witness. During the war, General Hermann von Kuhl (who was the Chief of the General Staff for the army of Crown Prince Rupprecht of Bavaria) has become known for his detailed report for the parliamentary Committee. His remarks demonstrate that he is a follower of the *Dolchstoßlegende* with the unique perspective based upon his [personal] knowledge of the situation. He believes that the army was stabbed-in-the-back in the staging areas and that prevented it from continuing the war. Note of the following [statement by General von Kuhl concerning] that, "victory was not possible for Germany after the March 1918 offensive was thwarted." The general further stated that,

> We cannot assert that we only lost the war through the subversion of the Army ... By the summer of 1918 we were seemingly at the end of our ability to give meaningful orders. We had to dissolve battalions and decrease the manpower of each company. Therein lies the primary cause of the defeat. This manpower shortage came from the exceptional sacrifices of the summer battles of 1918 ... We had between January 1918 and the armistice lost a total of 420,000 men kill or wounded and a further 340,000 men were taken prisoner or were missing ... By 10 November all militarily hope was lost. It was no longer possible to carry on the war. [Still], I am strongly convinced that we could have fought for better peace terms had there not been a revolution ... We had not thought of victory since the summer of 1918.

10.8 "THE CLOSE OF THE DOLCHSTOSS TRIAL," NOVEMBER 21, 1925[10]

After five contentious weeks, the *Dolchstoß* Trial concluded with the three-hour testimony of the indicted comrade Gruber. Gruber emphasized [that] Cossmann, in his closing remarks, has said nothing worth refuting but [Cossmann] had leveled the greatest possible insult towards the Social Democratic Party and its leadership by accusing them of treason against their country. Cossmann should not be surprised that the Munich Post has struck back strenuously against his mudslinging accusations.

The two *Dolchstoß* issues of the *Süddeutsche* Monatshefte had another purpose. They were meant to be used by the German National and anti-Semitic parties as election materials against the Social Democratic Party ...

The entire trial has had the effect of a cleansing thundershower. Whoever speaks after [the trial] of a *Dolchstoß* is an unscrupulous slanderer.

Contrast the *Vorwärts* appreciation of the trial with the matter-of-fact statement of *The Times* on the verdict.

10.9 "END OF THE MUNICH LIBEL ACTION. SOCIALIST EDITOR FINED," DECEMBER 10, 1925[11]

Judgment in what has been called the "Stab-in-the-Back" libel case was delivered in Munich this morning. The defendant, Herr Gruber, the responsible editor of the *Münchener Post*, was sentenced to a fine of 3,000 marks (£150), with the alternative of 30 days' imprisonment, and to bear all costs.

The charge arose out of the reply made by the *Münchener Post*, a Socialist daily newspaper, to a series of articles published in the *Süddeutsche Monatsheft*, a magazine edited by Professor Cossmann and devoted to expounding the extreme Nationalist point of view. Professor Cossmann's contributors were enlisted to prove that Germany lost the war as the direct result of Socialist agitation among the troops, the German Navy, and the workers in the munitions factories. Herr Gruber, in a review of these articles, accused Professor Cossmann of falsifying history.

The press and party response to the verdict—as was the case in the Ebert Libel Trial—is best recounted by a non-partisan overview. The US consul in Munich did a much less thorough job than the deputy ambassador in

Berlin in the case of the Ebert trial. Fortunately, George Botjer has written summations of the national press response (Document 10.10) and the specific response of the Nazi party organ, the *Völkische Beobachter* (Document 10.11) similar to what one might have expected from the consul.

10.10 GEORGE BOTJER ON THE RESPONSE OF THE GERMAN PRESS TO THE VERDICT[12]

Independent German newspapers—those that did not function as outlets for specific political parties—generally took a jaundiced view of the [trial], regretting that it had to take place at all. This would indicate that such newspaper, which included some of the most reputable in the country, such as the *Berliner Tageblatt* and the *Frankfurter Zeitung*, considered the whole *Dolchstoß* question to be only a source of internal strife, which had to be laid to rest at the earliest possible moment. The much larger political press, on the other hand, representing parties of quite varied outlook, followed the day-to-day proceedings in the Munich ... with gusto. In spite of the fact the that law forbade the distorted reportage of court proceedings, the political newspapers abandoned themselves to the most unabashed distortion of what went on in the courtroom.

An example of the jaundiced view taken by the independent newspapers, *par excellence*, is provided by the Munich evening newspaper, *Allgemeine Zeitung*. One of the city's oldest newspapers, whose appeal at this time was mainly to artists and intellectuals, *AZ* expressed its misgivings about the whole enterprise in a mocking poem ... The *Berliner Tageblatt* took a more sombre stance toward the proceedings in Munich, and limited coverage to regular but generally brief summaries in the back pages. On November 11, however, a front page article appeared under the headline, "Who Stabbed the Fleet in the Back?" The tenor of the article was revealed in a subheading that introduced Noske's testimony about his experiences during the Kiel mutiny. It referred to "the helplessness of the officers" in the face of the uprising. Noske's claim that the officers had in effect abdicated their responsibility were reported as fact. The unsigned article then concluded with the observation that the sailors had genuine grievances, not the least of which was the Channel attack plan. The *Tageblatt* gave the distinct impression that it considered the mutiny to have been justified.

The evening edition of the *Berliner Tageblatt* on December 9, 1925, the day on which the verdict and sentence were given by Judge Frank, featured an article titled, "The End of the *Dolchstoß* Legend" by Dr. Karl Eugen Müller. The article stated that Martin Gruber was entirely justified in his verbal attacks on the plaintiff. Was it a crime, the author asked, to call a hooligan an honest man? The writer was implying, apparently, that the same answer applied to the converse of that situation. Müller also claimed that the defendant was protected under Article 193 of the Criminal Code, for his remarks were made not as an individual but as a spokesman for an institution, the SPD. It was then alleged that the verdict was not directed at Gruber alone, but against the German people. The verdict was also condemned as a blow to objectivity in historical research, and Judge Frank was held to be unqualified to judge historical issues. Since the [trial] however, had provided a unique forum for presentation, in a debating situation, of both sides of the *Dolchstoß* question, it had provided a valuable service to the German people.

10.11 GEORGE BOTJER ON NAZI COVERAGE OF THE TRIAL[13]

The trial often received front page coverage in the *Völkischer Beobachter*, under headlines like, "On the Trail of the Traitors." ... Jewish witnesses for the defense were always identified as such, e.g., "the Jew Kuttner." ... The fact that Dr. Cossmann, currently the lead spokesman for the *Dolchstoß* theory, had been born a Jew was not to be overlooked, either. He was habitually referred to as "the Jew Cossmann," whose inherited Jewish nature showed through in his failure to denounce "the shabbiest, most fraudulent and most cowardly party of the Jews," the SPD ... The testimony of Philipp Scheidemann provoked a stronger reaction from the *Völkischer Beobachter* than that of any other witness. An account of his role in securing the abdication of the Kaiser appeared under the headline, "Scheidemann Required to Administer the Backstab." The chief perpetrators of treasonous acts during the war, however, were identified as Independent Socialists. The Nazi newspaper also followed the Cossmann line by condemning the reconciliation of the Independents with the Social Democrats in 1922. Another conspicuous aspect of *Völkischer Beobachter's* coverage of the trial was the fact that derogatory remarks were sometimes made about the late SPD leader and the president of the Republic, Friedrich Ebert. One headline proclaimed, "Ebert stands in Defense of the Traitors."

The Munich *Dolchstoß* trial was important for another reason: it was the first public airing of confidential testimony taken *in camera* before the Subcommittee investigating the causes and the Collapse. Many of the important specialists who drafted reports for the Subcommittee had been called to testify. In Document 10.12, the General Secretary of the

Subcommittee, Dr. Eugen Fischer, describes how he attended the trial to see if there was anything new that he could learn. His report described the military testimony in some detail, particularly regarding the fleet, which the Subcommittee had not yet heard. In Fischer's opinion, Groener's testimony was clearly the highpoint and contained three bombshells.

10.12 DR. EUGEN FISCHER ON THE TRIAL[14]

The Groener testimony was the high point of the trial. An air of historical revelation blew through the hall as Groener made his statement. Groener seemed much more purely factual than the other witnesses. I would like to highlight three points from the proceedings.

The first point is that deputy Haase was invited by Groener to a meeting immediately prior to May 1, 1917. At the close of this meeting, Haase shook Groener's hand and promised him that there would be no more strikes. He requested that Groener tell no one that they had spoken …

The second point regarded domestic policy. Groener maintained that the laws regarding the state of siege and the powers of the Deputy Commanding Generals were out-date and had to be curtailed in favor of accountability by the civil authorities. He maintained that the gradual failure of the civilian authorities was due to the fact that at the beginning of the war all responsibility was taken out of their hands. When the willingness to take responsibility and the energy of the civil bodies lessened, Groener came to believe that concessions had to be made relative to the Prussian suffrage and that the profits of the arms industry had to be lessened so that they did not cause public complaint. He wrote a long memorandum on these matters and was consequently removed from office [and reassigned to the Russian Front]. He never has learned who demanded his dismissal. He also believed that it was necessary to make arrangements in the event that Germany lost the war. This was not accepted as Ludendorff refused to believe that the war could be lost.

Lastly—and this was of paramount importance—Groener detailed the "Pact" that he reached on 10 November with Ebert regarding the secret line of communications between the *Reich* Chancellery and military headquarters for the suppression of the revolution, the gradual displacement of the Independents from the government and the agreement to hold elections for a National Assembly. A huge murmur ran through the hall as he spoke these words. Some listeners understood Groener as saying that he had reached an agreement with Ebert to reintroduce the monarchy. This was misunderstanding was clarified after a short break; the agreement was to act against the radical leftists who wanted to force Bolshevism on Germany. It was an agreement between the Supreme Command and with the national government, which was in the hands of Ebert and his friends. Groener put special emphasis on the word "Bündnis."

Groener then described the impact of the alliance with Ebert in detail. Some parts were amusing, such as his portrayal the state of affairs on December 23–25. At that critical time (when the Free Corps were suppressing the Red Naval Division) Ebert had not a single bodyguard and the two machine guns that looked out of the windows of the *Reich* Chancellery could not shoot. Ebert telephoned Groener and asked, "What should I do? If Liebknecht comes to arrest me, I can not stop him." Groener replied, "My volunteers will not arrive prior to January." "Well," said Ebert,

> I've worked a lot in the last few days. I am going to go to sleep. I will take leave of the *Reich* Chancellery and make sure that no one knows where I am. If Liebknecht comes, he will be punching air as he won't find me; afterwards we create the government in Kassel, or anywhere else, and the thing goes on.

Ebert did so. But Liebknecht and his followers were celebrating Christmas and missed their favorable moment.

Conclusion

The secondary literature mentions the Munich *Dolchstoß* Trial more frequently than the Ebert trial in Magdeburg. Why might this be the case? It was surely not because the sources are richer. Was it the poignancy of an ethnically Jewish nationalist who was to die in Theresienstadt promoted what became such a potent Nazi myth? As Botjer pointed out, the quality press ignored the trial until its conclusion. So did the Communist *Rote Fahne*, with the exception of Groener's testimony about the agreement that he made with Ebert to put down the revolution. Much of the surviving record, save in the actual trial transcript or the reporting of the *Münchner Post* (as Hans Delbrück made clear) was deeply politicized. Nor was it because the Munich trial was more clearly about the generally ignored navy, whose officer corps displayed gross incompetence.

It seems, rather, that part of the significance of the *Dolchstoß* Trial lay in the fact that it was the first time that the evidence prepared for the Subcommittee on the Collapse by its expert was revealed to the public. Rather than being presented as part of a unified whole, discussed and debated by both participants in the events and the people's representatives, aspects of Subcommittee's work was leaked out in an unedited and unscientific fashion. Partisan newspapers latched on to elements of the testimony that they found congenial and distorted those with which they disagreed. By refusing to give column space to the "sensationalist" trial in Munich, the quality newspapers abrogated their duty to provide their better-educated readers with information that they could use to put partisan distortions into context. As a result, the mass of middle-class voters who were inclined toward nationalist arguments rationally expressed and suspicious of the Left, were left with an unchallenged narrative written by the radical right.

FIGURE 10.3 *DNVP May 1924 election (Bundesarchiv Bildarchiv).*

A brave soldier advancing against the background of the black-red-white imperial flag is stabbed in the back by a masked villain dressed in red with the hat always used to designate Social Democrats. The text reads,

In the World War, who stabbed the German army in the back? Who is responsible for sinking our People and Fatherland so deeply into misfortune? The Magdeburg Social Democratic party secretary Vater has said: "We sent our people to the front to encourage desertion. We organized the deserters, fitted them out with false papers, money and untraceable leaflets. We sent these people in all directions but especially to the Front to work with the soldiers there and encourage their unhappiness. These encouraged the soldiers to desert thus brought about the fall gradually but surely." Who supported the Social Democrats in this? The Democrats and the people around Erzberger. These people want to stage a second stab-in-the-back [as the result of this election] and make us slaves of the Entente and keep us permanently subservient. If you don't want this, vote German National

Some interesting conflation was going on here. Vater in 1918 had been an Independent. When the two Social Democratic parties reunited, he again became a Social Democrat. His statement was made in 1920 at a USPD conference where he was bragging about the role of the party in the revolution. Thus the Nationalists hoped to tar the SPD with the stick of those they opposed in 1918 but were now in league with. The Democrats and the Erzberger people (the Center Party) were part of the coalition that controlled the Prussian state government from 1919 to 1932.

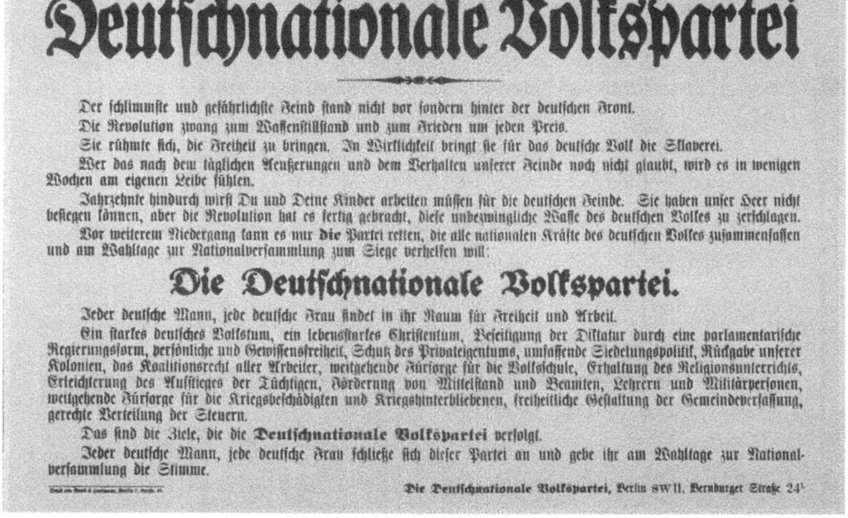

FIGURE 10.4 *DNVP 1920 election (Bundesarchiv Bildarchiv).*

A visually unsophisticated poster created by the German National People's Party for the *Reichstag* election of 1920. "The worst and most dangerous enemy stood not before but behind the German army's front lines. The revolution brought about an Armistice and Peace purchased at any price. They promised to bring you freedom. In reality, they brought the German people slavery."

Thought questions

1 Compare the Magdeburg and the Munich trials—which was the fairer of the two?
2 Prior to the Munich Trial, much of the evidence collected by the Subcommittee of the *Reichstag* investigating the collapse had been confidential. In the course of the trial, experts who advised the committee were called to testify. Should they have been allowed to do so before the Subcommittee's work was completed?
3 Although the *Südedeutsche Monatshefte* published its *Dolchstoß* issues in April and May of 1924, the Social Democratic satirical magazine *Lachen Links* published the cartoon of Cossmann and von Müller sifting through trash looking for evidence of a Stab-in-the-Back in November 1924. What was going on at that time? What does the cartoon suggest about the nature of Cossmann's evidence?
4 *Ulk*, the satire magazine published by the progressive *Berliner Tageblatt*, suggests that Peace was stabbed in the back. What does this say about the universality of the notion of a *Dolchstoß*?
5 One of the most famous depictions of a Stab-in-the-Back was published by the German National People's Party for the May 1924 national election. The Social Democratic Party offered its own take on betrayal in Figure 10.5, prepared for the Prussian state election in December 1925. Based on this second poster, who was betrayed and who was doing the betraying?

FIGURE 10.5 *SPD December 1924 Prussian election (Bundesarchiv Bildarchiv).*

"The true Stab-in-the-Back. Protect him! Vote Otto Braun!" A young man holding the republican black-red-gold flag with the words "peace-work-education" is stabbed in the back by an ominous military figure carrying the black-white-red shield of the monarchists. Note that the black figure does not wear the helmet or uniform of the Reichswehr so that the publishers cannot be held liable for defaming the military. Instead, it is suggestive of militarism in general and monarchist opposition to the Republic. Perhaps the black alludes slightly to the Social Democrats' coalition partners the Center Party (always depicted as black) who were opposed to the SPD's education reforms.

11

A *Dolchstoß* Consensus?

Institutional context

By the time that the Subcommittee had collected its sources, debated their worth and issued their final report, much of the public fire had gone out of the *Dolchstoß* debate. The issue had figured prominently in the national elections held in May and December 1924. Two sensational trials had brought a vast array of evidence—much of it provided by experts advising the Subcommittee—before the public. The controversial first president of the Republic was dead and a prominent propagator of the *Dolchstoßlegende* had been elected in his stead. The Dawes Plan and the end of the hyperinflation seemed to bring a period of calm and stability to a country badly in need of both. One might argue that a tortured sort of consensus—an agreement to disagree—had been reached. Having been victorious in the 1924 elections, the German Nationals were so internally divided over issues such as participation in the government that talk of a Stab-in-the-Back could only aggravate their situation. The now reunited Social Democrats needed to damp down resentments between former Majority and Independent constituents and fend off Communist incursions into their working class base. It was the Communists and Nazis who continued to use the rhetoric of their own variants of the *Dolchstoß* Myth to keep their followers within their camps.

We can see the development of this "consensus" in the progression from the original experts' depositions, to the attempt by Myth opponent Hans Delbrück to find common ground with Myth proponent Hermann von Kuhl, to the surprising unanimous agreement on the internal causes of the Collapse.

The expert depositions

Karl Helfferich's outburst before the larger *Reichstag* Committee in November 1919, followed the next day by the Hindenburg/Ludendorff testimony and the attendant popular demonstrations, convinced the

Reichstag leaders that the work of the investigation could no longer take place in public with the interrogation of live witnesses. It was decided instead that subcommittees—working with document specialists seconded by the military and the state archives—would commission depositions from acknowledged experts and receive written reports from interested individuals. As these depositions and reports were completed, they were read and discussed by the Subcommittee. The Subcommittee also reached out and took verbal testimony from individuals across the political spectrum. Because of the idiosyncratic way that the Subcommittee findings were published, the discussion of the experts' depositions and the collection of verbal responses to them were recorded in Volumes 4 and 5 while the depositions themselves were in Volume 6.

The Subcommittee met 42 times between 1920 and 1925. In June 1925 it picked up pace, meeting 80 times between June 16, 1925 and November 3, 1927. The first three volumes published by the Subcommittee dealt with the military Collapse. Volume 4 featured the Subcommittee's conclusions on the internal Collapse. This volume featured considerable input from non-committee members. Volume 5 was a continuation of the proceedings in Volume 4, with appendices by Ludwig Bergsträsser and a collection of letters from the front. Volume 6 was devoted exclusively to the *Dolchstoß* question. It featured long depositions from Kuhl, Delbrück, Katzenstein, Herz, and Volkmann, excerpts from which are featured later.

The experts provided a balance of opinions. Some of the depositions were long and detailed; others were more cursory. The longest was contributed by Berlin Superior Court judge Dr. Ludwig Herz. Other contributors included a nationalist former *Freikorps* member, Erich Otto Volkmann (a general staff officer in the war, and since 1920 an archivist at the Imperial Archives in Potsdam) and Simon Katzenstein, a Social Democratic writer and editor who taught at the party school in Berlin.

11.1 SUMMARY OF THE DEPOSITION OF DR. HERZ[1]

The analysis of the *Dolchstoß* falls into two camps. One group believes that the defeat came about because the fighting spirit of the Army was worn down by revolutionary agitation and the mood of the country. The other believes that a revolution from above—not the revolution from below—brought an end to the war.

It is true that the revolution made the rejection of the armistice conditions impossible and that the army was threatened by the dissolution of order behind the front. But it is a contradiction to believe that the army was so contaminated by anti-War agitation that it was defeated, while at the same time believing that it was possible to continue the war in spite of the deterioration of the fighting capacity of the army. It is illogical to claim that the hunger for peace on the home front was delusional because our enemies never wanted a negotiated peace, and to say in the same breath, that the Revolution led to the destruction of peace. It is a historical misrepresentation of the course of events to say that without the revolution the Entente would not have expected of us to surrender. It is a *hysteron proteron* to portray the defeat as a consequence of the revolution when in fact the revolution was the consequence of defeat; revolutionary agitation in the army and at home were not successful until defeat became apparent.

It is true that the mood of the home front became worse and ultimately failed when the tonic of victory in the field no longer worked its magic. The military leadership miscalculated the risk that the blockade of the Central Powers posed. It was a psychological error that it allowed the notion of a defensive war to be distorted into a war of conquest.

It is true that there was agitation at home and in the army. It is not possible to determine with mathematical exactitude how much of this was for a peace of understanding or how much was calculated to provoke a revolution. We can say, however, with certitude that it had a fatal influence on the soul of a starving people and an exhausted army. It is certain that without the grievances in the army and on the home front, the handful of revolutionaries would never have managed to gain influence even after the loss of the war.

It is dishonest, when discussing the collapse, to ignore the impact of the tactical and strategic errors of the Army leadership, the supremacy of our enemies in men and material that was growing by the hour, and the physical condition of our restless, scantily fed troops. Even if the spirit of the army and the replacement troops suffered from revolutionary propaganda, no evidence has been produced to show that it resulted in either the failure of the Offensive or loss of the war .... The story that the front was stabbed in the back is a fable.

11.2 SUMMARY OF THE DEPOSITION OF ARCHIVRAT VOLKMANN[2]

From the socialist side, the view is often expressed ... that the disagreement between the Majority Social Democrats and the Independents were only over tactics. Unfortunately, Professor Delbrück uncritically accepts this perspective in his own deposition to this Subcommittee.

The Independent Social Democrats had an unshakable distrust of the skill and power of the Supreme Command. This attitude sprang from their conviction that if the Supreme Command succeeded, it would implement annexationist and imperialist plans. Furthermore, the Independents believed that when they voted against war credits, the Socialists of enemy countries would follow their example, paving the way for a peace of understanding. The Majority Socialists thought this hope was utopian. Although they were skeptical about the annexationist goals of the Supreme Command, they felt that they must support the war effort and voted in 1916 to grant further credits to the government to prosecute the war. The concept of an intra-Socialist division appears strong on the surface .... It revolved around the key question of which path the movement should follow to achieve the final goal: natural and gradual evolution or the path of revolutionary violence.

In my view, however, the conflict within the Social Democratic Party during the war and in the months of the revolution was a matter of feeling and strategy, even if adherents of socialist ideology want to talk about tactical options .... Radical Marxists from the beginning advanced the idea of continuing the international struggle for the liberation of the proletariat during the war without regard to their own people. In this light, their actions have been clear and logical. They lead in a straight line from Liebknecht's anti-military propaganda before the war through the revolutionary activities of the Spartacus League during the war and ended with violence at the end of the war ....

In my opinion, the impact of the Independents on the war is that they significantly weakened the power of the army and the warlike spirit of the people. They accelerated the collapse and caused the war to be ended in a way that was not worthy of a brave people. Some might dispute whether the army could have continued to fight without the outbreak of the Revolution and without the previous subversion. From the patriotic-nationalist point of view, it is indisputable that the German people were in the grip of a delusion when they dropped their weapons at the very moment that the Armistice negotiations began.

11.3 SUMMARY OF THE DEPOSITION OF KATZENSTEIN[3]

Just as it would be inaccurate to say that the revolution brought about the defeat in the field, so it would also be wrong to depict the German people acting in a herd-like, revolutionary fashion in response to defeat.

> The spark for revolt was popular outrage over the deliberate dissemination of untruthful news ... and the systematic suppression of the true situation. Think of the propaganda about how the arrival of the Americans would not matter in the course of the war and the shattering effect on popular opinion when the truth came to light.
>
> *British Major-General Maurice—who's never-written words about the "stabbing of the front in the back" have done such effective agitational service [for the opponents of the Republic]*—accurately described the situation when he wrote, "The policy of deception was, I believe, one of the reasons the suddenness of the collapse when things started to go bad. The soldiers and the people realized that their rulers had either lied about the facts or had hopelessly misjudged the true state of affairs. They just lost confidence in the time when the trust was most needed." It was the sudden collapse of the confidence of the people in the military and government empowered revolutionary sentiment ....
>
> I assert that:
>
> 1. The defeat of the German army can be attributed to the military power relations and the strategic advantage of the Entente.
> 2. The cohesion of both Army and people were reprehensibly shaken by selfish and domineering abuses of class privilege that contributed to the final Collapse.
> 3. As a last resort, politically radical aspirations inspired by the abuses described above found a fertile breeding ground.

Delbrück contra Kuhl

The two main intellectual lights of the Subcommittee were Hermann von Kuhl and Hans Delbrück. Kuhl was introduced in Chapter 5, where we read his assessment on the status of the German forces and the Supreme Command's considerations regarding the arrival of the Americans. Hans Delbrück, the father of modern military history, taught at Berlin University and was editor of the influential *Preußischen Jahrbücher* until 1919. He was a politically active moderate conservative, serving from1882 to 1885 in the Prussian House of Deputies and from 1884 to 1890 in the *Reichstag*. Given his stature, he was from the beginning of the war involved in strategic discussions with Supreme Command. He opposed unrestricted submarine warfare, the demand for the annexation of conquered territory and Ludendorff's conduct of the war. Document 11.6 is a condensation of a written argument between Delbrück and Kuhl in which the former suggested that there was in fact considerable common ground between their two positions. Kuhl heatedly rejected Delbrück's compromise. One can only imagine what their face-to-face confrontation was like.

11.4 SUMMARY OF THE DEPOSITION OF GENERAL VON KUHL[4]

The concept of the "Stab-in-the-Back" has violently aroused public opinion since the end of the World War. There is hardly an issue in which the views facing each other so harshly. Some say we lost the war by the home front stabbing the undefeated army in the back. From the other side of the "Stab-in-the-Back" is rejected as a vicious and stupid myth. In this view, the army had not been betrayed by the home front or undermined by revolutionary propaganda. Those who hold this view maintain that there was no systematic revolutionary propaganda in the army and that the revolution was not responsible for the military collapse but resulted from it.

When the expression Stab-in-the-Back is used in the sense that the victorious Army only lost because it was betrayed on the Home Front, it is wrong. We lost the war for many reasons. It is indisputable that a pacifist, internationalist, anti-militarist and revolutionary subversion of the army had taken place and contributed to the injury and the decomposition of the army. The civilians that endured superhuman sacrifice for four and a half years of war are not to blame. Instead it was the rabble-rousers and those who sought to harm our people and destroy our army, who sought to poison the brave fighting army for political reasons. The effect of their sinister activity emerged mainly after the failure of our offensive in the summer of 1918, but the subversive work had been going on for a long time. One should define this less as a stab-in-the-back, but instead as a poisoning of the army.

The expression "stab-in-the-back" may, however, be applied to the sudden and devastating effects of the revolution itself. It was literally an attack on the Army from the rear. It disorganized the lines of communication, prevented the movement of supplies to the front, and put an end to all order and discipline as if at one blow. It made all further fighting impossible and compelled us to accept an armistice on any terms the enemy demanded. The revolution was not the result of the collapse of the offensive, although that substantially furthered its outbreak and its effects.

The revolution threatened to completely break-up of the Army during the retreat. This would have precipitated an even greater catastrophe. This danger was averted only with the greatest difficulty.

11.5 SUMMARY OF THE DEPOSITION OF DR. DELBRÜCK[5]

The agreements and the differences between Mr. v. Kuhl and I have felt in our original Depositions is notable, especially as they regard the question of the *Dolchstoßlegende*. Kuhl believes that for many Germans the will for victory (*Siegeswillen*) was compromised by the belief that they thought peace could only be achieved if Germany renounced territorial ambitions. He wrote, "That a resolute will to destruction lived in the hearts of our enemies, was not considered." I believe conversely, that a resolute, unified fighting spirit on our side would have been greatly increased if the government and Supreme Command had declared in a timely manner that Germany was conducting the war solely for defensive purposes and renounced all territorial expansion .... I do not dispute that our enemies possessed a determined will to destroy us. But it is also indisputable that there was a large desire for peace in England at a decisive point during the war. If we had engaged it in a timely fashion we might have achieved an honorable peace.

Kuhl asserts that anti-militarist agitation began before the failure of our offensive. This is certainly true and I do not think anyone asserts the opposite. What is certain is that this anti-militarist agitation was not successful before the summer of 1918. With what confidence in victory, the German people welcomed the Offensive! And when the German troops began to retreat after August, hardly anybody doubted that the front would hold. Both public opinion and our leaders were caught up in a totally erroneous assessment of our military situation. When General Ludendorff's nerves collapsed on 29 September and he demanded an immediate Armistice, it was a psychological disaster that plunged the whole German people into the abyss of despair.

In reality the war was already lost on 27 March, when it was clear that the tactical success of the great offensive was not sufficient to develop it into a strategic victory. The question is whether one can assume that support for the war at home or in the army would have existed if people had not believed that we were fighting a defensive war.

I argue that the German people's determination to continue the war was in the end paralyzed (1) by the military and economic supremacy of the enemy and the hunger blockade, (2) by the conversion of defensive war in the war of conquest, (3) the continuation of the war was after it had long since become hopeless, (4) the generation of an optimistic mood by untruthful war reports, and (5) the sudden destruction of this optimism by the request for an armistice. The last stroke was the insane plan of a great naval battle in the midst of negotiations for an armistice.

I also agree entirely with Kuhl that "the rabble-rousers and those who exploited the plight of the people for their own political purposes should be pilloried." But I would also ask that judgment be passed on all the persons whose unbridled ambition spilled the blood of the German people for war aims that the vast majority of our people did not desire and were not in the true interests of the German people …. Our offensives in March and April, while tactically successful, failed strategically. Revolutionary activity had nothing to do with this failure. On the contrary, it has been convincingly shown that despite shortages of food, clothing and equipment, the troops fulfilled their duty admirably.

Major Volkmann, in his book on the *Dolchstoß* and in his Deposition, gives the impression that the dissolution of military discipline and the revolution was the result of Marxist ideology …. Marxist doctrine was certainly not unimportant, but it was not a crucial or decisive factor in the turn of German history in November 1918. It was not the motive force. It was only a vehicle for the discharge of forces that had formed as a reaction against the country's disastrous leadership. Other reports prepared for the Subcommittee have demonstrated that Marxist agitation within the army was ineffective, so it is not correct to seek the ground of the German collapse in 1918 within Marxism or Marxist ideology.

The remnants of the army and the civil service rescued what could be salvaged of the old Germany when they offered their services to the new Council of Peoples' Deputies. This saved the country from falling into chaos and Bolshevism. Field Marshal v. Hindenburg, advised by General v. Groener, made the decisive decision to enter into an alliance with Ebert and the Majority Social Democrats, as did the … other ministries along with all their officials in the knowledge that it was required for the good of the country.

The true culprit for the collapse was the Emperor—who refused to voluntarily renounce the crown when the national interest demanded it—and the circle of people around him whom he trusted. This fact is intentionally obscured by talk of a "Stab-in-the-Back."

These facts force me to label the "Stab-in-the-Back" a fable.

11.6 BACK-AND-FORTH BETWEEN DELBRUCK AND KUHL[6]

Delbrück:

After the differences of opinion between General von Kuhl and myself have been discussed in detail, it may serve to elucidate completely the situation if I summarize the essential points on which we are in agreement.

I agree with Kuhl that the equipment of the German Army in the spring of 1918 was inadequate in many respects, that the numerical proportion was only approximately balanced, and that the Supreme Command nevertheless conceived the idea of a massive offensive with the object of completely defeating the enemy.

I agree with Kuhl that the Supreme Command prepared the attack, as regards both the training of the troops and choosing the best moment for taking the enemy by surprise, in a masterly manner with the greatest energy and circumspection.

I agree with Kuhl that, as regards the distribution of the troops for the offensive, the defensive wing was strong enough but the offensive wing too weak .... The dispersal and the incorrect distribution of our forces not in accordance with the plan resulted in the loss of the battle. In spite of tactical success, strategic success was not achieved. Kuhl does not express himself in this way—but this seems to be the logical conclusion to be drawn from his technical statements—so that I believe I may say that we are also agreed with regard to this point.

Kuhl and I and also agree that on August 14, General Ludendorff did not inform the political authorities about the military situation with the necessary clearness.

Kuhl's reply to Delbrück:

In his report, Professor Dr. Delbrück has asserted, "that there is hardly any difference between his and my technical criticism of Ludendorff's strategy." In a special summary entitled "Agreement between General von Kuhl and myself" he attempts to enumerate those points where agreement is supposed to exist.

I will begin by stating that he has often presented my opinions inaccurately or incorrectly. In particular, I have never asserted that the March offensive in 1918 was lost owing to the dispersal and incorrect distribution of our forces.

I must protest very strongly against any attempt to artificially construe agreement between my views and those of Professor Delbrück regarding Ludendorff's strategy. In my report, I have always strongly emphasized the contrast between Delbrück's views and my own. In particular, I must strongly protest against his opinion of General Ludendorff's personality and character and the way in which Ludendorff conducted the war, as his entire report mainly consists of a personal attack on the General.

The resolutions

On May 26, 1925, the Subcommittee first drafted a set of resolutions on various aspects of the collapse. It met a further 79 times to debate and refine these resolutions and to receive further input. The entire process entered it final stages in the autumn of 1927 and on November 3 the Subcommittee met for the last time to formally vote on the resolutions.[7] Regarding the military collapse, the Subcommittee was able to reach unanimous agreement on five points.

11.7 REGARDING THE MILITARY COLLAPSE, THE SUBCOMMITTEE AGREED ON 5 POINTS[8]

Point 1 Regarding the relationship between the Emperor, the civilian government, and the Supreme Command.

Regarding the relationship between the Emperor, the civilian government, and the Supreme Command, the Subcommittee unanimously agreed to the following:

- As the highest court of appeal, the Kaiser made the final decisions on all military and political questions. Under him, the political responsibility rested with the Imperial Chancellor (Count von Hertling and Prince Max of von Baden) and with his departmental representative, the Secretary of State for Foreign Affairs (von Kuhlmann, von Hintze, and Dr. Solf); in addition to these, the post of responsible Vice-Chancellor (von Payer) had been created.
- Responsibility for the conduct of the war rested with the Chief of the General Staff of the Field Army (General Field Marshal von Hindenburg); he was given a collaborator in the person of the First Quartermaster General (General Ludendorff); when appointed, the latter was assured of a full share of co-responsibility with the Chief of the General Staff.
- No omissions have been ascertained in the organization of communications between the Imperial government and the Supreme Command or between either of these bodies and the Kaiser.
- After the resignation of Imperial Chancellor, von Bethmann Hollweg, the dominance of the Supreme Command over the Imperial government became more and more pronounced. This predominance continued even after the Kaiser came to a decision in January 1918 that recognized the exclusive conduct of political affairs lay with the Imperial Chancellor and laid this down for the future.

Point 2 Regarding the possibilities of peace at the beginning of 1918

Regarding the possibilities of peace at the beginning of 1918, the Subcommittee unanimously agreed to the following:

- Colonel von Haeften's efforts, made at The Hague in March 1918, to get into touch with the Americans lacked significance. They

were undertaken without the previous knowledge of the Supreme Command or the German government, and were allowed to drop.
- The increasing effects of the food blockade decreased the inclination of the enemy for a peace by mutual agreement, since it was hoped that, even in the event of military defeat, success might be attained by starvation.

Point 3 Regarding the decision to go on the offensive in 1918
Regarding the decision to go on the offensive in 1918, the Subcommittee unanimously agreed to the following:

- At the beginning of 1918, the Imperial government was faced by the question whether it ought to continue the struggle or to endeavor to obtain peace at the price of sacrificing German-held territory. In view of the then existing situation it rejected the latter alternative. Hence the decision of the Supreme Command to undertake the spring offensive of 1918—a decision in which the Imperial government concurred—was due, on the one hand, to the conviction that peace could not be attained without sacrifices in the West, and, on the other hand, to the confidence of the Supreme Command in final victory. The Imperial Chancellor expressed his satisfaction that the Western Powers had declined to participate in peace negotiations on the basis of the Russian proposals.
- The Supreme Command reckoned correctly with the arrival of the American troops in the spring of 1918 and took this into consideration in deciding to start an offensive as soon as possible. The expectations of success were bound to diminish as time went on. The difficulty of replacing casualties also urged an early decision. The spirit of the German troops in the spring of 1918 fully justified risking the offensive. The losses occasioned by defensive engagements, as well as the physical and mental suffering of troops on the defensive, pressed for the offensive.

Point 4 Regarding the situation in July 1918 and the failure of the offensive
Regarding the situation in July 1918 and the failure of the offensive, the Subcommittee unanimously agreed that:

- In the middle of July 1918, i.e., before assuming office as Secretary of State, Herr von Hintze understood the answer given by General Ludendorff to a question of his to mean that, with the then (Rheims) offensive, the enemy would be successfully and finally vanquished; for the time being, he used this statement in determining his policy.

- Up to July 15, 1918 the Supreme Command rejected the point of view that the campaign could no longer be won by force of arms, and gave no incentive to peace negotiations on the basis of a military "draw," although General Ludendorff approved of the contents of Colonel von Haeften's memorial dated June 3, 1918, which was based on this presupposition. The Supreme Command considered any public mention of the stand taken in von Haeften's memorial to be fatal from both a military and a political point of view.

Point 5 Regarding the situation after August 8
Regarding the failure of the situation and the situation after August 8, the Black Day of the German army, the Subcommittee unanimously agreed that:

- The failure of the whole offensive, which became clear after the reverse of August 8, is explained by the fact that the unprecedented and continuous engagements had exhausted the mental and physical energy of the troops and that, on the front, the reserves to replace casualties and the supplies of war material were no longer sufficient.
- The Chancellor, Count von Hertling, adhered to his optimistic view of the entire situation, even after the deliberations in the Crown Council of August 14, which followed a confidential discussion between General Ludendorff and Secretary of State von Hintze on August 13. In harmony with General Field Marshal von Hindenburg's statement at this Crown Council that "he hoped that we should after all succeed in remaining on French soil and thereby in finally enforcing our will upon the enemy." He believed even then in a termination of the war favorable to Germany and endeavored to influence public opinion accordingly.
- The efforts made by the German government, even after August 8, to arrive at a peace by mutual agreement were overshadowed by the military events. From August 14 onward Secretary of State von Hintze—in accordance with his view of the entire situation—took every feasible diplomatic step to bring the war to an end. He tried every conceivable means but, owing to the military situation, without success.
- The offensive, which in March, April, and May resulted in great tactical successes but no strategic decision, came to a standstill in July 1918, not owing to any failure on the part of the troops but because the forces of the opponents at the front steadily increased while our own were decreasing.
- The war was lost from a military point of view when, during the withdrawal on the German Western front in September 1918, the

Bulgarian collapsed, followed by Austria-Hungary. This completely changed the position of the German army in the field. From then onward every effort to obtain a peace by military means alone seemed useless.
- On September 29, the Supreme Command told the government that to save the military situation, it was necessary to arrange an armistice as quickly as possible.
- The request of the Supreme Command for an armistice came as a complete surprise to the government; the latter however was not in a position to check the question whether the Supreme Command's estimate of the military situation was perhaps too unfavorable. All the other information the government had received confirmed the opinion of the Supreme Command. From then onward every effort made by the government to bring about a bearable peace seemed hopeless.
- State Secretaries von Hintze and Count Roedern acted in accordance with the instructions given them by the Kaiser at Spa on September 29, 1918 and also in accordance with the wishes of the Supreme Command, when they made efforts in Berlin to form a new government on the basis of the parliamentary system, in order to make possible the early dispatch of a note to Wilson.
- Imperial Chancellor Prince Max of Baden exhausted all the means at his disposal in order to avoid the immediate offer of a truce, which he regarded as an inappropriate move.
- After the dispatch of the armistice offer, the military situation justified the hope that, in view of the difficulties encountered by the advancing enemy, it would still be possible for us to remain on the defensive on the Western front for some time, in spite of the insufficient positions in the rear.

In summarizing its findings, the Subcommittee unanimously agreed that

- The government relied upon the judgment of the Supreme Command until the latter acknowledged the impossibility of victory. It had at its disposal no personality capable of opposing the will of the Supreme Command.
- The German front did everything in its power until the last moment.

The Subcommittee majority, with the three Social Democratic members and the one Communist member dissenting, agreed that:

- The Supreme Command always acted under the full conviction that they were serving the welfare of the entire country. It accorded with their military views that, as long as it appeared at all feasible,

they voiced the idea of a militarily advantageous and, afterwards, at least a bearable peace.
- It arrived at no conclusions with regard to the questions of the German military collapse in 1918 dealt with by it that would justify the apportioning of blame to any particular quarter.

Beyond their dissent with the summary of the Subcommittee's findings, the commission's three Social Democratic and one Communist members could not agree on one major area: the particulars of 1918 offensive.

The majority of the Subcommittee held that:

- No facts have been brought forward from whom the Subcommittee couldn't deduce a neglect of duty on the part of the Supreme Command during the preparation and the carrying out of the offensive of 1918.
- Although owing to the Peace of Brest-Litovsk and the occupation of the Ukraine strong military forces were still tied up in the East, we managed to have more men than our opponents on the battlefront in the West. Owing to the difficulties in the East there could be no question of any further substantial transfer from that quarter of forces suitable for offensive warfare.
- The supply of arms and munitions was sufficient for the offensive. There was a lack of horses and fuel.
- In view of the entire military situation it did not seem possible to the Supreme Command in the spring of 1918 to bring Austro-Hungarian forces to the Western front in addition to the heavy batteries already there.
- Everything possible had been done to equip and train the German troops with a view to the offensive.
- The lack of second-line positions is explained by the fact that all the effective troops and military workers were being used at the front, and by the impossibility of drawing more workers from home.
- Lack of munitions and other war material exerted no decisive influence on the course of the offensive until July 1918.
- The building of more tanks in 1918 would have been possible only if the manufacture of other war material, in particular of motor-driven material, had been restricted.
- The physical energy of the troops was indeed not as great as it had been before, especially owing to short rations, but it came up to expectations.
- The progress of the offensive was doubtless influenced in some cases by some troops remaining, contrary to orders, in provision and liquor stores, but on the whole it was not definitely hindered by this.

> The majority of the Subcommittee, with the one Communist member dissenting, agreed that:
>
> - The Supreme Command brought about the resignation of Secretary of State von Kuhlmann. The decisive factor was Kuhlmann's statement of in his speech in the *Reichstag* on June 24, 1918 to the effect that the war could not be decided by force of arms alone, a statement extracted from the memorial of Colonel von Haeften dated June 3, 1918.

Documents 11.8–11.10 are dissenting opinions from three different perspectives.

11.8 SOCIAL DEMOCRATIC RESOLUTION REGARDING THE CAUSES OF THE MILITARY COLLAPSE[9]

The inquiries of the Subcommittee ... have shown that the overweening annexationist program submitted to the government in May 1915 by the six large industrial and agricultural associations still dominated the political views of the Supreme Command in 1918. To subordinate Belgium as completely as possible to Germany—in both a military and a political sense—was still the war aim of the military leadership. Moreover, they had not abandoned the intention of annexing the littoral adjoining Belgium about as far as the Somme .... Even more consequential than the plans for annexations in the West was the peace brutally imposed upon the Russian Soviet Republic under strong pressure from the Supreme Command. Poland, Lithuania, Latvia, and Courland were separated from Russia in order to bring them under German sovereignty, as part of the imperialistic aim of establishing German hegemony over Eastern Europe. From both a political and a military point of view, it was particularly self-defeating that after the signing of the Treaty of Brest-Litovsk no real peace ensued in the east of Europe. Russia as far as the Dvina River in the north and the eastern frontier of the Ukraine in the south was still occupied by German troops.

The inquiry has demonstrated that when one considers the entire economic situation of Germany (a situation which entailed a terrible lack of food in the towns and the manufacturing districts) and when one recognized the much reduced moral fighting value of the troops (who were aware of the condition of their starving women and children at home), the great offensive of 1918 ought to have been risked only with the rear free in the East. This would have been accomplished through a peace treaty with Russia that involved slight corrections of the frontier and, otherwise restored full freedom to the territory occupied in Russia. A further essential political element of a successful offensive aimed at bringing about a peace by mutual agreement with the Western Powers was the renunciation of all annexationist intentions in the West. Most importantly this included the clear renunciation of all Germany's claims to Belgium. If these two things had been done (peace by mutual agreement in the East and the renunciation of claims to Belgium) even if the planned offensive in the spring of 1918 should fail, it would have been possible to obtain a tolerable peace. It would then have been very difficult for the enemy governments to continue the war with their war-weary troops, who, according to the testimony of French military men, could only be induced to attack under the "shadow of the tanks."

The investigations of the Subcommittee have shown that the main roadblock to the realization of these two conditions was the opposition of General Ludendorff and Field Marshal von Hindenburg. Under the spell of the above-mentioned annexationist program of the great industrial associations, both men strove for an economic affiliation of Belgium with Germany, to the effect which they regarded the occupation of Belgian territory for several years after the conclusion of peace as inevitable. In addition, Field Marshal von Hindenburg thought it was necessary that Liege remain under German military occupation. The stubbornness with which these two military leaders clung to their demands is proved by the testimony of General Hoffmann. According to Hoffmann, Ludendorff demanded that the Kaiser dismiss him because he had argued that a peace by mutual agreement with Russia and the surrender of Belgium was the only way to save Germany.

As far as the military preparation of the offensive is concerned the Subcommittee should have accepted the opinion of those military experts who ... believe that Field Marshal von Hindenburg and Quartermaster-General Ludendorff made serious errors when they insufficiently reduced the number of troops remaining on the Eastern front, when they declined an offer of Austro-Hungarian troops, when they failed to construct strong positions for the army to retire to in the event that the 1918 offensive was not successful, and their failure to ensure that sufficient numbers of tanks were built for offensive and defensive purposes. As a result of these errors of judgment, the failure of the offensive was a catastrophe for the German army.

11.9 COMMUNIST RESOLUTION ON THE CAUSES OF THE MILITARY COLLAPSE[10]

The Subcommittee was assigned the task of ascertaining the causes of the military collapse in the year 1918.

As war is only a special manifestation of general politics, the inquiry could not be limited to investigating merely the technical military reasons for the failure of the offensive in 1918. Such a limitation would result in obscuring the final causes of the collapse, which lie not so much in technical military mistakes as in a despotic political system serving the interests of the capitalist classes and supported by a military hierarchy.

It is indisputable that all capitalistic states have pursued a policy of military force in order to extend their economic and political power, enlarge their sphere of influence, and outdo their competitors or bring them under their sway. Like others, the war of 1914–18 was an outcome of this policy of force. The final collapse of German military power in 1918 was merely the result of exaggerated war aims on the part of the Supreme Command and the government; the Supreme Command prevented a timely termination of the war on the basis of a peace by mutual agreement.

The war was, from the start, not a purely defensive war on the part of Germany. As early as 1915 this fact became clearly manifest in the unrestrained annexationist demands of the big industrial firms, demands which were supported by representatives of science and leaders of the large bourgeois parties. These demands were not abandoned until after the collapse of the 1918 offensive. These annexationist demands met with no opposition in the government. Although the expression "defensive war" recurred in all official speeches made by representatives of the government, no pronouncement against the annexationist demands was ever issued by any responsible government body. Almost without exception the political parties and their representatives in the *Reichstag* made these demands their own. Even from the Social Democratic Party voices were heard in favor of open or covert annexation.

The Supreme Command acted as pacemaker of the policy of conquest. When in July 1917, after three years of war, a powerful majority in the *Reichstag* finally aroused themselves and proposed a modest resolution that aimed at a peace by mutual agreement, the Supreme Command replied with the renewed demand for the annexation of the whole of Belgium (Kreuznach Conference of August 9, 1917). In the Crown Council held in Bellevue Palace on September 11, 1917 General Ludendorff demanded the seizure of the French ore basin and also of Belgian territory, as well as an economic affiliation and military occupation of Belgium equivalent to complete annexation. In the East his plans for annexation included Courland and large parts of Poland

Under the pressure of the war situation, the Kaiser decided to renounce the annexation of Belgium. The Supreme Command, however, demanded that the government should not publish this renunciation.

In December 1917 the Supreme Command declare that the renunciation of the annexation of Belgium had lost its validity because no peace had been reached by the end of 1917, stating that the Kreuznach demands, i.e., the annexation of Belgium, must be maintained.

The Peace of Brest-Litovsk, forced on Russia a few months later, was in accord with this policy of conquest. The invasion of the Ukraine on the pretext of obtaining better supplies of food for Germany represented an act of conquest. The imports of foodstuffs from the Ukraine were quite insignificant.

With the help of the proclamation of martial law, the military had, from the outset secured great predominance over the political leaders and the civil authorities. In the course of time the Supreme Command usurped unlimited dictatorial power.

Bethmann Hollweg and Secretary of State von Kuhlmann were dismissed from office at the demand of the Supreme Command, which determined what men were to be given office in the government. Any opposition in government circles to the Supreme Command's scheme of conquest was ruthlessly suppressed. The Foreign Office was eliminated. It neither could nor was it allowed undertaking anything independently for the realization of peace. The Supreme. Command demanded the right to exercise decisive influence in the peace negotiations.

The Supreme Command systematically deceived the German government, the *Reichstag*, and the people about the real state of the war. It ruthlessly suppressed opinions that ran contrary to its wishes by means of the severest censorship. Opponents of the policy of conquest were subjected to police and judicial prosecution; advocates of a peace by mutual agreement were treated as traitors. Colonel von Haeften, who endeavored to bring about a peace by mutual agreement, was reproached with being a "defeatist" and the Ministry of War endeavored to get him removed from his post ....

It is wrongly denied that peace possibilities existed. When the Russian Soviet government made overtures for peace in November 1917, an opportunity for a general peace by mutual agreement would have occurred if only the Supreme Command had been willing wholeheartedly to renounce all annexations. Peace possibilities existed even later, as is proved by Professor Delbrück's report. But for General Ludendorff the very thought of peace by mutual agreement was a "crime." The Supreme

Command rejected efforts made by Colonel von Haeften in March 1918 to get into touch with American diplomats at The Hague with the object of promoting peace from the government.

Thus all attempts to arrive at a peace by mutual agreement were thwarted by the Supreme Command, though at the same time General Ludendorff informed his intimates of his readiness to agree to such a peace. This duplicity resulted from the desire of the Supreme Command to burden the German government with the responsibility for peace and to represent themselves as the undaunted and heroic champions of Germany's greatness. If the Supreme Command declined to create the preliminary conditions necessary for a peace by mutual agreement and to give their support to such a peace, there remained no alternative but to crush the enemy powers so completely that peace could be dictated to them.

A proper appreciation of the situation ought to have made it clear to the Supreme Command that, in view of the complete economic and military exhaustion of Germany after four years of war, it was beyond the range of possibility to break the resistance of the enemy powers, whose troops were constantly increasing in number and whose opposition had been lashed to the utmost pitch by their knowledge of Germany's war aims.

Instead of recognizing this and of drawing the only possible conclusion—a timely peace offer accompanied by the renunciation of conquests—the Supreme Command speculated on an improbable victory, and even continued the war after they had themselves acknowledged that it was no longer possible to obtain by force of arms a decision favorable to Germany. This criminal presumption of infallibility on the part of the Supreme Command lightheartedly consigned thousands of soldiers to an untimely death.

The final verdict can therefore only be as follows: Irrespective of the annexationist war aims approved of by the Government and by the *Reichstag* down to the end of 1917 and tolerated by them in self-incurred impotence against the Supreme Command, the latter bear the main responsibility for Germany's collapse.

11.10 RESOLUTION OF FORMER COMMITTEE MEMBER DEERMANN (BAVARIAN PEOPLE'S PARTY)[11]

In the winter of 1917–18, the whole military and political situation demanded that a purposeful and energetic attempt should be made to end the war by the summer of 1918 in a form bearable to Germany ....

Opposed to this was France's unbroken determination to prosecute the war, inspired by hate and spurred on by the Peace of Brest-Litovsk. A peace by mutual agreement was rendered impossible by the war terms in the East and in particular by General Ludendorff's armies in Belgium. The Supreme Command stood in the way of a declaration of complete renunciation of claims to Belgium by Secretary of State von Kuhlmann (representing the political leadership in Germany). Such a statement was valueless without the unconditional approval of the Supreme Command .... After the great tactical successes in the March and April offensives, Germany could still have tried to achieve a bearable peace with some prospects of success. Since General Ludendorff was aware of the strategic failure and of the impossibility of solving the difficult question of replacing casualties, he ought to have explained the real situation to the political leaders with the goal of paving the way for a peace by mutual agreement. At the same time he should have completely abandoned his designs on ... Belgium. But even on July 3, General Ludendorff still adhered firmly to his demands with regard to Belgium and did not even drop them after the reverse on August 8, in particular during the discussions on August 13 and 14, 1918 with government representatives ....

If the offensive of 1918 was to bring about the end of the war in a manner favorable or even only bearable to Germany, there ought to have been the closest conceivable touch between the Supreme Command and the men in charge of the political side before it was started ....

The Supreme Command did not co-operate frankly with those responsible for foreign policy, not even with Secretary of State von Hintze, with whom they maintained good personal relations during the greater part of his period of office .... At the beginning of August 1918 the war was definitely lost. Political negotiations ought not to have been postponed any longer. But in spite of General Ludendorff's personal recognition of this fact, the Supreme Command did not accurately inform the Kaiser and the political leaders on August 13 and 14 on the true state of the military situation. Indeed, General Ludendorff, by substantially changing the text of General Field Marshal von Hindenburg's words, represented the military situation as quite favorable and hopeful. This attitude cannot be excused on the ground of military reasoning .... It was not until September 10 that the Supreme Command, in order to forestall Austrian peace feelers, communicated to Secretary of State von Hintze their agreement to start discussing an end to the war with the enemy through a neutral power. But it was then too late.

On August 13 and 14, the Kaiser and the political leaders did their duty in accordance with the information supplied to them .... The *Reichstag*, as a constitutional and political factor, was almost completely ignored by the Supreme Command, although it was necessary to enlist its co-operation in order to bring such a war to a successful conclusion .... "The armistice demands of the Supreme Command on September 29, were equivalent to hoisting the white flag .... The German military leaders themselves confirmed the victory of the Entente." (Report of the expert, Schwertfeger.) Confidence in the Supreme Command, especially in General Ludendorff, and faith in the qualities of leadership of the old state broke down.

Owing to this shock, the revolution that had been unscrupulously prepared for several years was able to force its way forward with success .... International anti-militaristic endeavors, increased enemy propaganda and the revolutionary undermining of the Army, the lines of communication and the country in general are jointly responsible for the collapse on the Western front in 1918, but they are by no means the decisive factors. For these forces were not yet perceptible during the offensive in March and April and had not even assumed dimensions worth mentioning. It was only after the breakdown of the offensive that they became effective ....

The political and state system and its autocratic war-time structure were out of date. It broke down at the hour of its supreme trial because the man who held the autocratic conduct of the war in his hands [the Kaiser], acted as he did because he was not correctly advised and because he did not possess a necessary knowledge of mankind. The Kaiser is not free from the responsibility of having before the war assumed the leadership given to him by the constitution and—although he recognized his own inadequacy when the time of trial came—of not having discerned and effectuated the constitutional consequences.

11.11 SUBCOMMITTEE CONCLUSIONS ON THE INTERNAL CAUSES OF THE COLLAPSE[12]

I. Preconditions

There were manifold conflicts present within Germany before the war that prevented the formation of a unified national character. There was increasing tension between the existing system of government and civic consciousness of many groups within the population. The outbreak of war temporarily removed the urgency of these problems, although inwardly they remained.

Under the influence of war profiteering and serious abuses in the food supply, the idea of class antagonism and the will to class struggle rose once again among the working masses. This discontent found its strongest expression in the formula that the war was being conducted in the interests of propertied classes.

Discontent grew with the unexpectedly long duration of the war, with the massive loss of human life and national strength through the blockade, with the apparently growing conflict between military and political leadership as well as in wide circles of the bourgeoisie .... This opposition was directed against the fading of the idea of a defensive war, against the application of censorship, and against the underestimation of the value of democratic reforms as a result of general war duty. These oppositional circles even came to believe that some individuals in the Supreme Command and in certain economic sectors sought to obstruct efforts to bring the war to a peaceful conclusion.

II. The propaganda for peace and revolution

The widespread dissatisfaction was directed into three political currents, whose members by various means and for various purposes fundamentally sought to alter the domestic balance of power and end the war. The first current consisted of the parties, which later came together on the basis of the [1917] Peace Resolution—the Majority Social Democrats, the Center Party, and Progressive People's Party. The second current was dominated by the Independent Social Democrats, the third, the Spartacus League and the radical left.

The parties supporting the Peace Resolution and the masses behind them did not want to jeopardize the national defense, but their confidence in the political and military leadership continued to diminish over time. They sought to democratize the government. Therefore, they approved all attempts directed at increasing parliamentary rule. Without the oppositional attitude within the masses of the Social Democratic workers and the bourgeois middle parties, the revolution on the home front would not have succeeded.

The Independent Social Democrats represented the belief that a peace without annexations and indemnities could and must be forced upon the warring governments. They thought that it was the obligation of the proletariat of each country to force their governments to make such a peace. Their goal was to achieve this by influencing the masses and sponsoring oppositional opinion in the workforce.

The Spartacus League and the left-wing radicals, although few in number, worked towards the violent overthrow of the system and sought by all means to bring about world revolution. Its members remained part of the Independent Socialist Party until the end of 1918 for legal purposes. Its role model for the realization of the revolution was the Russian Revolution. Workers and soldiers councils on the Russian model were created that drafted revolutionary operational plans with advice and help of individual Russian Bolsheviks.

III. The November revolution

After years, the confidence of the German people in its leadership collapsed when it was announced that the war for Germany was militarily unwinnable. The desire to end the war as soon as possible under any circumstances now came over the masses who stood behind both Social Democratic parties and the bourgeois parties who had supported the Peace Resolution.

President Wilson's rejection of the German peace proposals even further depressed the general mood in Germany, although many hoped that it was still possible to achieve a tolerable peace through the satisfaction of all the demands of the President.

The mutiny of some crews of the High Seas Fleet on October 30, 1918 when given the order to set sail for battle, was the clarion call for the seizure of power in conjunction with the rebel army units throughout the entire Empire. Dynastic rulers were overthrown; the ability of officers to demand obedience from their troops was challenged. Soldiers' and Workers' Councils after the Russian model were formed and took over the public power. The outbreak of the revolution in November surprised the leaders of the Majority Socialists. Which individuals and groups in each case took the initiative cannot everywhere be determined.

The question of whether Germany's enemies refused to moderate their ceasefire conditions when the German people had shown that they were not willing to fight to the last man remains unclear. The adoption of the armistice resulted in the Treaty of Versailles. Whether political resistance would somehow have moderated the terms of the Versailles peace when Germany was the militarily defenseless remains contested.

Conclusion

It is ironic that by the time the Subcommittee completed its work and published its report, public opinion on the Stab-in-the-Back had hardened. Most people had already made up their minds, if not before then during the two high-profile trials discussed in Chapters 9 and 10. Even so, the Subcommittee was able to reach a remarkable degree of unanimity. To some extent this was due to the care with which the resolutions were worded. Any document about which both Communists and Nationalists could agree was clearly worded with great delicacy, but this did not mean that the documents consisted of vague generalities. Instead, these were rather startling in their

CHART 11.1 *Members of the Subcommittee, 1919–1927*

National Assembly		Reichstag I		Reichstag II		Reichstag III	
Party	Member	Party	Member	Party	Member	Party	Member
USPD (1)				KPD (1)		KPD (1)	
	Eichhorn				Fröhlich		Eichhorn
							Rosenburg
							Höllein
SPD (3)		SPD (3)		SPD (2)		SPD (3)	
	Landsberg		Hellmenn		Quessel		Quessel
	Katzenstein		Radbruch		Moses		Dittmann
	Kahmann		Kaiser				Moses
	Krüger		Henke				Schnabrich
	Meerfeld		Mehrhof				
	Hellmann		Moses				
DDP (1)		DDP (1)		DDP (1)		DDP (1)	
	Heile		Korell		Goetz		Bergstrasser
Z (2)		Z (1)		Z (1)		Z (1)	
	Diez		Spahn		Bell		Spahn
	Schwarz						Joos
		BVP (1)					
			Merck				
			Deermann				
		DVP (1)		DVP (1)		DVP (1)	
			Kahl		Schneider		Hoff
							Rheinbaben
							Brüninghaus
DNVP (1)		DNVP (1)		DNVP (2)		DNVP (2)	
	Philipp		Philipp		Philipp		Philipp
					Westarp		Schulenburg
							Eulenburg
							Treviranus
				NSFP (1)		WVg (1)	
					Wulle		Bredt
							Bachmeier

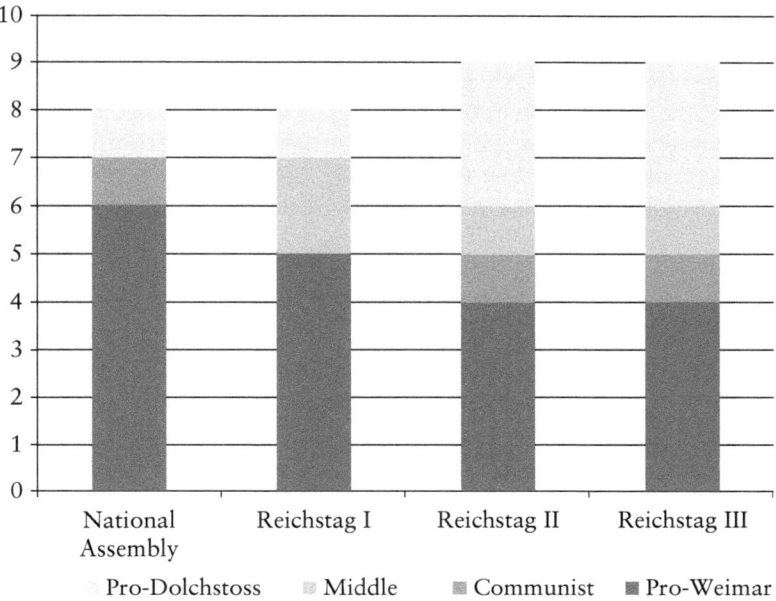

CHART 11.2 *Subcommittee membership by party bloc.*

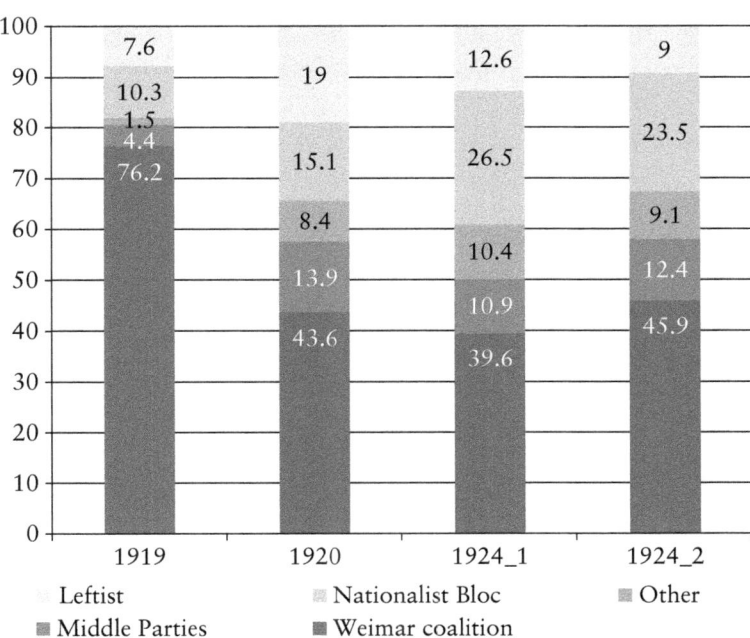

CHART 11.3 *Election results 1919–24 by party bloc.*

specificity. The cause is to be found in the differing meaning the competing parties attached to the same words and the memories these words invoked for each group. What was one group's treason was another's common sense. What the internal Subcommittee debates on the resolutions make clear is that each party required above all else that their interpretation of events be given due credence. Once that was achieved, the resolutions could be passed and the entire eight volumes of evidence be sent to the printer.

Thought questions

1. What issues regarding the military collapse found unanimous approval? Where were the areas of disagreement?
2. How did both Social Democrats and Communists critique the majority resolutions on the military collapse? Do they share a common critique?
3. What dissent did former Subcommittee member Deermann make? Why do you think he did not share in either the Social Democratic or Communist dissents?
4. Why was the Subcommittee able to reach a unanimous agreement on the causes of the internal collapse in Document 11.1? Try to look at the document from both a Nationalist and a Communist perspective. Why would each side be happy with the wording? How would a Social Democrat be able to be happy with the same words?

12

The *Dolchstoßlegende* and the Fall of the Weimar Republic

The Stab-in-the-Back Myth did not directly bring about the fall of the Weimar Republic. It was not constantly at the center of political discussion. There were a raft of substantive policy issues to be argued; the quotidian jostling of cabinet politics consumed a large amount of the attention of the press; the hyperinflation and stabilization impacted the daily lives of Germans in ways that dominated political discourse. As Rainer Sammet has convincingly shown, the multiple versions of the *Dolchstoßlegende* surfaced and resurfaced as a burning political issue at certain moments, especially 1919–20 and 1924–25, when it was a useful political tool to consolidate the nationalist electorate and divide the socialists; otherwise it was in the background and by 1928 had disappeared from the routine political vocabulary of all save the obsessive National Socialists.

While it might not have caused the fall of the Weimar Republic, the *Dolchstoßlegende* did play a vital role in political self-definition and group cohesion. The German National People's Party, a new and internally fractured coalition of interests, was divided by acceptance of the Dawes Plan and the question of whether to enter government. Karl Helfferich, who had done so much to gather the kindling that would flame into the hyperinflation, proposed a gold loan that was at the center of the Dawes Plan. The successful implementation of the Plan required Nationalist participation in republican cabinet formation. So too did the looming return of German freedom to set tariffs. Most farmers were eager to reintroduce the protective tariffs that had existed before the Great War; industrialists were already contemplating a trade treaty with Poland that would favor German industrial exports in exchange for keeping the German market open to the import of Polish pigs.

Even the strong undercurrent of antisemitism present in most versions of the nationalist Myth was not problematic for German Nationals, who defined their party in exclusively "Christian" terms and refused to admit Jews into the party membership. In the 1924 elections, the German Nationals burnished their anti-Jewish credentials and ran advertisements in county newspapers disputing the claims of the Hitler/Ludendorff alliance that they were not sufficiently antisemitic. A focus on the Stab-in-the-Back—a theme that united nationalists of all stripes—was therefore to the party's advantage in 1924 and 1925.[1]

The radical essays contained in Cossmann's *Dolchstoßhefte* fueled the emerging consensus within the nationalist movement. The dark "victory was ours until the Jews and Socialists stole it" view of the Collapse left little room for more "moderate" proponents of the Stab-in-the-Back Myth such as Hermann von Kuhl. Kuhl's complex dialectic of military and non-military factors was displaced by a National Socialist vision of the collapse as the result of a Jewish conspiracy.

Keeping alive the leftist version of the *Dolchstoßlegende* also served the interests of the new Communist Party.[2] Scrolling through the issues of the party newspaper, *Die Rote Fahne*, headlines describing the Social Democrats as "strike breakers," "grandees," and "Social Fascists" abound. When negotiations for a union of the Independents and the Communists broke down, the party adopted a clear policy of winning over the Independent membership. By focusing on Ebert and Scheidemann's "betrayal" of the revolution, they were able to appeal to the still-vibrant revolutionary spirit of radical workers. Every ill—up to and including the suspension of the forty-hour week—could be ascribed to the Majority Social Democratic refusal to accept council-style governance in 1918. The need to harp on "distant chords of memory" became even more essential with the ongoing Bolshevization of the party after 1925. As with the German Nationals, the Stab-in-the-Back Myth served to reinforce cohesions within a disparate Communist party alliance.

One might imagine that after the Majority and Independent Social Democrats reunited in 1922, the new party would seek to minimize past disputes over wartime actions and the revolution. Surprisingly, this was not the case. The reunified party rejected the Stab-in-the-Back Myth in all its versions. When Friedrich Ebert filed suit against Erwin Rothardt and Martin Gruber was forced to defend himself against charges of libel, the entire panoply of socialist leaders testified on their behalf, including not only Ebert-supporter Philipp Scheidemann but also former Independent Wilhelm Dittmann. The Social Democratic press of the period was filled with articles on the *Dolchstoß* "lie"—vastly preferring that term to "fable" or "legend." Martin Gruber's ill-considered attacks on Paul Nicholas Cossmann were but one manifestation of that full-court-press. One is tempted to observe that there was almost a cottage industry for Social Democratic publicists seeking to refute both nationalist and communist versions of the Myth. Erich Kuttner not only published *Der Sieg*, he went on to edit the party's satirical monthly *Lachen Links*. One of the first issues to appear under his direction was a *Dolchstoßheft* devoted to mocking the Stab-in-the-Back conspiratorialists.[3]

Attitudes toward the Stab-in-the-Back played a more divisive role within German liberalism. The German Democratic Party "owned" the revolution.[4]

They were the "Gold" in the "Black-Red-Gold" Weimar coalition and a consistent member of the Social Democratic-led coalition that governed Prussia from the revolution until June 1932. At their core, the Democrats defined themselves as anti-nationalist and anti-militarist, favoring a policy of class reconciliation and rule of law. Their contemptuous attitude toward the purveyors of the Stab-in-the-Back Myth was exemplified by Theodor Wolff's savage editorial on the Ebert libel judgment. The liberals of Stresemann's German People's Party straddled the nationalist/republican divide. The party was initially monarchist and only after 1924 became "republicans of necessity." A famous December 1924 cartoon in *Kladderadatsch* depicts Stresemann standing before a black board. With his right hand he is writing "we are monarchists" while with his left he is writing "we are republicans." A member of the appreciative audience remarks, "isn't he skillful?" It was in the People's Party interest that the Stab-in-the-Back discussion go away. It styled itself the sole party of "sensible" national assertion, willing to "move beyond" the past to solve issues common to all Germans.[5]

What about the Center Party—the Black in Black-Red-Gold? The Center ignored the issue, or perhaps it would be best to say, "rose above" the Myth. Center labor unions had not backed the strikes of 1916–1918, but the party had voted for the Peace Resolution and was firmly in the anti-Annexationist, compromise peace camp. Center Party leader Mathias Erzberger has signed the Armistice and served as finance minister before his assassination by a nationalist death squad. Throughout, the party's interests had always been to protect its individual members and institutional interests of the Catholic Church. This required that it work with parties and forces with which it did not agree. Stirring up animosity served no purpose. Two posters from the early 1930s (available on our website) illustrate how the party positioned itself. In one, the Center is pictured as a strong tower holding out against waves of anarchy breaking against it. A second depicts a deep valley filled with Nazis and Communists killing each other and looting villages. Above the chasm, a bridge labeled "Center" is crossed by a peaceful procession following a banner displaying a white Christian cross.

The National Socialists were most committed to a Stab-in-the-Back Myth of the most profoundly antisemitic variety. In their imagination, the victorious German army was betrayed by a hydra-headed Jewish conspiracy. The Nazis did not need the *Dolchstoßlegende* to cement the elements of their party together as antisemitism already served that function, but they were all deeply committed to their special version of the Myth. On our website, we explore how Adolf Hitler experienced and articulated the events, describe Nazi attempts to use of the *Dolchstoßlegende* as part of their propagandistic arsenal, and suggest ways that this thinking might have influenced Nazi policy-making before and during Hitler's war.[6]

The death of Friedrich Ebert in February 1925 and the election of Paul von Hindenburg as his successor three months later marked an important turning point in the Stab-in-the-Back discussion.[7] Hindenburg was already on record with his opinion about the collapse. Twice in his brief *Reichstag* testimony in 1919 he referenced "an English general" as the originator the Stab-in-the-Back. As this was clearly and demonstrably a lie, a thoroughgoing *Dolchstoß* discussion could only harm his reputation. Better now that the matter was settled in the public mind, to let the matter lay.

Social Democratic publicists also had reason to be more discrete in their pronouncements. They could be quite certain that public prosecutors would be more strenuous in prosecuting any perceived libel of a President Hindenburg than they had been of a President Ebert. Could a book like Erich Kuttner's *Der Sieg war greifbar im Nähe*—where he clearly calls Hindenburg and Ludendorff liars—have been published after May 1925? Even the issue of *Lachen Links* published under Kuttner's editorial direction in October 1925 was circumspect about Hindenburg. Gone were the days of the red bathing suit and verbal attacks on the Head of State.

The national election in May 1928 indicated that the Stab-in-the-Back Myth was beginning to exceed its sell-by date. Led by a *Dolchstoß* "moderate," Kuno Westarp, the German National People's Party won only 14.2 percent of the votes cast, its lowest since January 1919. The *Schwarz-Rot-Gold* parties won 46.8 percent of the votes cast. A Social Democrat, Hermann Müller, formed a Socialist-Center-Democrat coalition cabinet with Gustav Stresemann as Foreign Minister. Among the anti-Republican radicals, the Communists won 10.6 percent of the vote and fifty-four seats in the new *Reichstag*, while the radical antisemitic parties were thoroughly defeated. (The Nazis experienced something akin to a near-death experience, wining only 2.6 percent of the votes cast.) A foreign observer might be forgiven for thinking that the Republic had now stabilized into parliamentary system that would experience alternating center-left and center-right governance.

This vision evaporated in October 1928 when Alfred Hugenberg ousted Westarp as German National leader. Hugenberg, a leading press magnate whose wire service provided news to all of the country's center-right newspapers, was fundamentally opposed to the Republic and turned all his efforts toward creating a nationalist, anti-republican alliance that would bring an end to the hated "system." Hugenberg's plan included bringing the marginalized and routed National Socialists into his anti-republican coalition, giving them press space and favorable national exposure. An important ideological underpinning of this alliance was a rejection of "moderate" Stab-in-the-Back school and full-throated support for the Nazis' radical, antisemitic version of the *Dolchstoßlegende*.

The attractiveness of the Nazis' radicalized view of the *Dolchstoß* was that it moved Jews to the center of all of the problems experienced by the Republic. Each individual problem—whether it was foreign or domestic, social, economic, or cultural—could be traced back to the "system" created by the "November criminals" and therefore to the Jews. This served to spread political antisemitism beyond the marginal and stigmatized position it had occupied before the Great War. Witness the horrific cartoon by Werner

Hahmann that appeared in *Kladderadatsch* at the time of the Hindenburg testimony. *Kladderadatsch* had published mild, mocking cartoons poking fun at Jews before the war, just as it other social groups, but the Hahmann caricature was new.

When prices on the New York Stock Exchange tumbled (the same month Hugenberg took over the German National leadership), Germany stood on the precipice of economic ruin. The economic and political stability attained with such care in the second half of the 1920s was almost exclusively dependent upon the Dawes Plan and the American gold loans that followed. After the collapse of share prices on the New York Stock Exchange in the third week of October 1929, American banks would struggle to stay afloat. There was no excess capital to lend to German businesses and municipalities. The downward cycle put great pressure on the Müller government to reduce expenditures and curtail union rights won in the course of the revolution. When his party would not accept a deal that he had reached with Heinrich Brüning of the Center, he was forced to resign. Brüning was appointed Chancellor.

The September 1930 election was a disaster for the supporters of the republic, as the Nazis emerged as the second largest party with 18.3 percent of the vote and 107 seats. The Communists also surged, with 13.1 percent of the vote and seventy-seven seats. The Black-Red-Gold parties dropped from a combined 46.8 percent of the vote to 36.3. With 289 votes needed to form a cabinet and 184 votes held by the radical left and right, parliamentary government could no longer effectively function. Brüning was forced to continue to rule with President von Hindenburg's sufferance, trying to cope with the deepening depression through an austerity program of tightened credit. As the post-Dawes republic lived on borrowed money, after September 1930 it was living on borrowed time. Although the Stab-in-the-Back party *par excellence* – the National Socialists – would ultimately triumph, it did so because of conditions after 1930 and not because of events in 1918–20.

One fact through this entire discussion is clear: the attractiveness of the notion of Stab-in-the-Back. The need for victim status, shared by all actors and institutions, was palpable. It was as if after the defeat, all segments of German society shared a need to scream, "it wasn't my/our fault! My/our actions did not bring about the Collapse." The Myth—whichever version an individual believed—filled an entirely understandable social psychological void. The seeming swiftness of the Collapse and the shock of loss after so much personal sacrifice required an explanation. The truth, as is so often the case, was a complicated matter with multiple moving parts, contingent upon the unfolding of events over time and the unrelated actions of multiple participants. Some analysts, such as "moderate" *Dolchstoß* proponent Hermann von Kuhl, were able to recognize this. It was Germany's tragedy that a sophisticated understanding of the events of 1914–20 was ultimately beyond the comprehension of the *deutsche Michel*.

NOTES

Preface

1. *Die Ursachen des Deutschen Zusammenbruches im Jahre 1918* (Berlin: Deutsche Verlagsgesellschaft für Politik und Geschichte, 1928), 8 vols.
2. Ralph Haswell Lutz, ed., *The Fall of the German Empire, 1914–1918* (Stanford: Stanford University Press, 1932) and Ralph Haswell Lutz, *The German Revolution 1918–1919* (Stanford: Stanford University Press, 1922).
3. Major German newspapers of the period all had morning and evening editions, with as many as three midday "extras" as news and material warranted. All citations, unless otherwise specified, are to the morning edition. Newspapers, such as *Vorwärts*, that were published by political parties operated on a distinctly different basis. Each had a special board consisting of the paper's editors and representatives of the party leadership. This board would meet in the late evening, set the morning edition's editorial line, and choose lead articles, making the morning edition the "authoritative" expression of the party's opinion. The material in the midday and evening editions was usually at the discretion of the paper's managing editor.

Introduction

1. Friedrich Freiherr Hiller von Gaertringen, "'Dolchstoß'-Diskussion und 'Dolchstoß Legende' im Wandel von der Jahrzehnten," in *Geschichte und Gegenwartsbewusstein*, eds. Waldemar Besson and Friedrich Freiherr Hiller von Gaertringen (Göttingen: Vandenhoeck & Ruprecht, 1963), p. 138.
2. Manfred Hülsewede, *Die Propstei* (Leer: Verlag Grundlagen und Praxis, 2002), vol. 2, pp. 206–229.
3. Laird Easton, Review of Boris Barth, *Dolchstoßlegenden und politische Desintegration: Das Trauma der deutschen Niederlage im Ersten Weltkrieg, 1914–1933* (Düsseldorf: Droste, 2003); *Journal of Modern History*, 77 (2005), pp. 1145–1147.
4. Gaertringen, "'Dolchstoß'-Diskussion," pp. 134–135 describes where term comes from and how it changed over time.
5. Scholars use the term *Dolchstoss/Dolchstoß* interchangeably with Stab-in-the-Back. The preferred German term for what in English is called the Stab-in-the-Back Myth is the *Dolchstoßlegende*.

6. The army was not *siegreich* (victorious), but it was *im Felde unbesiegt* (unconquered on the field of battle). Kuhl and the "moderates" never could explain how a "poisoned" army, if that poisoning was serious and effective, was able to maintain cohesion for so long.
7. Admiral von Trotha would make this assertion in the infamous Munich *Dolchstoß* Trial, providing the judges with detailed plans of exactly how German ships would be deployed and the Royal Navy would be defeated.
8. A perhaps apocryphal story has Ludendorff muttering at the time of his resignation, "the politicians have made this soup. Now we shall make them eat it."
9. The *Deutsche Tagezeitung* was partially owned and edited by the reactionary Agrarian League. Before the war, it frequently expressed antisemitic views but the full range of its Jew-hatred was constrained by government disapproval and censorship. Elke Kimmel, *Methoden antisemitischer Propaganda im Ersten Weltkrieg. Die Press des Bundes der Landwirte* (Berlin: Metropol, 2001) best tells the story of how its controlled prejudice intensified and was unleashed by military censors in the course of the war.
10. Frequently left out of this Left narrative is Groener's claim that Independent Social Democratic leader Hugo Haase had also secretly pledged to work against the Spartacists and those in his own party who advocated revolution.
11. Gerd Krumeich, "Die 'Dolchstoß-Legende', Deutscher Errinerungsort?" in *Deutsche Erinnerungsorte*, eds. Etienne Francois and Hagen Schulze (Munich: C.H. Beck, 2000), p. 596.
12. Gaertringen, "'Dolchstoß'-Diskussion," pp. 121–160.
13. Joachim Petzold, *Die Dolchstoßlegende. Eine Geschichtsfälschung im Dienst des deutschen Imperialismus und Militarismus* (Berlin: Akademie-Verlag, 1963).
14. *Der Gewaltfrieden*, 2010. Director: Bernd Fischerauer. Writers: Bernd Fischerauer and Klaus Gietingen. Telux Films. The videos would be an excellent addition to the classroom experience, but the DVD lacks either German or English subtitles, the large and mostly unidentified cast of characters is superficially drawn, and the political bias of the screenwriters in the portrayal of certain personalities is quite marked.
15. Decidedly outside the consensus were the remarks made to one of the co-authors by a German colleague that "the men who shot Liebknecht and Luxemburg deserved the *Bundesverdienstkreuz*."
16. See Bernd Ullrich and Benjamin Ziemann, eds. *Frontalltag im Ersten Weltkrieg. Wahn und Wirklichkeit. Quellen und Dokumenten* (Frankfurt: Fischer Taschenbuch, 1994); Bernd Ullrich, "'Militärgeschichte von Unten.' Anmerkungen zu ihren Ursprüngen. Quellen und Perspektiven im 20. Jahrhundert," *Geschichte und Gesellschaft*, 22, no. 4 (1996), pp. 473–503; Wolfgang Kruse, "Krieg und Klassenheer. Zur Revolutionierung der deutschen Armee im Ersten Weltkrieg," *Geschichte und Gesellschaft*, 22, no. 4 (1996), pp. 530–561; John Horn, "Kulturell Demobilmachung 1919–1939," *Geschichte und Gesellschaft*, 21 (2005), pp. 129–150; Christopher Jahr, *Gewöhnliche Soldaten: Desertion und Deserteure im deutschen und britischen Heer,*

1914–1918 (Göttingen: Vandenhoek & Ruprecht, 1998). Also see the excellent collection of essays, Jörg Duppler and Gerhard P. Groß, *Kriegsende 1918. Ereignis, Wirkung, Nachwirkung* (Munich: Oldenbourg, 1999).

17. Krumeich, "Die 'Dolchstoß-Legende', Deutscher Errinerungsort?" pp. 585–599. Students interested in Krumeich's work on memory are directed to Gerd Krumeich, "The First World War in the History of the Weimar Republic," in *The Legacies of Two World Wars. European Societies in the Twentieth Century*, eds. Lothar Kettenacker and Torsten Riotte (New York: Berghahn, 2011), pp. 77–89.

18. Barth, *Dolchstoßlegenden und politische Desintegration*; Rainer Sammet, *"Dolchstoß:" Deutschland und die Auseinandersetzung mit der Niederlage im Ersten Weltkrieg (1918–1933)* (Berlin: Trafo, 2003).

19. Neither Laird Easton (see note 3 above) nor Harold Marcuse, Review of Barth, *Dolchstoßlegenden und politische Desintegration*, H-German (December 2006), were particularly taken with Barth's work.

20. Boris Barth, "Dolchstoßlegende und Novemberrevolution," in *Die vergessene Revolution von 1918/19*, ed. Alexander Gallus (Göttingen: Vandenhoeck & Ruprecht, 2010), pp. 117–139

21. Eric D. Weitz, *Weimar Germany. Promise and Tragedy* (Princeton: Princeton University Press, 2007), p. 20, 98, 333.

22. Richard Evans, *The Coming of the Third Reich* (New York: Penguin, 2004), pp. 60–61.

23. Larry Eugene Jones, "Conservative Antisemitism in the Weimar Republic: A Case Study of the German National People's Party," in *The German Right in the Weimar Republic. Studies in the History of German Conservatism, Nationalism, and Antisemitism* (New York: Berghahn, 2014), p. 80.

24. Richard Bessel, *Germany after the First World War* (Oxford: Clarendon Press, 1993), p. 263.

25. For a comprehensive review of the literature, see Belinda Davis, "Experience, Identity and Memory: The Legacy of World War I," *Journal of Modern History*, 75, no. 1 (2003), pp. 111–131.

26. Jeffrey Verhey, *The Spirit of 1914: Militarism, Myth and Mobilization in Germany* (Cambridge: Cambridge University Press, 2000). See also Gerhard Hirschfeld, "'The Spirit of 1914': A Critical Examination of War Enthusiasm in German Society," in *The Legacies of Two World Wars. European Societies in the Twentieth Century*, eds. Lothar Kettenacker and Torsten Riotte (New York: Berghahn, 2011), pp. 29–40

27. Belinda Davis, *Home Fires Burning: Food, Politics, and Everyday Life in World War I Berlin* (Chapel Hill: University of North Carolina Press, 2000); Scott Stephenson, *The Final Battle: Soldiers of the Western Front and the German Revolution of 1918* (Cambridge: Cambridge University Press, 2009); and Thomas Weber, *Hitler's First World War* (Oxford: Oxford University Press, 2010).

28. Peter Applebaum, *Loyalty Betrayed: Jewish Chaplains in the German Army during the First World War* (Portland: Vallentine Mitchell, 2014; Peter Applebaum, *Loyal Sons: Jewish Soldiers in the German Army in the Great*

War (Portland: Vallentine Mitchell, 2014). Brian E. Crim, *Antisemitism in the German Military Community and the Jewish Response, 1914–1938* (Lanham, MD: Lexington, 2014) and Tim Grady, *The German-Jewish Soldiers of the First World War in History and Memory* (Liverpool: Liverpool University Press, 2011).

29. Benjamin Ziemann, *War Experiences in Rural Germany, 1914–1923*, translated by Alex Skinner (New York: Berg, 2007) and Benjamin Ziemann, *Contested Commemorations: Republican War Veterans and Weimar Political Culture* (Cambridge: Cambridge University Press, 2013).

30. Bernd Ulrich and Benjamin Ziemann, *German Soldiers in the Great War: Letters and Eyewitness Accounts*, translated by Christian Brocks (Barnsley: Pen & Sword Military, 2010).

31. Pierre Broué, *The German Revolution, 1917–1923* (Historical Materialism, 2006); Ralf Hoffrogge, *Working Class Politics in the German Revolution. Richard Müller, the Revolutionary Shop Stewards and the Origins of the Council Movement* (Leiden: Brill, 2015); and Gabriel Kuhn, *All Power to the Councils! A Documentary History of the German Revolution of 1918–1919* (Oakland, CA: PM Press, 2012).

32. Harold Marcuse, Review of Barth, http://www.history.ucsb.edu/faculty/marcuse/publications/reviews/BarthRev069.htm (accessed May 1, 2015).

Chapter 1

1. *Die Ursachen des Deutschen Zusammenbruches im Jahre 1918* (Berlin: Deutsche Verlagsgesellschaft für Politik und Geschichte, 1928), vol. 4, p. 1. Food policy had been a recurring source of domestic conflict since the introduction of agricultural tariffs in 1878. Social Democrats and left-leaning liberals favored lower tariffs, convinced that high tariffs raised price of food. Conservatives, most of whom were food producers, wanted protection from lower-priced (American, Canadian, and Argentinian) competition. They rationalized this policy on military grounds, arguing that the country needed a strong agricultural sector to feed the country in the event of war. The fact that Germany could not feed itself even with this pre-war sacrifice was a cause of enormous resentment among middle and working class urbanites.

2. The amount provided for with the ration cards in most states amounted to only half of the needed weekly per capita total. The remainder had to be purchased on the "unofficial" market at unregulated prices.

3. The predictable result was a temporary glut of pork followed by meat shortages in subsequent years.

4. *Vossische Zeitung*, February 11, 1915, evening edition, p. 4.
5. *Vorwärts*, January 27, 1915, p. 5.
6. *Berliner Tageblatt*, February 2, 1915, evening edition, p. 5.
7. *Frankfurter Zeitung*, July 15, 1915, evening edition, p. 1.
8. *Vorwärts*, October 16, 1915, p. 5.

9. *Stenographische Berichte über die Verhandlungen des Preussischen Hauses der Abgeordneten*, February 16, 1916, pp. 432–436.
10. Ralph Haswell Lutz, *The Fall of the German Empire, 1914–1918* (Palo Alto: Stanford University Press, 1932), pp. 166–168.
11. *Norddeutsche Allgemeine Zeitung*, May 23, 1916, evening edition, p. 1.
12. *Vossische Zeitung*, August 23, 1916, p. 1.
13. Lutz, *Fall*, pp. 187–188.
14. Lutz, *Fall*, pp. 188–191.
15. *Vorwärts*, November 19, 1917, pp. 1–2.
16. *Vorwärts*, May 17, 1918, p. 1.

Chapter 2

1. See Geoff Eley, *Reshaping the German Right: Radical Nationalism and Political Change After Bismarck* (New Haven: Yale University Press, 1980).
2. The classic study on the topic, Paul M. Kennedy, *The Rise of the Anglo-German Antagonism 1860–1914* (London: Allen & Unwin, 1980) can still be profitably read. Students will also find two books by Robert Massie, *Dreadnought: Britain, Germany and the Coming of the Great War* (New York: Random House, 1991) and *Castles of Steel: Britain, Germany and the Winning of the Great War at Sea* (New York: Random House, 2003) eminently readable.
3. On the American response, see Justus D. Doenecke, *Nothing Less Than War: A New History of America's Entry into World War I* (Lexington: University of Kentucky Press, 2011). Under the rules of war as they existed in 1914 regarding neutral shipping, submarines had to notify neutral ships of their presence, then board and search them for contraband. If war materials were found, the ship's crew must be safely removed before the ship was sunk. This was both time-consuming and dangerous for the submarine crews. Further, the German Supreme Command would argue that even food aided the enemy; hence their insistence on unrestricted submarine warfare.
4. Only sixteen of these Americans were ever interned. The German government had found from its treatment of French and British nationals after August 1914 that it was a waste of resources to intern civilians who, unlike POWs, could not be forced to work. The Germans preferred to let Americans leave voluntarily.
5. Reports extracted from US Department of State, *Records Relating to the Internal Affairs of Germany* (National Archives Microfilm Publication M 336, rolls 82–83); Record Group 59; National Archives at College Park, MD.
6. Leading military figures and their apologists throughout the 1920s refused to accept that Germany's ever-worsening nutritional state had anything to do with the Collapse.
7. *Frankfurter Zeitung*, January 10, 1919, p. 1.

8. Ibid.
9. William Carl Mathews, "The Economic Origins of the *Noskepolitik*," *Central European History* 27, no. 1 (1994) pp. 65–86.

Chapter 3

1. *Vorwärts*, July 26, 1916, p. 1.
2. *Vorwärts*, April 17, 1917, pp. 1–2.
3. *Norddeutsche Allgemeine Zeitung*, April 27, 1917, pp. 1–2
4. *Norddeutsche Allgemeine Zeitung*, April 27, 1917, evening edition, p. 1.
5. Ibid., p. 1.

Chapter 4

1. As a side-note, Scheidemann's many enemies on both Left and Right referred to his associates and followers as *Scheidemänner*, a cute play on words that was not meant kindly. Scheidemann is a compound noun: *scheide* (cut or divide) and *mann* (man or person). The plural noun "männer" can mean "men," so Scheidemann's men or the dividers (of the Social Democratic Party). Scheidemann remains a controversial figure among both scholars and Social Democrats, eclipsed perhaps only by Gustav Noske. Those interested in how and why this is so can access http://www.dolchstosslegende.com/short-biographies. Thanks to Richard Levy for his insight regarding Scheidemann.
2. *Chicago Daily Tribune*, January 26, 1918, p. 2.
3. *Norddeutsche Allgemeine Zeitung*, January 29, 1918, evening edition, p. 1
4. *Vorwärts*, January 29, 1918, p. 1.
5. *Chicago Daily Tribune*, January 31, 1918, pp. 1–2.
6. *Chicago Daily Tribune*, February 1, 1918, pp. 1–2.
7. *Chicago Daily Tribune*, February 3, 1918, pp. 1–2.
8. Ibid.
9. *Vorwärts*, February 16, 1918, pp. 1–2.
10. *Verhandlungen des Deutschen Reichstags*, no. 134, February 26, 1918, pp. 4162–4171. The *German Reichstag Session Reports* have been digitized by the Bayerische Staatsbibliothek and are available at http://www.reichstagsprotokolle.de/en_index.html. The online search aid is in German and English; the *Protokolle* and Appendices (*Anlagen*) themselves are the original German *Fraktur*.
11. *Verhandlungen des Deutschen Reichstags*, no. 134, February 26, 1918, pp. 4162–4171.

Chapter 5

1. *Die Ursachen des Deutschen Zusammenbruches im Jahre 1918* (Berlin: Deutsche Verlagsgesellschaft für Politik und Geschichte, 1928), vol. 2, pp. 125–128, and Ralph Haswell Lutz, ed., *The Causes of the German collapse in 1918; Sections of the Officially Authorized Report of the Commission of the German Constituent Assembly and of the German Reichstag, 1919–1928* (Palo Alto: Stanford University Press, 1934), pp. 28–31. We have based our translations on the German original and provided citations to the English translation for the benefit of those who would like to look at more of the documents.
2. *Die Ursachen*, vol. 3, pp. 6–8; 37–43 and Lutz, *The Causes*, pp. 53–61.
3. *Die Ursachen*, vol. 3, pp. 73–74 and Lutz, *The Causes*, pp. 66–67.
4. The question of desertion from the colors was extremely controversial. Both Nationalist proponents of the *Dolchstoßlegende* and Communists/Independent Social Democrats preferred for their own purposes to inflate the extent of this problem. For a detailed consideration of the problem, see Stephenson, *Final Battle*, pp. 46–50.
5. Gaertringen, "'Dolchstoß'-Diskussion," p. 148 states that Philipp was regarded as a fair-minded chair. His statements—understated for political purposes—suggest that he firmly shared the Nationalist belief that Jews circumvented their duties. It should be noted as well that he drafted this report solely on the basis of Kuhl's deposition without reference to the deposition of Hans Delbrück, the other "military expert" advising the Subcommittee.
6. The infamous *Judenzählung* was instituted by the military at the insistence of Antisemites hoping to prove that German Jewish soldiers shirked frontline duty and were mostly to be found in the rear echelon or in desk jobs. For more on the "Jewish census," see http://www.dolchstosslegende.com/Judenzählung; Tim Grady, *The German-Jewish Soldiers of the First World War in History and Memory* (Liverpool: Liverpool Press, 2011); David J. Fine, *Jewish Integration in the German Army in the First World War* (Berlin and Boston: De Gruyter, 2012).
7. *Die Ursachen*, vol. 4, pp. 6–36 and Lutz, *Causes*, pp. 167–175. Philipp's first paragraph (on shirking) is an absolute lie. Not only was the *Judenzählung* instituted at Antisemitic (not Jewish) insistence, but it is widely believed that it was not published because it showed the opposite of what the Antisemites believed.
8. *Die Ursachen*, vol. 3, pp. 52–58 and Lutz, *Causes*, pp. 61–66.
9. *Die Ursachen*, vol. 3, pp. 213–215 and Lutz, *Causes*, pp. 86–88.
10. The Communists were much more interested in the actions of the naval high command and the mutinies by the sailors and marines of the High Seas Fleet, no doubt because they and the Independents had played an active role there. One is also tempted to think that since the navy stayed inert after 1916, its activities require less military expertise to critique.
11. *Die Ursachen*, vol. 6, pp. 85–98.
12. *Washington Evening Star*, January 24, 1919, p. 12.

Chapter 6

1. *Die Ursachen*, vol. 5, p. 116.
2. Ibid., pp. 117–121.
3. Ibid., pp. 151–71 and Lutz, *Causes*, pp. 113–131.
4. *Die Ursachen*, vol. 4, pp. 6–16 and Lutz, *Causes*, pp. 167–175.
5. *Die Ursachen*, vol. 4, pp. 208–209.
6. On our website we have posted a second photograph that depicts Ebert, wearing his reading glasses, actually reading the speech.
7. Friedrich Ebert, *Schriften, Aufzeichnung, Reden* (Dresden: Carl Reissner Verlag, 1926), vol. 4, pp. 126–127.
8. Ebert, *Schriften*, vol. 2, pp. 127–130.
9. See "Freikorps" under "Other Stories" at http://www.dolchstosslegende.com.

Chapter 7

1. W. Pyta, *Hindenburg. Herrschaft zwischen Hohenzollern und Hitler* (Berlin: Siedler, 2007), p. 404.
2. *Deutsche Tageszeitung*, December 18, 1918, p. 1. In German, the headline reads: "*Die 'erdolchte' deutsche Armee.*"
3. *Neue Zürcher Zeitung*, December 17, 1918, 4th edition, p. 1.
4. *Daily News*, November 17, 1918, p. 1.
5. Frederick Maurice, *The Last Four Months; the End of the War in the West* (London: Cassell, 1919), pp. 216–232.
6. Trained as a lawyer, Kuttner joined the SPD in 1910. He volunteered for military service and was discharged after being severely wounded at Verdun. In 1916 he was named editor of *Vorwärts* and was later the founding editor of *Lachen Links*, a Social Democratic satirical weekly created in 1924. See our website for a short biography.
7. Erich Kuttner, *Der Sieg War zum greifen Nahe!* (Berlin: Verlag für Sozialwissenschaft, 1921), pp. 5–6.
8. *Die Ursachen*, vol. 4, p. 3.
9. Ibid., p. 33–35.
10. D. J. Goodspeed, *Ludendorff: Genius of World War I* (Boston: Houghton Mifflin, 1966), pp. 279–280.

Chapter 8

1. Those seeking more on Wilhelm II should see John Röhl, *Wilhelm II: Into the Abyss of War and Exile, 1900–1941*, translated by Sheila de Bellaigue and Roy Bridge (Cambridge: Cambridge University Press, 2014).

2. Hindenburg lacks a recent scholarly biography in English. The most commonly cited, John Wheeler-Bennett, *Hindenburg: the Wooden Titan* (London: Macmillan, 1936), is badly dated. Students with reading knowledge of German are directed to Wolfram Pyta, *Hindenburg: Herrschaft zwischen Hohenzollern und Hitler* (Munich: Siedler, 2007).
3. John Williamson, *Helfferich, 1872–1924: Economist, Financier, Politician* (Princeton: Princeton University Press, 1971).
4. *Deutsche Tageszeitung*, November 11, 1919, p. 1. The only deputies named by the *Tageszeitung* were Jewish, either Independents or Majority Social Democrats. In the case of Georg Gothein, he was a long-time Progressive *bête noir* of the newspaper's Agrarian readership.
5. Pyta, *Hindenburg*, pp. 406–409.
6. *The Times*, November 17, 1919, p. 12.
7. Ibid.
8. *The Times*, November 19, 1919, p. 12.
9. Ibid.
10. Ibid.
11. *Chicago Daily Tribune*, November 13, 1919, p. 4.
12. *Chicago Daily Tribune*, November 16, 1919, p. 6.
13. *The Times*, November 17, 1919, p. 12.
14. *New York Times*, November 17, 1919, p. 17.
15. Ibid.
16. Paul von Hindenburg, *Aus Meinem Leben* (Leipzig: S. Hirzel, 1918), p. 302. See Wheeler-Bennett, *Wooden Titan* for the story of how this publication came about and its intended purpose and audience.
17. *Stenographischer Bericht über die öffentlichen Verhandlungen des 15. Untersuchungsausschusses der verfassungsgebenden Nationalversammlung*, vol. 2. Berlin, 1920, pp. 700–701.
18. *The Times*, November 20, 1919, p. 12.
19. Charles B. Dyar, "Memorandum on the Political Situation in Germany." U.S. Department of State, Records Relating to the Internal Affairs of Germany (National Archives Microfilm Publication M336, roll 14, p. 2) Record Group 59; National Archives at College Park, MD.

Chapter 9

1. A typical example, although not made with ill intent, was the publication of a picture of Ebert and Gustav Noske in bathing suits on their summer vacation. It exposed the president to constant ridicule and disturbed those Germans who wanted their chief of state to be an aristocratic, glorified figure. Read more at http://www.dolchstosslegende.com/Ebert.
2. Bernhard Fulda, *Press and Politics in the Weimar Republic* (Oxford: Oxford University Press, 2009), pp. 81–89.

3. Ibid., p. 82.
4. *The Times* provides a much more readable and coherent narrative than that available in any of the German newspapers, so we have let its coverage tell the story of the trial.
5. *The Times*, December 11, 1924, p. 13.
6. Ibid.
7. Ibid.
8. *The Times*, December 12, 1924, p. 13.
9. Ebert, *Schriften*, pp. 348–352.
10. *The Times*, December 13, 1924, p. 11.
11. *The Times*, December 15, 1924, p. 13.
12. Ibid.
13. *The Times*, December 18, 1924, p. 11.
14. *The Times*, December 24, 1924, p. 10.
15. Ebert, *Schriften*, p. 353.
16. Alanson B. Houghton to Secretary of State, "Report on the Ebert Trial." U.S. Department of State Records Relating to the Internal Affairs of Germany (National Archives Microfilm Publication M336, roll 22, p. 353) Record Group 59; National Archives at Collage Park, MD.
17. Rather than translating the newspapers ourselves, we have used Hanna's expert translation, with minor changes to suit contemporary English usage.
18. First Secretary Matthew E. Hanna, "Weekly Press Report." U.S. Department of State, Records Relating to the Internal Affairs of Germany (National Archives Publication M336, roll 22, pp. 9–14) Record Group 59; National Archives at College Park, MD.
19. Ibid., unpaginated.
20. Ibid., unpaginated.
21. Ibid., unpaginated.
22. Ibid., unpaginated.
23. Ibid., unpaginated.
24. *Sandusky Star-Journal*, December 12, 1925, p. 1.
25. *Portsmouth Daily*, March 3, 1925, p. 1.
26. Werner Maser, *Hitler's Letters and Notes* (New York: Harper & Row, 1974), pp. 310–311.

Chapter 10

1. Cossmann's partner in this venture was Karl Alexander von Müller. Son of a Bavarian minister of religion, Müller was an accomplished historian who taught at the university in Munich. He organized and taught sections in the special course created to train "education officers" for the Reichswehr after

the suppression of the Munich soviet. A young Adolf Hitler was one of his pupils in the course.
2. Consul General C.B. Curtis, "Report on Bavarian Political Conditions, October 1924." U.S. Department of State, Records Relating to the Internal Affairs (National Archives Microfilm Publications M336, roll 24, pp. 1–2) Record Group 59; National Archives at College Park, MD.
3. *The Times*, October 20, 1925, p. 13.
4. *The Times*, October 22, 1925, p. 11.
5. George F. Botjer, "A Judicial Effort to Determine the Causes of the German Defeat in 1918: Dolchstossprozess Cossmann-Gruber (1925)," Diss. Florida State University, 1973, p. 5.
6. Eyre was the Berlin correspondent of the paper and one of the best-known American newspapermen in Europe. Writing for the *World*, he followed the retreating German army in October 1918 and was the first newsman to interview Hindenburg after the Armistice. He was in Berlin during the revolution and was later stationed in Moscow before returning to Berlin.
7. *New York Times*, October 30, 1925, p. 2.
8. *New York Times*, November 3, 1925, p. 11.
9. *Vorwärts*, October 27, 1925, p. 1.
10. *Vorwärts*, November 21, 1925, p. 3.
11. *The Times*, December 10, 1925, p. 15.
12. Botjer, "A Judicial Effort," pp. 244–246.
13. Ibid., pp. 258–260.
14. *Die Ursachen*, vol.4, pp. 74, 83–85.

Chapter 11

1. *Die Ursachen*, vol. 6, pp. 99–248.
2. Ibid., pp. 249–306.
3. Ibid., pp. 85–98.
4. Ibid., pp. 1–39.
5. Ibid., pp. 57–80.
6. Ibid., pp. 345–346 and Lutz, *Causes*, pp. 89–91.
7. A complete list of these meetings and the participants is accessible at http://www.dolchstosslegende.com/Subcommittee.
8. *Die Ursachen*, vol. 1, pp. 19–21 and Lutz, *Causes*, pp. 3–8.
9. *Die Ursachen*, vol. 1, pp. 31–32 and Lutz, *Causes*, pp. 11–13.
10. *Die Ursachen*, vol. 1, pp. 27–29 and Lutz, *Causes*, pp. 8–11.
11. Lutz, *Causes*, pp. 13–15.
12. *Die Ursachen*, vol. 4, pp. 1–2b and Lutz, *Causes*, pp. 188–189.

Chapter 12

1. The paucity of English-language literature on the German Nationals is saddening. Students desiring an introduction to the topic should consult the bibliography in Larry Eugene Jones, *The German Right in the Weimar Republic*.
2. The literature on the German Communist Party is more complete. See Eric Weitz, *Creating German Communism, 1890–1990: From Popular Protests to Socialist State* (Princeton: Princeton University Press, 1997), David Morgan, *The Socialist Left and the German Revolution: A History of the German Independent Social Democratic Party, 1917–1922* (Ithaca: Cornell University Press, 1975), and Curt Geyer, *Die revolutionäre Illusion: Geschichte des linken Flügels der USPD: Erinnerungen an Curt Geyer*, eds. Wolfgang Benz und Hermann Graml (Stuttgart: Deutsche Verlags-Anstalt, 1976).
3. The most recent monograph on the end phase of Weimar Social Democracy is Donna Harsch, *German Social Democracy and the Rise of Nazism* (Chapel Hill: University of North Carolina Press, 1993). See our website for the extensive German-language literature.
4. The standard German-language work on liberals and the German revolution is Lothar Albertin, *Liberalismus und Demokratie am Anfang der Weimarer Republik; eine vergleichende Analyse der Deutschen Demokratischen Partei und der Deutschen Volkspartei* (Düsseldorf: Drost, 1972). In English, see Larry Eugene Jones, *German liberalism and the dissolution of the Weimar Party System* (Chapel Hill: University of North Carolina Press, 1988) and Bruce Frye, *Liberal Democrats in the Weimar Republic: the History of the German Democratic Party and the German State Party* (Carbondale: Southern Illinois University Press, 1985).
5. Jonathan Wright, *Gustav Stresemann: Weimar's Greatest Statesman* (Oxford: Oxford University Press, 2002).
6. See http://www.dolchstosslegende.com/Hitler.
7. See Peter Fritzsche's chapter on the "Hindenburg" election in *Germans into Nazis* (Cambridge: Harvard University Press, 1998).

BIBLIOGRAPHY

Archives

U.S. Department of State, Records Relating to the Internal Affairs of Germany. Record Group 59. National Archives Microfilm Publication M 336, Rolls 14, 22, 24, 82, 83. National Archives at College Park, MD.

Newspapers

Berliner Tageblatt
Chicago Daily Tribune
Daily News
Deutsche Tageszeitung
Frankfurter Zeitung
Neue Zürcher Zeitung
New York Times
New York World
Norddeutsche Allgemeine Zeitung
Portsmouth Daily
Sandusky Star-Journal
The Times
Vorwärts
Vossische Zeitung
Washington Evening Star

Document collections

Bane, S. and R. Haswell Lutz, eds., *The Blockade of Germany after the Armistice, 1918–1919; Selected Documents of the Supreme Economic Council, Superior Blockade Council, American Relief Administration, and Other Wartime Organizations*, Stanford: Stanford University Press, 1942.
Bell, A., *A History of the Blockade of Germany and the Countries Associated with Her in the Great War*, London: Her Majesty's Stationary Office, 1961.
Kuhn, G., ed., *All Power to the Councils! A Documentary History of the German Revolution of 1918–1919*, Oakland, CA: PM Press, 2012.
Lutz, R., *The German Revolution 1918–1919*, Stanford: Stanford University Press, 1922.

Lutz, R., ed., *The Fall of the German Empire, 1914–1918*, Stanford: Stanford University Press, 1932.
Lutz, R., ed., *The Causes of the German Collapse in 1918; Sections of the Officially Authorized Report of the Commission of the German Constituent Assembly and of the German Reichstag, 1919–1928*, Stanford: Stanford University Press, 1934.
Maser, W., ed., *Hitler's Letters and Notes*, New York: Harper & Row, 1974.
Philipp, Albrecht, Eugen Fischer, and Walther Bloch, *Die Ursachen des Deutschen Zusammenbruches im Jahre 1918*, Berlin: Deutsche Verlagsgesellschaft für Politik und Geschichte, 1928, 8 vols.
Stenographischer Bericht über die öffentlichen Verhandlungen des 15. Untersuchungsausschusses der verfassungsgebenden Nationalversammlung, vol. 2. Berlin, 1920.
Verhandlungen des Deutschen Reichstags, www.reichstagsprotokolle.de/index.html.

Memoirs and collected writings

Barth, E., *Aus der Werkstatt der deustsche Revolution*, Berlin: Hoffmanns Verlag, 1919.
Delbrück, H., *Vor und nach dem Weltkrieg*, Berlin: O. Stollberg, 1926.
Dittmann, W., *Erinnerungen*, J. Rojahn (ed.), Frankfurt: Campus Verlag, 1995.
Ebert, F., *Schriften, Aufzeichnung, Reden*, vol. 2, Dresden: Carl Reissner Verlag, 1926.
Geyer, C., *Die Revolutionäre Illusion: Geschichte des Linken Flügels der USPD: Erinnerungen an Curt Geyer*, edited by Wolfgang Benz und Hermann Graml, Stuttgart: Deutsche Verlags-Anstalt, 1976.
Groener, W., *Lebenserinnerungen: Jugend, Generlstab, Weltkrieg*, H. von Gaertringen (ed.), Göttingen: Vandenhoeck und Ruprecht, 1957.
Hindenburg, P., *Aus Meinem Leben*, Leipzig: S. Hirzel, 1920.
Hitler, Adolf, *Mein Kampf*, Boston: Houghton Mifflin, 1999.
Hitler, Adolf, *Reden, Schriften, Anordnugen*, edited by K. Klee, C. Hartmann, and K. Lankheit, Munich: K.G. Saur, 2003.
Kessler, H., *Berlin in Lights: The Diaries of Count Harry Kessler (1918–1937)*, C. Kessler, New York: Grove Press, 2002.
Lambach, W., *Ursachen des Zusammenbruchs*, Hamburg: Deutschnationale Verlagsanstalt, 1920.
Lewinsohn, L., *Die Revolution an der Westfront*, Charlottenburg: Mundus Verlaganstalt, 1919.
Ludendorff, E., *Ludendorff's Own Story, August 1914-November 1918*, New York: Harper, 1919.
Lüttwitz, W., *Im Kampf gegen die November-Revolution*, Berlin: Verlag Otto Schlegel, 1934.
Mühlhausen, W., *Friedrich Ebert und seine Familie: Private Briefe, 1909–1924*, München: R. Oldenbourg, 1992.
Noske, G., *Von Kiel bis Kapp*, Berlin: Verlag für Politik und Wirstschaft, 1920.

Oehme, W., *Damals in der Reichskanzlei: Erinnerungen aus den Jahren 1918/1919*, Berlin: Kongress-Verlag, 1958.
Scheidemann, P., *The Making of New Germany: the Memoirs of Philipp Scheidemann*, translated by J. E. Michell, New York: Appleton and Company, 1929.
Streseman, G., *Vermächtnis Der Nachlass in Drei Bänden*, Berlin: Ullstein Verlag, 1932.
Thaer, A., *Generalstabdienst an der Front und der O.H.I.*, Gottingen: Vandenhoeck und Ruprecht, 1958.

Secondary literature in English

Applebaum, Peter, *Loyal Sons: Jewish Soldiers in the German Army in the the Great War*, Portland: Vallentine Mitchell, 2014.
Applebaum, Peter, *Loyalty Betrayed: Jewish Chaplains in the German Army during the First World War*, Portland: Vallentine Mitchell, 2014.
Bessel, R., *Germany after the First World War*, Oxford: Clarendon Press, 1993.
Botjer, G., "A Judicial Effort to Determine the Causes of the German Defeat in 1918: Dolchstossprozess Cossmann-Gruber (1925)." PhD diss. Florida State University, 1973.
Broue, P., *The German Revolution, 1917–1923*, translated by J. Archer and edited by I. Birchall and B. Pierce, Leiden: Brill, 2005.
Cox, M., "Hunger Games: Or How the Allied Blockade in the First World War Deprived German Children of Nutrition, and Allied Food Aid Subsequently Saved Them," *The Economic History Review*, 68, no. 2 (2015), pp. 600–631.
Crim, B., *Antisemitism in the German Military Community and the Jewish Response, 1914–1938*, Lanham, MD: Lexington, 2014.
Davis, B., *Home Fires Burning: Food, Politics and Everyday Life in World War One Berlin*, Chapel Hill: University of North Carolina Press, 2000.
Davis, B., "Experience, Identity and Memory: The Legacy of World War I," *Journal of Modern History*, 75, no. 1 (2003), pp. 111–131.
Deist, W., "The Military Collapse of the German Empire: The Reality Behind in the Stab-in-the-Back Myth," translated by E. Feutchtwanger, *War in History*, 3, no. 2 (April 1996), pp. 186–207.
Dorpalen, A., *Hindenburg and the Weimar Republic*, Princeton: Princeton University Press, 1964.
Evans, R., *The Coming of the Third Reich*, New York: Penguin, 2004.
Easton, L., "Review of Boris Barth, *Dolchstoßlegenden und politische Desintegration: Das Trauma der deutschen Niederlage im Ersten Weltkrieg, 1914–1933* (Düsseldorf: Droste, 2003)," *Journal of Modern History*, 77 (2005), pp. 1145–1147.
Feldman, G., *Army, Industry, and Labor in Germany, 1914–1918*, Princeton, NJ: Princeton University Press, 1966.
Fine, D., *Jewish Integration in the German Army in the First World War*, Berlin and Boston: De Gruyter, 2012.
Fritzsche, P., *Germans into Nazis*, Cambridge: Harvard University Press, 1998.
Frye, B., *Liberal Democrats in the Weimar Republic: The History of the German Democratic Party and the German State Party*, Carbondale: Southern Illinois University Press, 1985.

Fulda, B., *Press and Politics in the Weimar Republic*, Oxford: Oxford University Press, 2009.
Geyer, M., "Insurrectionary Warfare: The German Debate about a *Levée en Masse* in October 1918," *Journal of Modern History*, 73 (2001), pp. 459–527.
Grady, T., *The German Jewish Soldiers of the First World War in History and Memory*, Liverpool: Liverpool University Press, 2011.
Goodspeed, D. J., *Ludendorff: Genius of World War I*, Boston: Houghton Mifflin, 1966.
Harmer, H., *Friedrich Ebert*, London: Haus Pub, 2008.
Harsch, D., *German Social Democracy and the Rise of Nazism*, Chapel Hill: University of North Carolina Press, 1993.
Hering, R., "Academics and Radical Nationalism: The Pan-German League in Hamburg and the German Reich," in L. Jones (ed.), *The German Right in the Weimar Republic. Studies in the History of German Conservatism, Nationalism, and Antisemitism*, New York: Berghahn, 2014.
Heussler, H., *General Wilhelm Groener and the Imperial German Army*, Madison: University of Wisconsin Press, 1962.
Hirschfeld, G., "'The Spirit of 1914': A Critical Examination of War Enthusiasm in German Society," in L. Kettenacker and T. Riotte (eds.), *The Legacies of Two World Wars. European Societies in the Twentieth Century*, New York: Berghahn, 2011.
Hoffrogge, R., *Working Class Politics in the German Revolution. Richard Müller, the Revolutionary Shop Stewards and the Origins of the Council Movement*, Leiden: Brill, 2015.
Jackisch, B., *The Pan-German League and Radical Nationalist Politics in Interwar Germany, 1918–39*, Burlington, VT: Ashgate, 2012.
Jones, L., *German Liberalism and the Dissolution of the Weimar Party System*, Chapel Hill: University of North Carolina Press, 1988.
Jones, L., *The German Right in the Weimar Republic. Studies in the History of German Conservatism, Nationalism, and Antisemitism*, New York: Berghahn, 2014.
Jones, L., "Conservative Antisemitism in the Weimar Republic: A Case Study of the German National People's Party," in Larry Eugene Jones (ed.), *The German Right in the Weimar Republic. Studies in the History of German Conservatism, Nationalism, and Antisemitism*, pp. 79–107, New York: Berghahn, 2014.
Krumeich, G., "The First World War in the History of the Weimar Republic," in L. Kettenacker and T. Riotte (eds.), *The Legacies of Two World Wars. European Societies in the Twentieth Century*, pp. 78–79, New York: Berghahn, 2011.
Marcuse, H., Review of Boris Barth, *Dolchstoßlegenden und politische Desintegration: Das Trauma der deutschen Niederlage im Ersten Weltkrieg, 1914–1933*, Düsseldorf: Droste, 2003. http://www.history.ucsb.edu/faculty/marcuse/publications/reviews/BarthRev069.htm (accessed April 1, 2015).
Mathews, W., "The Economic Origins of the *Noskepolitik*," *Central European History*, 27, no. 1 (1994), 65–86.
Maurice, F., *The Last Four Months; the End of the War in the West*, London: Cassell, 1919.
Maehl, W., *The German Socialist Party: Champion of the First Republic, 1918–1933*, Philadelphia: American Philosophical Society, 1986.

Morgan, D., *The Socialist Left and the German Revolution: A History of the German Independent Social Democratic Party, 1917–1922*, Ithaca: Cornell University Press, 1975.
Offer, A., *The First World War: An Agrarian Interpretation*, Oxford: Oxford University Press, 1989.
Osborne, E., *Britain's Economic Blockade of Germany, 1914–1910*, New York: Frank Cass, 2004.
Pyta, W., "Hindenburg and the German Right," in Larry Eugene Jones (ed.), *The German Right in the Weimar Republic. Studies in the History of German Conservatism, Nationalism, and Antisemitism*, New York: Berghahn, 2014.
Röhl, J., *Wilhelm II: Into the Abyss of War and Exile, 1900–1941*, translated by Sheila de Bellaigue and Roy Bridge, Cambridge: Cambridge University Press, 2014.
Rosenberg, A., *The Birth of the German Republic*, translated by I. Morrow, New York: Oxford University Press, 1965.
Stephenson, S., *The Final Battle: Soldiers of the Western Front and the German Revolution of 1918*, Cambridge: Cambridge University Press, 2009.
Stibbe, M., *Germany, 1914–1933: Politics, Society, and Culture*, New York: Longman, 2010.
Tooze, A., *The Deluge. The Great War, America and the Remaking of the Global Order, 1916–1931*, New York: Viking, 2014.
Ulrich, B. and Benjamin Ziemann, *German Soldiers in the Great War: Letters and Eyewitness Accounts*, translated by C. Brocks, Barnsley: Pen & Sword Military, 2010.
Verhey, J., *The Spirit of 1914: Militarism, Myth and Mobilization in Germany*, Cambridge: Cambridge University Press, 2000.
Vincent, C., *The Politics of Hunger. The Allied Blockade of Germany, 1915–1919*, Athens: Ohio University Press, 1985.
Watson, A., *Enduring the Great War: Combat, Morale and Collapse in the German and British Armies, 1914–1918*, Cambridge: Cambridge University Press, 2008.
Watson, A., *Ring of Steel: Germany and Austria-Hungary in World War I*, New York: Basic Books, 2014.
Weber, T., *Hitler's First World War*, Oxford: Oxford University Press, 2010.
Weitz, E., *Creating German Communism, 1890–1990: From Popular Protests to Socialist State*, Princeton: Princeton University Press, 1997.
Weitz, E., *Weimar Germany. Promise and Tragedy*, Princeton: Princeton University Press, 2007.
Wheeler-Bennett, J., *Hindenburg: The Wooden Titan*, London: Macmillan, 1936.
Williamson, J., *Helfferich, 1872–1924: Economist, Financier, Politician*, Princeton: Princeton University Press, 1971.
Wright, J., *Gustav Stresemann: Weimar's Greatest Statesman*, Oxford: Oxford University Press, 2002.
Yaney, G., *The World of the Manager: Food Administration in Berlin during World War I*, New York: Peter Lang, 1994.
Ziemann, B., *War Experiences in Rural Germany, 1914–1923*, translated by A. Skinner, New York: Berg, 2007.
Ziemann, B., *Contested Commemorations: Republican War Veterans and Weimar Political Culture*, Cambridge: Cambridge University Press, 2013.

Select secondary literature in German

A complete list of German works on the *Dolchstoß* can be found at http://dolchstosslegende/Resources.

Albrecht, N., "Die Macht einer Verleumdungskampagne Antidemokratische Agitationen der Presse und Justiz gegen die Weimarer Republik und ihren ersten vom 'Badebild' bis zum Magdeburger Prozeß Reichspräsidenten," PhD. diss. Bremen, 2002.

Barth, B., "Dolchstoßlegende und Novemberrevolution," in Alexander Gallus (ed.), *Die vergessene Revolution von 1918/19*, Goettingen: Vandenhoeck & Ruprecht, 2010.

Barth, B., *Dolchstoßlegenden und politische Desintegration: Das Trauma der deutschen Niederlage im Ersten Weltkrieg, 1914–1933*, Düsseldorf: Droste, 2003.

Beckmann, E., *Der Dolchstoßprozess in München vom 19. Oktobr bis 20. November 1925*, Munich: Süddeutsche Monatsheftes, 1925.

Brammer, K., *Der Prozess des Reichspräsidenten*, Berlin: Verlag für Socialwissenschaft, 1925.

Duppler, J. and Gerhard P. Groß, *Kriegsende 1918. Ereignis, Wirkung, Nachwirkung*, Munich: Oldenbourg, 1999.

Foerster, W., *Der Feldherr Ludendorff im Unglück. Eine Studie über seine Hältung in der Endphase des ersten Weltkrieges*, Wisebaden: Limes Verlag, 1952.

Gärtringen, F., "'Dolchstoß'-Diskussion und 'Dolchstoß Legende' im Wandel von der Jahrzehnten," in W. Besson and F. Hiller von Gaertringen (eds.), *Geschichte und Gegenwartsbewusstein*, pp. 121–160, Göttingen: Vandenhoeck & Ruprecht, 1963.

Horn, J., "Kulturell Demobilmachung 1919–1939," *Geschichte und Gesellschaft*, 21 (2005), pp. 129–150.

Hülsewede, M., *Die Prosptei*, vol. 2, Leer: Verlag Grundlagen und Praxis, 2002.

Jahr, C., *Gewöhnliche Soldaten: Desertion und Deserteure im deutschen und britischen Heer, 1914–1918*, Göttingen: Vandenhoek & Ruprecht, 1998.

Krumeich, G., "'Die Dolchstoß-Legende', Deutscher Errinerungsort?" in E. Francois and H. Schulze (eds.), *Deutsche Erinnerungsorte*, pp. 585–599, Munich: C.H. Beck, 2000.

Kuttner, E., *Der Sieg War zum greifen Nahe!* Berlin: Verlag für Sozialwissenschaft, 1921.

Lipp, A., *Meinungslenkung im Krieg: Kreigserfahrungen deustscher Soldaten und ihre Deutung 1914–1918*, Göttingen: Vandenhoeck und Ruprecht, 2003.

Miltenberger, M., *Der Vorwurf des Landesverrats gegen Reichspräsident Friedrich Ebert. Ein Stück deutscher Justizgeschichte*, Heidelberg: Decker & Müller, 1989.

Petzold, J., *Die Dolchstoßlegende: Eine Geschichtsfaelschung im Dienste des deutschen Imperialismus und Militarismus*, Berlin: Akademie-Verlag, 1963.

Pyta, W., *Hindenburg. Herrschaft zwischen Hohenzollern und Hitler*, Berlin: Siedler, 2007.

Sammet, R. *"Dolchstoß:" Deutschland und die Auseinandersetzung mit der Niederlage im Ersten Weltkrieg (1918–1933)*, Berlin: Trafo, 2003.

Seiler, B., "'Dolchstoß' und 'Dolchstoßlegende,'" *Zeitschrift für Deutsche Sprache*, 22 (1966), pp. 1–20.

Ulrich, B., "'Militärgeschichte von Unten.' Anmerkungen zu ihren Ursprüngen. Quellen und Perspektiven im 20. Jahrhundert," *Geschichte und Gesellschaft*, 22, no. 4 (1996), pp. 473–503.

Ulrich, B., *Die Augenzeugen. Deutsche Feldpostbriefe in Kriegs—und Nachkreigszeit 1914–1933*, Essen: Klartext-Verlag, 1997.

Ulrich, B. and B. Ziemann, eds., *Frontalltag im Ersten Weltkrieg. Wahn und Wirklichkeit. Quellen und Dokumenten*, Frankfurt: Fischer Taschenbuch, 1994.

INDEX

antisemitism
   antisemitic origins of
      Dolchstoßlegende 2, 112–13,
      124–6
   antisemitism and the
      Dolchstoßlegende 203–6
   Jews as deserters and shirkers 68,
      214

Cossmann, Paul
   biography 159
   Munich *Dolchstoß* Trial 162–4,
      168–70

Delbrück, Hans
   biography 181
   Munich *Dolchstoß* Trial testimony
      166–7
   Subcommittee deposition 183–5
desertion and shirking 68, 71–3, 161

Ebert, Friedrich
   biography 50
   January Strike 52, 57–9, 61, 132–4,
      137–8
   origin of *Dolchstoßlegende* 86–90
   revolution 82, 90, 139–40, 165–6

Groener, Wilhelm 4, 7, 16, 46–7, 63
   biography 44
   Ebert Libel Trial 140, 145
   January Strikes 44–7
   Munich *Dolchstoß* Trial 165–6,
      171–2
   revolution 79, 86, 89, 90–1

Helfferich, Karl
   biography 111–13
   choreographing the *Dolchstoß* 113,
      118–21

Hindenburg, Paul von 44, 46–7, 95
   biography 109–11
   Ebert Libel Trial 139–40
   origin of *Dolchstoßlegende* 103, 113
Hitler, Adolf 3–6, 147, 204–5
   on Ebert and the January Strike 157

Kuhl, Hermann von 104–5, 167
   biography 66
   on the military situation in 1918 66–72
   Subcommittee deposition 181–2, 185

Ledebour, Georg 77, 80–2
Ludendorff, Erich
   on the food situation 19–20
   Hindenburg testimony 111–13,
      121, 125
   origins of *Dolchstoßlegende* 105–6

Maurice, Sir Frederick 93–4, 98–103
Müller, Richard 77, 79
myth (political uses of)
   conflict within Left parties 1–3, 6–7,
      61, 115–16, 150–1, 156–7, 177,
      205–7
   conflict within Right parties 7,
      115–16, 170, 172, 177, 203–7
   elections of 1924 3, 157, 159, 168,
      176–7, 201, 203

naval mutinies 49, 91, 163–4, 169, 172, 214

revolutionary propaganda 65–6, 71, 73,
   83–4, 162, 166–7, 170, 178–82, 197–8

Scheidemann, Philipp
   biography 51
   January Strike 60, 132–9
   revolution 84, 90–1

Wolff, Theodore 152–5

www.ingramcontent.com/pod-product-compliance
Ingram Content Group UK Ltd.
Pitfield, Milton Keynes, MK11 3LW, UK
UKHW021907220326
469204UK00008B/227